WRITTEN BY
HERSELF

Blacks in the Diaspora

Darlene Clark Hine, John McCluskey, Jr., and David Barry Gaspar
General Editors

WRITTEN BY HERSELF

Literary Production by
African American Women,
1746–1892

FRANCES SMITH FOSTER

INDIANA UNIVERSITY PRESS
Bloomington and Indianapolis

The paper used in this publication meets the minimum requirements of American
National Standard for Information Sciences—Permanence of Paper for Printed
Library Materials, ANSI Z39.48-1984.

⊚ ™

Manufactured in the United States of America

Library of Congress Cataloging-in-Publication Data

Foster, Frances Smith.
   Written by herself : literary production by African American
women, 1746–1892 / Frances Smith Foster.
      p.   cm. — (Blacks in the diaspora)
   Includes bibliographical references and index.
   ISBN 0-253-32409-2 (cloth : alk. paper). — ISBN 0-253-20786-X
(paper : alk. paper)
      1. American literature—Afro-American authors—History and
   criticism.   2. American literature—Colonial period, ca. 1600–1775—
History and criticism.   3. American literature—Women authors—
History and criticism.   4. American literature—19th century—
History and criticism.   5. Afro-American women—Intellectual life.
6. Afro-American women in literature.   7. Afro-Americans in
literature.   I. Title.   II. Series.
PS153.N5F68   1993
810.9'9287—dc20   92-23916

1 2 3 4 5   97 96 95 94 93

For Mama,
Who saved her books for me

Contents

Acknowledgments

A lot of good things have happened during the dozen years that I've been working on this book. Literary archeological projects such as the Schomburg Library of Nineteenth Century Black Women Writers, the Black Periodical Fiction Project, and the Project on the History of Black Writing have made it much easier to identify and to study the material. Recent movements in theory and methodology have provided the tools and validated many of the assumptions through which more authentic and authoritative discussions of this literature may flourish. And, the resultant renaissance of interest in early African American literature and in African American women's literature has begun to produce a visible and vital scholarship in the subject matter.

But in 1980 when I began to investigate the literature published before 1892 by African American women, the enterprise was considerably different. Bibliographies on early African American literature were relatively slight and scarce and the books, once identified and located, were generally noncirculating. Though woman's literature and early black literature were gaining academic respectability and claiming more scholarly attention, critical discussion of early African American women writers was virtually nonexistent. A study such as I proposed required time and texts, serious consideration and rigorous discussion. Thus, my year in residence at Atlanta University as a member of Richard Long's seminar in Afro-American Studies and as a visiting research associate with the Center for African and Afro-American Studies was crucial, and my first thanks must go to the National Endowment for the Humanities which funded Professor Long's proposal and to those who selected my application to participate. I am grateful especially to Charles P. Henry and the other members of that group who taught and listened; to Loretta Henry and Ceretha Cartwright and the other colleagues and friends at the Atlanta University Center and in the Atlanta community who did what had to be done so I could do what I needed to do.

The object of my study was uncharted territory and I had to make my way through daunting and seemingly impenetrable overgrowth of books and papers, attitudes and assumptions. Without the support, advice, and labor of my colleagues and friends, without the money and time offered by San Diego State University, University of California, San Diego, and the Harvard Divinity School, without the suggestions and commitment of Joan Catapano and the reader she selected for this manuscript this book would not have been completed. Had my computer not crashed during the final stages of this preparation, I would insert here a long list of individuals who supported and contributed to this project. But I lost that file and cannot readily recall the many who deserve acknowledgment. I can, however, easily identify certain colleagues who never fail to make time to challenge and correct, to bolster and caution me: Elsie B. Adams, Nellie McKay, Roy Harvey Pearce, Sherely Anne Williams, Richard Yarborough, Jean Fagan Yellin, and Bonnie Zimmerman. Among the libraries and archives that preserved the material and made it available to me are the Atlanta University Center Woodruff Library; the Library Company of Philadelphia; the Moorland-Spingarn Research Center, Howard University; the Schomburg Center for Research in Black Culture, New York Public Library; San Diego State University Love Library; the Charles P. Brockson Collection, Temple University; the Central Library, University of California, San Diego; the Rembert E. Stokes Library Resource Center, Wilberforce University; the Ohio Historical Society; the Pennsylvania Historical Society; and the Harvard University Libraries. The professional staff at these institutions were without exception helpful and courteous but among those who became what I consider friends and fellow explorers are Esme Bhan, Jacqueline Brown, Paul Coates, Philip Lapsansky, Jean Mulhern, and Janet Sims-Wood.

Permission to quote from the Francis Grimke papers is by courtesy of the Moorland-Spingarn Research Center, Howard University, Washington, D.C.

WRITTEN BY
HERSELF

ONE

Testing and Testifying

The Word, the Other, and African American Women Writers

> Being a sensible intelligent woman, and having a good memory, . . . [Alice] would often make judicious remarks on the population and improvements of the city and country; hence her conversation became peculiarly interesting, especially to the immediate descendants of the first settlers, of whose ancestors she often related acceptable anecdotes.[1] (Isaiah Thomas 1803)

> Men of eminence have mostly risen from obscurity; nor will I, although a female of a darker hue, and far more obscure than they, bend my head or hang my harp upon willows; for though poor, I will virtuous prove.[2] (Maria W. Stewart 1833)

> It is because I believe the American people to be conscientiously committed to a fair trial and ungarbled evidence, and because I feel it essential to a perfect understanding and an equitable verdict that truth from each standpoint be presented at the bar.—that this little Voice has been added to the already full chorus. The 'otherside' has not been represented by one who lives there. And not many can more sensibly realize and more accurately tell the weight and the fret of the 'long dull pain' than the open-eyed but hitherto voiceless Black Woman of America.[3] (Anna Julia Cooper 1892)

Quiet as it's kept, black women have been recording and influencing American history since their earliest arrival upon these shores. They used English because they were denied the use of the languages of their African ancestors and because they needed to communicate with people from diverse linguistic backgrounds. Defying the laws and customs that imposed silence upon them,

African American women testified to their personal experiences and perceptions and to those they shared with their communities. Those who converted to Christianity (and virtually every extant text was written by a professed Christian) took seriously the biblical injunction to "write the vision, and make it plain" (Hab. 2:2). They used the Word as both a tool and a weapon to correct, to create, and to confirm their visions of life as it was and as it could become.

Not only did African American women appropriate the English language to record their truths, but assuming prerogatives to its literary traditions, they consciously revised that tradition to more accurately conform to their truths and their visions. In so doing, they were testifying to the fact of their existence and insisting that others acknowledge their existence and their testimonies. They were consciously creating new criteria against which the testimonies of others might be judged. And they were testing ways in which the English language and its literature might better serve them as African American women writers. Before discussing the ways in which their understanding of the Word, their status as the Other, and their shared identity as African American women created and informed their writings, I will sketch a basic outline of what one may now recognize as the early African American women's literary tradition and of the context within which it developed. To represent the tradition at critical points in its development, I submit the examples of Alice, Maria W. Stewart, and Anna Julia Cooper.

The role of Alice in the women's literary tradition is similar to that of Adam in the development of the slave narrative. "Adam Negro's Tryalls" is the earliest written account of an individual black person's life in North America.[4] It encompasses only a fragment of Adam's life. We know that he was an adult in 1694 when he was promised his freedom after seven years of service and that in 1701 that promise was not honored. Adam sued and in 1703 won his freedom. Though some of his actions are described, Adam's own words are not recorded. "Adam Negro's Tryall" is really a conglomeration constructed from a series of personal and public documents recorded during the first twenty years of the eighteenth century. Still, it demonstrates the basic patterns of bondage and of resistance to that bondage that are found in later autobiographical writings by African Americans. It demonstrates, also, the early testimony of African Americans to alternative visions of the world and the early testing of the power of language to bring those alternatives into being. "Adam Negro's Tryall" comes to us through the pens of others but it stands as a precursor to the published works of later African Americans who sought similar ends.

The situation of Alice is similar. Hers is the earliest extant example of an African American woman who testified to her experience in this country and thereby tested the ability of language to influence the society within which she lived. Alice's life in slavery and her attempts to create an increment of freedom within that condition are briefly reported by Isaiah Thomas in *Eccentric Biography; or, Memoirs of Remarkable Female Characters,*

Ancient and Modern (1803). Alice was born into slavery in Philadelphia in 1686. Unlike Adam, she did not sue for her legal freedom, but she, as he, was known as an especially independent and resourceful individual. As a ferriage collector, Alice had to possess considerable verbal and quantitative skills. She had to be authoritative, responsible, and diplomatic. Alice successfully created a certain amount of individual freedom. She used her abilities and compensated for her weaknesses. For example, since she could not read, she would have friends read the Bible to her. But once she had heard the written word, Alice did not hesitate to interpret and to "often make pertinent remarks" (Thomas 2) upon its lessons.

The story of Alice is particularly important because it demonstrates an African American woman's very early command of language and linguistic authority. Alice was recognized as a "sensible intelligent woman" whose "judicious remarks" were valued. Isaiah Thomas writes, "Being a sensible intelligent woman, and having a good memory, . . . [Alice] would often make judicious remarks on the population and improvements of the city and country; hence, her conversation became peculiarly interesting, especially to the immediate descendants of the first settlers, of whose ancestors she often related acceptable anecdotes. She remembered William Penn, the proprietor of Pennsylvania, Thomas Story, James Logan, and several other distinguished characters of that day" (1–2). This eighteenth-century African American slave woman not only freely interpreted the Holy Scriptures but she also presumed to teach about the secular past and to analyze and to judge the present. Since she was a valued source of information, both familial and civic, for the descendants of the Philadelphia colonists, this slave woman may be considered one of the earliest American historians and social commentators. Alice is one of the earliest examples of an African American woman who testified to her experiences in this country and commented upon the society within which she lived. However, there is no reason to believe that Alice was the only African American or woman to merit such distinction during that period.

Twenty-eight years after Thomas's eulogy to Alice, Maria W. Stewart, another African American woman, dared to speak publicly on issues commonly considered beyond the sphere of any woman. Two months after Nat Turner's insurrection had alerted the nation, once again, to the discrepancies between white and black ideas of democracy and religious responsibilities, Maria W. Stewart introduced herself to William Lloyd Garrison and presented him with a manuscript called "Religion and the Pure Principles of Morality: The Sure Foundation on Which We Must Build." In this essay, Stewart warned white Americans that the souls of black Americans "are fired with the same love of liberty and independence with which your souls are fired" (40). Unlike Nat Turner, Maria W. Stewart was not advocating violence. This essay and her subsequent writings argue for a revival of Christian morality and for social advancement through education and moral suasion. However, Stewart's was a militant Christianity which assumed that in building the sure foundation, some might have to fight and to die. "We are not afraid of them that kill the body, and after that can do no more" (40), she proclaimed.

Like Alice, Maria W. Stewart assumed the prerogative of making "judicious remarks on the population and improvements of the city and country." Unlike Alice, whose words are described but not preserved, Stewart's actual language has survived. Not only was she a pioneer in women's public speaking but, as Marilyn Richardson has informed us, Stewart is generally considered to be the "first American woman to lecture in public on political themes and leave extant copies of her texts."[5] Although Isaiah Thomas considered Alice a "Remarkable Female Character," one can only speculate on the specifics of her remarks and, for example, how she compared herself to other women. With Stewart, however, one no longer need conjecture. Maria W. Stewart frequently used autobiographical examples.

In her remarks to audiences integrated by race, sex, and class, Stewart frequently addressed particular remarks to particular segments of that audience. For example, in "Religion and the Pure Principles of Morality," an essay that she convinced William Lloyd Garrison to print and which was obviously intended for a mixed audience, Stewart addressed her black sisters directly saying, "O, ye daughters of Africa, awake! Awake! Arise! No longer sleep nor slumber, but distinguish yourselves. Show forth to the world that you are endowed with noble and exalted faculties. O, ye daughters of Africa! What have you done to immortalize your names beyond the grave?" (30). In her "Lecture at Franklin Hall," she challenged her "fairer sisters, whose hands are never soiled, whose nerves and muscles are never strained, go learn by experience!" (48) what it is like for other women. She advised them that "had we had the opportunity that you have had, to improve our moral and mental faculties," African Americans would not be struggling to survive as manual laborers and servants but they would also be contributing to the intellectual and social refinement of the nation.

Maria W. Stewart believed passionately that women had the responsibility of speaking out and into history. She acted upon her beliefs by writing and lecturing. Her published words show that her arguments were well reasoned and she had comprehensive command of the language in which she wrote. Unfortunately, Stewart could not long withstand the social pressure that denied women, of whatever color, the freedom of speech. Scarcely a year after her first public lecture, Maria W. Stewart retired from the podium. Though she was giving up on the public lecture circuit, Stewart continued to challenge the status quo. In her farewell address she vowed: "Men of eminence have mostly risen from obscurity; nor will I, although a female of a darker hue, and far more obscure than they, bend my head or hang my harp upon willows; for though poor, I will virtuous prove" (71). True to her promise, she abandoned the podium but she did not bend her head nor hang up her harp. Two years later, in 1835, she published *Productions of Mrs. Maria W. Stewart* and in 1879 she issued a revised version.

Alice, the oral historian and social commentator, was a precursor of the African American women's literary tradition. Maria W. Stewart, orator and essayist, was an early contributor to that tradition. Stewart was not the first African American woman to be published, but she was one of the first to proclaim herself a representative of and a model for others. For nearly fifty years, Maria W. Stewart fought for her right to participate in the public language and literature of the country. By the end of her career, she had been joined by other African American women, including Frances Harper, Mary Ann Shad, Charlotte Forten, and Elizabeth Keckley, who testified to the special experiences of American black women and who tested the power of the English language to record and to shape those experiences.

Theirs was a limited achievement. By the mid-nineteenth century, several African American women had established themselves as poets and essayists, as editors and publishers, but they were generally confined to the "women's pages" of periodicals, and their publications were discreetly acknowledged. When Maria W. Stewart wrote in the preface to the second edition of *Productions* that "The Christian public will undoubtedly be astonished at the humble source from which this work emanates" (87), it was in recognition that her candid language and her audacity in seeking a more general audience were still considered unusual. But Maria W. Stewart believed in her right and her obligation to speak out and she believed in the value of what she had to say. In that same preface, Maria Stewart continued boldly, "Nevertheless, it must be a God-send, as every one must be convinced who may read its pages" (87).

By 1879 when Maria W. Stewart published the second edition of *Productions,* African American women had established a viable literary tradition. But as Stewart's words suggest, that tradition was not yet commonly recognized. The writings of women during and before Maria Stewart's time have not been lost, but, unfortunately, what Marilyn Richardson has said of Maria Stewart is true of her contemporaries as well. Their words come "to us from a personal experience only faintly discernible through the mists of time" (xvi). Nonetheless, Stewart did write herself into history, and her writings do provide us not only the opportunity to know her private testimony but to recognize in her writings the testimonies of other writers who most influenced her own.

African American women continued to experiment with the literary techniques that would most effectively help them bear witness. In *A Voice from the South by a Black Woman of the South* (1892), Anna Julia Cooper wrote:

It is because I believe the American people to be conscientiously committed to a fair trial and ungarbled evidence, and because I feel it essential to a perfect understanding and an equitable verdict that truth from *each* standpoint must be presented at the bar,—that this little Voice has been added to the already full chorus. The "other side" has not been represented by one who "lives there."

And not many can more sensibly realize and more accurately tell the weight
and the fret of the "long dull pain" than the open-eyed but hitherto voiceless
Black Woman of America. (ii)

Cooper's declaration that African American women had until the moment of her writing been "voiceless" was more rhetorical than factual. Undoubtedly there were many in her audience who were not aware of that
tradition, but Cooper knew it well. As an avid reader and a member of the
Bethel Literary and Historical Association, Cooper knew the works of earlier writers such as Phillis Wheatley, Maria Stewart, Harriet Jacobs, and
Ann Plato. At Oberlin College, she had been the classmate of two black
women, Mary Jane Patterson and Mary Church Terrell, who at the time of
her writing were decidedly unquiet. And among her own friends and colleagues were African American women of letters such as Charlotte Forten
Grimke, Fannie Barrier Williams, Ida B. Wells, Josephine St. Pierre Ruffin,
and Victoria Earle Matthews.

In the chapter that she calls "The Status of Woman in America," Cooper
clarifies and qualifies the more ringing pronouncement with which her book
begins. Women in general, she says, have traditionally been "quiet observer[s]" who "whisper[ed] just the needed suggestion or the almost forgotten
truth" (138) and African American women specifically have been "not inferior in strength and excellence" (140) in this capacity. While they had been
effective in making changes, Cooper says their tactics had often been so
discreet that they had not been acknowledged for their contributions: "Not
unfelt, then, if unproclaimed has been the work and influence of the colored
women of America. Our list of chieftains in the service, though not long, is
not inferior in strength and excellence, I dare believe, to any similar list
which this country can produce" (140). A Voice from the South was intended
to modify that tradition of quiet whispers and to proclaim more forcefully
its ideas and perspectives.

The year 1892 marks the beginning of a new era in African American
women's literary tradition. It became less discreet, more visible. As Cooper
stated, the work of earlier women writers had been "not unfelt" but with
the notable exception of a few such as Phillis Wheatley and Frances E. W.
Harper, it had been "unproclaimed." By the time that Cooper published her
book, there was reason to believe that the situation was changing. By the
mid-nineteenth century, women writers had established a tradition of domestic literature which claimed a loyal following among the increasingly
literate and outspoken American women. Since Harriet Beecher Stowe's
resounding success with Uncle Tom's Cabin, American women writers had
increasingly commanded serious attention from the general reading public.
Writers such as Helen Hunt Jackson, Louisa May Alcott, Rebecca Harding
Davis, and Sarah Orne Jewett had proved that women could combine social
awareness and aesthetic ambitions without totally abdicating their claims to
ladyhood. African American women writers knew that they faced great

odds, that theirs was a particularly difficult test because they were confronting not only sexism but also racism. Still, they believed that it was time to clearly affirm their womanhood, their blackness, and their desire for full participation in American society.

A Voice from the South was a manifestation of Anna Julia Cooper's belief that the twentieth century would see a new America, one more prosperous and powerful than ever before. "The struggle with nature is over, the struggle with ideas begins" (132), she proclaimed. "In the era now about to dawn, [woman's] sentiments must strike the keynote and give the dominant tone" (133). Cooper further believed that the touchstone for this new society would be the African American woman. "The colored woman of to-day," declared Cooper, "occupies, one may say, a unique position in this country. . . . She is confronted by both a woman question and a race problem, and is as yet an unknown or an unacknowledged factor in both" (134). Her experience in the coming century would determine the success of the American ideal, for as Cooper had explained before, "Only the BLACK WOMAN can say 'when and where I enter, in the quiet, undisputed dignity of my womanhood, without violence and without suing or special patronage, then and there the whole *Negro race enters with me'*" (31).

Anna Julia Cooper was not alone in believing that a more democratic society was being born. Today, we recognize that the 1890s was the peak of the period known for its faith in social progress via philanthropy and self-help. It was, as John Hope Franklin has reminded us, "The Age of Booker T. Washington." Like Washington, most black Americans believed that through hard work and circumspection they could realize the American Dream, that the twentieth century would be a New Era. Though racial discrimination was being increasingly codified into law and violent attacks against blacks were rampant, many believed as Franklin says, that these were "the dying gasps of a reign of terror."[6] Most realized that Reconstruction had failed to accomplish the reforms necessary for a free and equal society, but they also knew that it had created the constitutional amendments upon which such a society could be based. Most African Americans were poorer and less educated than were Anglo-Americans but they too believed that industrialization and the movement towards populism promised a better future.

To be sure, there had been signs of progress. By 1892 African American society had a small but viable middle class. The few black Americans who had been educated at institutions such as Harvard, Oberlin, Amherst, and Bowdoin were joined by the far more numerous alumni of black schools and colleges such as Fisk, Howard, Atlanta, Talladega, and Tuskegee. Among the number was a sizeable group of women trained for professions that included medicine, law, social work, and education. There were several schools and at least two colleges, Spelman and Bennett, especially for African American women. African American women had begun to establish a national network of social service and literary organizations clearly based upon the foundation laid by their ancestors and their sisters in the struggle for women's rights. So exuberant were they about the promise of the future that some such as Gertrude Mossell grandly proclaimed that they were at the brink of the "woman's century."[7]

In retrospect, it is clear that these nineteenth-century African Americans were excessively optimistic. Writing the vision did not bring it into full being. It did not change the attitudes and actions of as many people as decisively as they had hoped. When they put their words to the test, they discovered that sexism and racism, conservatism, pragmatism, and greed were more formidable enemies than they had assumed. They discovered that negotiations with editors and publishers, appeasements of civic and religious leaders, and even justifications to family and friends were often protracted and frustrating experiences.

These women writers did not realize all that they had hoped, but their achievements are profound and are increasingly recognized as such by literary historians. Most studies of contemporary black women's literature acknowledge that it did not spring fully grown from the general African American literary tradition, but that writers such as Ann Petry, Margaret Walker, Gwendolyn Brooks, and Lorraine Hansberry were building both consciously and unconsciously upon the foundations of their literary forebears. Scholars of African American women's fiction, for example, generally began their studies with discussions of the 1890s because, as Barbara Christian points out, from that time forward, African American women were "successful in expressing their own ideas and feelings and were also pivotal in the development of the black novel."[8]

But few critics have spoken of the literature before 1892. Anna Julia Cooper intended her remarks about the "hitherto voiceless Black woman" to be rhetorical, to dramatize the relative silence with which earlier voices have been greeted. Yet Cooper's remarks pose questions that are not rhetorical. Why had the voices of African American women been unheard? Why was there an overwhelming silence before 1892? Why—to shift to the 1980s—for the majority of Americans, is there still so little recognition of their contributions? These are questions made more obvious by the fact that black women have a strong claim to being considered the founders of both the African American literary tradition and the American women's literary tradition. The earliest extant poem by a black in North America is Lucy Terry's "Bar's Flight" (1746). The first volume of poetry to be published by an African American, and the second volume published from the American colonies by a woman, is Phillis Wheatley's *Poems on Various Subjects, Religious and Moral* (1773). Frances Wright is usually cited as the first American woman to "pass through the curtain of silence" but Maria W. Stewart provides us with the earliest published lectures (1833). Maria Stewart's passionate writings for abolition and women's rights preceded those of the more famous Sarah and Angelina Grimke, Lucy Stone, Lydia Maria Child, and Margaret Fuller. African American women are among the pioneers in every major genre of early African American and women's literature. And this is despite the oft cited fact that to be a black woman writer in America from colonial times until the end of the nineteenth century was to be heir to multiple legacies of suppression, oppression, and repression. This is despite the not as often mentioned, but undeniable, fact that while these legacies informed their literary production and handicapped their efforts, they did not prevent African American women from writing testimonies to strength, courage, and self-esteem. With their writing, as with their lives, African American women probed the literary possibilities for changing their circumstances and for recording their endeavors. In many ways, the story of the African American woman is the quintessential enactment of the New World being, combining the religious faith of the Puritans and the Protestant evangelists with the Common Sense approach to social betterment of Paine, Jefferson, Franklin, and Lincoln. Why, then, have theirs been voices unheard and stories untold? To begin to answer such questions, one must consider the impact of race, gender, and class upon writing, upon the creation of literature, and upon its reception.

Though logical, such consideration is not easily accomplished. One problem is ascertaining the facts and another is applying those facts appropriately. In dealing with the past, we must depend on the records that have been preserved. Most often, these are legal documents, statistics, and accounts of public figures. While these documents may be adequate to sketch the theoretical or official framework of a society, they are inadequate for establishing the social ethos of a period. They do not, in particular, document the perspectives or record the failures and dreams of the silenced or ignored.

The problem of discovering the stories previously unheard requires that we look beyond what has been preserved as the official or privileged realities. We must become literary anthropologists, looking underneath the stated ideas and events to see what is not shown. We must discover and understand the context of the fragments left by those whose words were not valued or were devalued. We must, as Winthrop Jordan says, assume "the task of explaining how things actually were while at the same time thinking that no one will ever really know."[9] And we must do so with full knowledge that individual experiences vary and that the experiences of groups were not static over time or place.

This is especially relevant to the situations of African American women. We can only speculate about the numbers of African American women who wrote for publication, but the number of extant texts suggests there were more African American men and more Anglo-American women published than there were African American women. And again, compared to the writings by Anglo men, relatively few African American men or Anglo-American women were able to record their views. Moreover, those women and people of color who did publish were subjected to more criticism, skepticism, and censorship than their peers and their publications were haphazardly preserved and rarely cited. The scholarship to which one must turn to try to ascertain the circumstances under which African American women lived and wrote verifies the assertion in the title of what may be the only text designed for black women's studies that "All the women are white, all the blacks are men, but some of us are brave."[10]

The paucity of extant texts by African American women writers makes study difficult but not impossible. More texts are being discovered as interest grows. But we also can make headway because the texts that do survive often self-consciously reveal their context and intent. And African American women's experiences contain elements of other, more documented, experiences. Anna Julia Cooper's observation that in 1892 the African American woman was confronted by "both a woman question and a race problem" is true for those who lived before and those who came after her time. Thus, we can extrapolate much about the circumstances of African American women by examining the general conditions within which African Americans lived on the one hand, and within which American women lived, on the other, and by trying to understand how these conditions were manifested in African American women's experiences.

The African American experience is inextricably bound with racial discrimination. Historians indicate that white people's attitudes toward black people moved from curiosity to ethnocentrism to more insidious forms of racism. Before the eighteenth century, whites generally recognized blacks as different, as the Other. They stressed the obvious contrasts in color, religion, and lifestyle and they entertained notions that African people possessed an excess of "animality and a peculiarly potent sexuality" (Jordan 43). Little by little, difference and stereotype became reasons to devalue, and in this country, those attitudes created increasingly rigid and codified patterns of racial discrimination. By the mid-eighteenth century, the time of the earliest extant African American writings, "blacks," "slavery," and "subservience" were becoming synonymous, if not in practice, at least in the minds of the American colonists. Legislation began plainly to differentiate between rights and punishments for whites and for blacks. For example, black indentured servants no longer assumed the privileges of full citizenship upon the termination of their indenture. The English common-law practice in which the father's station determined that of the child was changed to make the mother's status determinative, thus consigning the children of slave women to perpetual slavery. By the nineteenth century, free blacks could no longer vote, live or travel as freely as had their parents.

Similarly, attitudes toward women and their roles in American society were not imported fully developed from the Old World but evolved in response to a complexity of needs and experiences in this developing nation. As were the Africans, the first significant numbers of white women were imported to serve the needs of the white male explorers and settlers. Both the white women and the Africans arrived in Virginia in 1619. In charting the history of women's roles in the North American colonies, Eleanor Flexner describes the development of class discrimination as well. Flexner writes,

There was little difference at first in the rigors endured by the women, gentle-born mistress, servant, artisan's wife, or indentured maid. . . . the women cared for one another in childbirth and sickness with no skill to call on save their own, . . . they toiled from sunup to sundown, converting the raw skins and meat brought home by the men into the necessary food and clothing, and planted and tended the ground the men had cleared. . . . To be a bondman or bondwoman was to be, for the time specified, little better than a slave. . . [but] As growth and increased wealth produced social stratification, generalization about "colonial women" became more difficult.[11]

From studies such as Jordan's and Flexner's, one realizes that as the settlers of the New World were declaring their independence from the Old, they were also in the process of creating a new form of bondage, one that far exceeded any feudality or indenture they may have experienced themselves. As the various colonies combined to become the United States, they also agreed to create a more stratified society, which reserved the privileges of the Constitution for a few. During this time of the founding fathers and their Declaration of Independence, white men began to seriously justify their physical domination by alleging their intellectual superiority. "What American intellectuals did in the post-Revolutionary decades," Jordan says, "was, in effect, to claim America as a white man's country" (xiii). This minority relegated the majority of the inhabitants of this country to second-class citizenship, renamed people of color as pagans and savages, and proclaimed black slaves to be only three-fifths human, outside the realm of humanity. In actuality, the founding fathers brought forth upon this continent a new nation dedicated to the proposition that all white men are created approximately equal. Women and people of color became the Other, the means by which white men could know what they were by asserting what they were not.

Recognizing the historical divisions by race, sex, and class as evolutionary processes that privileged a few against the many invites a comparative perspective that helps with the re-creation of the facts of the African American women writers' historical context. Given their identification as the Other, much of what we learn about the status of women, of African Americans, or of all those who were excluded by appearance, national origin, or class can be applied to our understanding of African American women and their literature.

For example, in *The Madwoman in the Attic,* a study almost exclusively based upon the literature of middle-class white women, Sandra M. Gilbert and Susan Gubar argue that men had usurped the word and its power and that the "striking coherence we noticed in literature by women could be explained by a common, female impulse to struggle free from social and literary confinement through strategic redefinitions of self, art, and society."[12] Gilbert and Gubar use "men" to mean "literate, white men." Their assertion of a common "impulse to struggle free" derives from study of literature almost entirely by middle-class white women. Yet much of their argument holds true for most Americans, male and female, who were not of the privileged race, sex, and class. Their conclusions about white women's literature may be readily expanded, for example, to declare that the literature of those who are not white, educated males is essentially concerned with testifying against that which would confine or repress their experiences and with testing the possibilities of language to replace rejected versions of self, art, and society with more accurate and positive representations.

Gilbert and Gubar also state that to understand the circumstances which created the literature as it exists one must confront "two separate but related matters: first, the social position in which nineteenth-century women writers found themselves and, second, the reading that they themselves did" (xi). Here, too, their findings hold true for more than those who make up their literary sample. The literature of the Other is not the obverse of the literature from which they are excluded. For the most part, their concepts of literature, its strategies, methods and possibilities are informed by the tradition established by and for white men.

From its beginnings, Anglo males dominated American literature. Women, and Others in general, were less privileged and consequently more illiterate than white men. Even as the rise of public education opened doors to more men of lower-class or non-European heritage, the schools did not generally accept women. Not only were women expected to remain decorously silent and to apply themselves within the domestic sphere but, as Eleanor Flexner explains, "It was almost universally believed that a woman's brain was smaller in capacity and therefore inferior in quality to that of a man" (23).

It was the second half of the nineteenth century before any significant number of women could claim a formal education. Even then, very few could garner the money, time, and permission to attend an institution of higher education. Those who did found themselves restricted to a special curriculum that consisted primarily of music, domestic arts, and china painting. Consequently, to encounter the "masterpieces" of western literature was an experience available to a small minority of women. They read authors such as Shakespeare, Milton, the British Romantics, the Fireside Poets, and various clergymen—these not particularly noted for their non-sexist views. Those women who had access to earlier literature studied the patriarchal mythology of the Old Testament, which was understood to be infallible, and the equally masculine lore of the Greek and Roman classics.

Until the mid-nineteenth century, then, the literature that women read was, for the most part, the literature created by and for American and British men. It reflected, in form and content, Anglo male perspectives, aspirations, and expectations. As Gilbert and Gubar have noted, women who read the literature of western culture discovered that the "text's author is a father, a progenitor, a procreator, an aesthetic patriarch whose pen is an instrument of generative power like his penis" (6). In such canonical texts, as many feminist critics have shown, "the sacred nature of the phallic order" is privileged and women's roles were limited. Sidonie Smith's categorization of the "four predominant life scripts available to women of the late medieval and Renaissance periods: the nun, the queen, the wife, and the witch"[13] is essentially true for American women until at least the end of the nineteenth century.

Women who aspired to belle lettres and women who simply wanted to be popular writers or journalists faced particular psychological barriers. As did men who would write, they had to face "the tensions and anxieties, hostilities and inadequacies writers feel when they confront not only the achievements of their predecessors but the traditions of genre, style, and metaphor that they inherit from such 'forefathers'" (*Madwoman* 46). But as Gilbert and Gubar also explain, the anxieties faced by a woman writer were complicated by the fact that "unlike her male counterpart, then, the female artist must first struggle against the effects of a socialization which makes conflict with the will of her (male) precursors seem inexpressibly absurd, futile, or even . . . self-annihilating" (49).

The description of the struggle that confronted women who would read and write within the dominant American literary tradition is generally applicable to women of all colors. And it is true, as Mary Dearborn asserts in *Pocahontas's Daughters: Gender and Ethnicity in American Culture,* that attempts to distinguish discrete gender and ethnic traditions involve "arbitrary and forced distinctions of ethnic group and chronology."[14] Moreover, as Amy Ling has noted in her essay "I'm Here: An Asian American Woman's Response," "the more we hear about the experiences of each particular group, the more we learn how much we share as a community of women and how often our commonalities cross cultural and racial barriers."[15] But, the similarities must not be allowed to obscure the significant differences. It is equally true that to gloss over differences, to argue, for example, as did nineteenth-century white feminists that the social situations between themselves and black slaves were parallel, is to grossly distort reality. Many of the facts of an African American woman's life—even that of a free-born, middle-class African American woman in the North who may have resided only a stone's throw away—would strain the limits of credibility for her white sister. Some of the commonalities shared by gender might "cross cultural and racial barriers" but many would not.[16] Amy Ling continued in the same essay, "white women are the grandmothers, mothers, wives, and sisters of white men; thus it would seem natural that granting equality and recognition to their own women would be the first, and a much easier, step for white men than to give respectful attention to descendants of former slaves, prostitutes, and aliens" (152).

The problem of ascertaining the ambiance within which early African American women lived and wrote may be partly solved by reconstructing the world of the Other during the eighteenth and nineteenth centuries, but the application of this general situation to a specific group must be done with great caution. Profound cultural differences existed among the descendants of European, Asian, and African heritages and they combine in myriad forms to impact the experiences of each group and of each individual within each group. The processes by which language and cultural changes have been forced upon those who have arrived in North America or, in the case of the Native Americans, who have been invaded, have been distinctly different. The position of the natives who lived in what are now the United States, Canada, and Mexico and who found themselves confronting hoards of invaders babbling of "manifest destiny" and "divine right" was different from that of Africans stolen, stripped of their language and cultural traditions, denied access to those of their new environment, and proclaimed subhuman because they then were not assimilated.

The history of oppression, exclusion, and social discrimination in the United States is not monolithic. There were, particularly in the southern colonies, many white people, for example, who were involuntarily removed to this country and sold into slavery. Because of their sex, national origin, or economic position, many whites were denied formal education and particularly any easy access to or participation in the English literary tradition. And yet they were rarely deprived of association with those who shared their ancestral languages. Rarely were they legally restricted from teaching or learning to read or to write the language of the dominant society. Nor were they regularly taxed to establish schools which they and their children had absolutely no chance of attending.

To cultural differences must be added the varieties of racisms and sexisms, not only as applied to the various groups which society thinks it can identify but as applied to the various configurations of kinship and national origin, economic and educational status, and era and geographical location. Hazel Carby summarizes the situation this way:

> racisms and sexisms need to be regarded as particular historical practices articulated with each other and with other practices in a social formation. For example, the institutionalized rape of black women as slaves needs to be distinguished from the institutionalized rape of black women as an instrument of political terror, alongside lynching, in the South. Rape itself should not be regarded as a transhistorical mechanism of women's oppression but as one that acquires specific political or economic meanings at different moments in history.[17]

Not only are there varieties of discrimination, but racism and sexism are evolving patterns of behavior and attitude. And contrary to popular notions, these patterns are not necessarily progressive. The situation of Alice, born a slave in the seventeenth-century frontier town of Philadelphia, is barely comparable to that of Charlotte Forten, the daughter of a free-born, wealthy black businessman in nineteenth-century Philadelphia. For example, Alice as a ferriage collector undoubtedly rode across the river on the same vehicle as her passengers. Charlotte Forten, on the other hand, found to her dismay that the white man who collected fares for the local streetcar would neither accept her money nor allow her to ride in the same conveyance as did white women of lesser economic status. While it is common to describe the situation of African American women as a simple matter of addition, to imply that their reality is the sum of racial and sexual discrimination is to use a simplistic formula which may well do more harm than good both to those it presumes to describe and those who would accept such definitions.

African American women's literature is a concourse wherein merge traditions of African Americans, women, the Other, and western civilization in general. The African American women's literary tradition, as is their history, is an amalgam, a mixture of diverse elements, some carefully and purposefully created and some a matter of coincidence or convenience. At the same time, this literature is an entity, an interstice, a nexus, and it is not deducible simply by identifying its components. It exists in its own right. In studying this literary tradition, it is not of prime importance to ascertain whether it is more "women's literature" or more "African American literature," more "American" or more "third world." As an amalgam it is more than the sum total of its parts. It transcends its elements even as it exists only because of them. As literature the productions of African American women may be subjected to the various theoretical perspectives. It may be analyzed structurally or poststructurally. It may be de- or re-constructed. But as literature it came into being and was shaped by the social and historical forces of its times. To attempt to comprehend it without attention to its context is to ignore the elements that its creators and its readers certainly did not ignore.

The three examples cited earlier to outline the African American women's literary tradition before 1892 are not the only ones that demonstrate the continuity of a tradition, the existence of the Word in and of black women since their first appearance on these shores. To avouch such a tradition is not to say that the women who wrote for publication were typical of all African American women. That would be foolish, historically inaccurate, and contrary to the role of writers in any culture. To suggest that artists are just plain people or to ignore distinctions among folk, popular, and elite literature is naive and insulting.

Yet to assume that literature written by African American women for publication is somehow less authentic than the oral literature or the material creations by their sisters, or that the African American women who wrote for publication ignored their folk heritage or their African American community is equally wrong. As Langston Hughes and Arna Bontemps noted in *The Poetry of the Negro,* the "articulate slaves belonged to a tradition of writers in bondage that goes back to Aesop and Terence."[18] To assert that those who adopted forms and techniques of western literature and addressed their remarks to an audience not confined to the African American community were really writing just to convince white people that they, too, could sing America is also an ingenuous and ignoble conclusion. It devalues the relationships between black writers and black readers and it disregards the vitality and versatility of African American culture. Melvin J. Herskovits's response in *The Myth of the Negro Past* to a similar idea is applicable here. Herskovits writes,

> It does not follow . . . that the training of those who operated and repaired sugar mills, or acted as house servants, or otherwise followed a routine different from that of the great body of field hands was in itself sufficient to cause them to give up their African modes of thought or behavior. Though greater personal contact with the masters was the direct route to greater taking over of European modes of behavior, the manner of life led by the whites, . . . was not such as to inculcate either love or respect for it on the part of those who viewed it closest."[19]

I suggest that the extant literature from 1746 to 1892, albeit small in quantity, proves that African American women, like African American men, deliberately chose to participate in the public discourse despite considerable Anglo-American resistance to their doing so. They appropriated the English literary tradition to reveal, to interpret, to challenge, and to change perceptions of themselves and the world in which they found themselves.

Their faith in the power of the Word came from sources religious and secular, African and American. While this should seem an obvious bit of common sense, many scholars have long pursued or been embarrassed by the signs of Anglo-American literary influences, while ignoring or slighting the Africanisms in our early literature. Yet our understanding of the earliest writings by African Americans is considerably enhanced when we consider what Africanists have told us about the primacy of *Nommo* or the Word. Africans in colonial America knew that *Nommo* is the life force, it produces all life, influences all things, or as Janheinz Jahn says, "All change, all production and generation are effected through the word."[20] "The central significance of the word in African culture," Jahn reminds us, "is not a phenomenon of one particular time. It was always there, an age-old tradition which has recently—and here only is the 'situation'—been carried on in European languages and will be carried on so long as and wherever African poetry makes its influence felt" (134).

Early African Americans treasured *Nommo* and certainly would have encouraged their children to do the same. Alice's role as historian and political commentator, which earned her inclusion in Isaiah Thomas's *Eccentric Biographies,* would not have been considered eccentric in many West African countries and was probably taken for granted by her African American community. As many scholars of African culture have pointed out, in traditional African life, virtually nothing is done without poetry and virtually every individual is "expected to have some competence in certain types of verse." Lucy Terry's 1746 poem in commemoration of the lives lost during the skirmish between the Native Americans and the American colonists and Phillis Wheatley's many "On the death of . . ." poems may stem as much from the African praise song, the Lau *nyatiti* or the Yoruba *rara,* for example, as from the European ballad or elegy.[21] Study of the various African literatures and customs, especially the praise songs, the autobiographical writings, and the emphasis upon proverbs, masking, and naming, may provide very salient explanations for the prevalence of poetry and political commentary in literature by African American women.

On the other hand, the experiences of African Americans in the New World invested profession of the Word with particular significances. At one time public announcements of a conversion to Christianity as taught in the Holy Scripture had been sufficient to release the convert from earthly bondage as well. Later, literacy gained African Americans access to other forms of freedom. Those who could read and write could find spiritual freedom, could write themselves passes or read their way to physical freedom, or could serve their people as interpreters, guides, and witnesses for both kinds of freedom.

Literacy and literature did have distinct significance to the Other, but it is important to recall that literacy and literature as empowerment was not a concept peculiar to the Other. In his study of the writings of the founding fathers, Robert A. Ferguson noted that they were very conscious of themselves as "men of letters." According to Ferguson, "In eighteenth-century America, the accomplished man demonstrates his worthiness for place and influence by writing about the world around him. . . . The eighteenth-century American work invariably alludes to its own importance as historical and intellectual event." Writers such as Thomas Jefferson, Thomas Paine, and Benjamin Franklin, Ferguson states, believed that "anything is possible with the proper word, which is desperately needed for a crisis at hand."[22]

There was, however, one important exception. The place and privileges of the founding fathers allowed them to assume the importance of their work and to assume that their readers would accept if not their personal eminence at least their right to argue public matters. But African American women writers knew, as did the Others, that the public was not inclined to grant such authority to those of their sex or race. African American women could not and did not overtly proclaim the importance of their speech as "historical and intellectual event." They knew that their very acts of writing tested social attitudes toward their intelligence and their historical situations. As black women they knew that their gender and their race infused their words with connotations which were complex, complicated, and difficult to control. In transgressing social conventions, they faced condemnation as "unnatural" beings. In publishing their thoughts and concerns, they also invited uncommonly stringent scrutiny of their diction, their form, and their content.

Phillis Wheatley's experience was not the only one but it is instructive. Wheatley's education was considered a noble experiment and her literary pretensions excited great curiosity. Her first submissions to local presses were accompanied by letters of recommendation from her mistress, Susanna

Wheatley. However, when an entire book was contemplated, the testimony of a woman, even a white woman, was apparently insufficient. Phillis Wheatley's manuscript was sent to the publisher along with an affidavit from Susanna's husband, John, who explained the circumstances and the scope of Phillis's formal education. Before her book was presented to the public, Phillis Wheatley had to submit to the examination of eighteen of the "most respectable Characters in *Boston,* that none might have the least Ground for disputing their *Original.*"[23] Their affidavit along with that of John Wheatley and of the publisher served as the introduction to *Poems on Various Subjects, Religious and Moral* when it was published in 1773. And even with all this, the Countess of Huntingdon requested that distribution be delayed until a picture of the author could be included in order that the last lingering doubts might be assuaged.

African American women knew what happened to Phillis Wheatley and to her work. They knew Wheatley's literary achievements may have facilitated her eventual freedom but they also knew that it had not protected her finally from the ravages of racial discrimination and poverty. They knew it took more than words to change society and they knew that their words would be subjected to interpretations engendered by non-literary expectations and assumptions. Yet African American women writers did not give up on the Word. They refused to entertain literary bigotry and they exercised their right to use the language of the country within which they found themselves to contribute to and create its literary traditions.

They wrote, as Phillis Wheatley's book is entitled, of "Various Subjects, Religious and Moral." And unlike the few white American women who published in those early years, African American women tended to write beyond their personal experiences. In her study of early American women's poetry, Emily Stipes Watts notes that Phillis Wheatley was not only the first American woman after Anne Bradstreet to have a volume of her poetry published, but she was the first to speak poetically of politics or other such "men's work."[24] Unfortunately, Watts does not explore the reasons for or the implications of this African slave woman's choice of subject. Watts limits her discussion to poetry, but Wheatley's subject matter is characteristic of black women's literature from its beginnings. Though they did write of "pious sentiments and domestic concerns," they, more than white women writers of that time, also display a particular interest in public occasions and historic events.

As William Andrews has so ably demonstrated in his study of the first century of African American autobiography, the quests and strategies of early African American writers in general were toward greater freedom in telling their stories. Though Andrews's study limits itself to autobiography and includes the works of both women and men, at least one of his conclusions is equally appropriate to the literature of black women in early America. To paraphrase Andrews, black women's writings were a very public way of declaring themselves free, of redefining freedom and then assigning it to themselves in defiance of their bonds to the past or to the social, political, and sometimes even the moral exigencies of the present.[25] These women saw their literature as both art and artifact. They recognized that their readers would evaluate their publications for their intellectual and aesthetic merit and their readers would judge both the author and the author's race by their success in meeting the prevailing literary standards. They believed that their contributions, by their very existence, served as artifacts, physical proof of their intellectual ability to contribute to the western literary tradition. They wanted to prove, as Janheinz Jahn phrases it, "that they could compose poetry and write novels just as well as any white writer" (130). Such concern did not relegate their work to being, in Leroi Jones's words, "always 'after the fact,' *i.e.,* based on known social concepts within the structure of bourgeois idealistic projections of 'their America,' and an emotional climate that never really existed."[26]

At the same time as they were demonstrating their linguistic capabilities, African American women were testing American literature for its ability to accommodate their own testimonies. And they were modifying that tradition, wherever necessary, to accommodate the inclusion of those testimonies. These women were familiar with their African American literary tradition as well as with leading authors of their day and they were, as Fannie Barrier Williams wrote, "ambitious to be contributors to all the great moral and intellectual forces that make for the greater weal of our common country."[27] The idea of a separate literary aesthetic was not a serious proposition in their minds. The oral literature and the spiritual and secular literature of the African American folk were not unknown to them and were, in fact, frequently incorporated into their texts. But for the majority of these writers, the work of the Word was as much an outreach program as it was a self-creating process. They chose to write, to sing the songs for their people, to a heterogeneous audience. Their melodies had to be somewhat familiar to their audiences' ears. And for that purpose, the Shakespearean sonnet sometimes was more useful than the blues. Not only could they compensate in this way for readers who like Frederick Douglass might have misunderstood the basic meaning of "sorrow songs," but the tradition and models of Shakespeare or Whittier, Pope and Stowe were as much the heritage of African Americans as were the laws and political structures within which they asserted their case for full participation.

Their appropriation of the western literary tradition is seen in their use of literary form, structure, and language. It is also obvious in the sources of many of their stories, for example, Wheatley's retelling of David and Goliath and Harper's epic, *Moses: A Story of the Nile.* Writers such as Henrietta Cordelia Ray wrote poems retelling myths such as that of Antigone and Oedipus and poems praising writers of Europe and of the New World. It is in Ray's poem "Milton," in fact, that one gets a glimpse of the aesthetic to which she and many others aspired. Milton, she says, had a divine gift that enabled him to "trace the rich outpourings of celestial grace mingled with argument" and thus solve the problem of redemption.[28] It is a commonplace that Milton's religion and politics were intertwined in his art. So too were the religion and politics of Ray and others.

Ann Plato, writing in the 1930s, was even more explicit about her literary goals. In "The Natives of America" her persona pleads for stories about her ancestors because she recognizes that the literature she reads is biased toward the whites. This particular poem deals explicitly with her "Indian fathers." It is clear, however, that the words, "In history often do I read, / Of pain which none but they did heed"[29] are applicable to her African ancestors as well. Ann Plato expected these comparisons would be made. She wrote for, and her book was marketed to, black people, especially young black girls. And in "To the First of August," Plato celebrates the emancipation proclamation of Britain and ends the poem with a statement of its intent and a call to "teach the rising race the way / That they may not depart" (115).

The ecumenism of early African American women's literature is verified by writers such as Charlotte Forten. Forten wrote in her journal that a poem such as Elizabeth Barrett Browning's "The Runaway Slave at Pilgrims' Point" was "most suitable to my feelings and to the times." "How powerfully it is written!" she exclaimed. "It seems as if no one could read this poem without having his sympathies roused to the utmost on behalf of the oppressed."[30] In another entry she shows her awareness of the multiple uses to which black women could put their literature. Forten notes, "This evening read 'Poems of Phillis Wheatley' an African slave, who lived in Boston at the time of the Revolution. She was a wonderful gifted woman, and many of her poems are very beautiful. Her character and genius afford a striking proof of the falseness of the assertion made by some that hers is an inferior race" (92). Forten wanted to continue the traditions of Browning and of Wheatley by combining powerful language that moved one's sympathies while refuting concepts of black inferiority. She worked earnestly to that end, writing and publicly reading her writing as often as possible. It was not easy but difficulty was no excuse for her or for other black women of her circle. In another journal entry Forten writes, "I do think reading one's composition, before strangers is a trying task. If I were to tell Mrs. R. this, I know she would ask how I could expect to become what I often say I should like to be—an Anti-Slavery lecturer" (91–92).

Another role model for Charlotte Forten was Frances Ellen Watkins Harper, poet, essayist, novelist, and anti-slavery lecturer. Harper, too, saw literature as a means of testimony and test. When her heroine in *Iola Leroy* says, "I wish I could do something more for our people than I am doing. . . . something of lasting service for the race," her companion, Dr. Latimer, replies, "Why not write a good, strong book?" and assures her that she has a "large and rich experience; . . . a vivid imagination and glowing fancy." With these assets, she could then "write, out of the fullness of [her] heart, a book to inspire men and women with a deeper sense of justice and humanity." Dr. Latimer continued, "Out of the race must come its own thinkers and writers."[31]

In her essay, "The Value of Race Literature," Victoria Earle Matthews confirms the ecumenical goals of testifying and testing. Matthews says that "race literature" will be a part of the literature of the world. It "will be a revelation to our people, and it will enlarge our scope, make us better known wherever real lasting culture exists, will undermine and utterly drive out the traditional Negro in dialect,—the subordinate, the servant as the type representing a race whose numbers are now far into the millions. It would suggest to the world the wrong and contempt with which the lion viewed the picture that the hunter and famous painter besides, had drawn of the King of the Forest."[32]

Matthews's statement says directly what many of her literary sisters and mothers conveyed more subtly—that is, their testimonies for themselves and for their people were done with an awareness, and an increasing articulation of that awareness, that their contributions were necessary for an authentic American literature. As Anna Julia Cooper has demonstrated in *A Voice from the South,* African American women were intent upon having their work and influence not only felt but proclaimed. Joining Harper, Matthews, and Cooper were other women, including Fannie Barrier Williams, whose speech at the World's Congress of Representative Women was published a year later as *The Present Status and Intellectual Progress of Colored Women.* Then Williams predicted that "In less than another generation American literature, American art, and American music will be enriched by productions having new and peculiar features of interest and excellence. The exceptional career of our women will yet stamp itself indelibly upon the thought of this country. American literature needs for its greater variety and its deeper soundings that which will be written into it out of the hearts of these self-emancipating women" (700).

Statements such as these invite us to reinterpret earlier writers. Phillis Wheatley, for example, wrote in the introductory poem to her volume that she intended to "snatch a laurel" from the head of Maecenas because Terence was certainly not the only African who could write in that tradition. Wheatley followed her invocation "To Maecenas" with "On Virtue." In that poem she petitioned Virtue, that "auspicious queen," saying:

> But guide my steps to endless life and bliss.
> *Greatness,* or *Goodness,* say what I shall call thee,
> To give an higher appellation still,
> Teach me a better strain, a nobler lay,
> O thou, enthron'd with Cherubs in the realms of day! (13–14)

The writing of these women who snatched a laurel and demanded the blessings of Maecenas, who petitioned Greatness or Goodness to learn even better strains and nobler lays, strongly suggests the intention to use standard written English in ways that extend and modify the tradition or that revise its original purposes and re-form the literary tradition. Insofar as their language demonstrated a sound education and singular poetic abilities, their writings were defiant statements that they too could, and would, sing. Given the racial attitudes of their times, these songs were not just songs of themselves but also songs for and songs of their people. In amalgamating the various examples of appropriate language and literature into their own creations, they became not reactors but actors redefining the uses and possibilities of literature and of language in ways that served their own purposes. These writers were not uniformly successful in achieving their intentions, but with their entrance into the tradition, it could not remain as it had been. They wrote defiantly or pleadingly, prayerfully or confidently, testifying to their lives and their experiences and testing the abilities of the language and their readers to convey and to understand the truths that—from the depths of their special experience—they knew. They, too, in their own ways, made it new.

TWO

"Sometimes by Simile, a Victory's Won"

Lucy Terry Prince and Phillis Wheatley

August 'twas the twenty-fifth,
Seventeen hundred forty-six;
The Indians did in ambush lay,
Some very valient men to slay,
The names of whom I'll not leave out.
Samuel Allen like a hero fout,
And though he was so brave and bold,
His face no more shall we behold.
Eleazer Hawks was killed outright,
Before he had time to fight,—
Before he did the Indians see,
Was shot and killed immediately.

. . . .

Eunice Allen see the Indians coming,
And hopes to save herself by running,
And had not her petticoats stopped her,
The awful creatures had not catched her,
Nor tommy hawked her on her head,
And left her on the ground for dead.
Young Samuel Allen, Oh lack-a-day!
Was taken and carried to Canada.[33]

The poem quoted above is "Bar's Fight," a straightforward, simply rhymed narrative commemorating an altercation between Indians and colonists in a frontier settlement. In what has been called "the fullest contemporary account" on record, the poet wrote into history an Indian attack that occurred August 25, 1746, in Deerfield, Massachusetts.[34] This skirmish was not one of colonial America's most significant battles; however, because of this writer, its victims are memorialized while countless others are not. The poem is not one of colonial America's most elegant either; but it is appealing enough to have become a ballad sung by several generations of New Englanders and to be published in the *History of Western Massachusetts* over one hundred years after its creation.

Like much poetry produced in colonial America, "Bar's Fight" was created to memorialize a particular event of local importance. Its narrator avoids direct commentary or analysis and focuses instead on describing a climactic episode. Its rhythm and its rhyme scheme are unpolished but adequate enough for easy comprehension and memorization. In short, "Bar's Fight" is a good example of eighteenth-century occasional poetry. Today, scholars might mention that *bar* was a colonial word for *meadow*. Some might observe that the poet used the word *men* for both males and females, but devoted the longest description to the fate of the female, Eunice Allen. There is little about this poem's content or style or language that seems unusual until one notes that its author was a sixteen-year-old slave girl, Lucy Terry.

With the introduction of the author's gender, race, and class, the readers' social attitudes and expectations influence their responses to the poem. For many modern critics, "Bar's Fight," like much early black literature, has been something of a problem. On the one hand, they are eager to embrace it as the earliest extant poem by a black person living in North America and as evidence that even when enslaved and systematically kept illiterate, black bards continued to sing. Yet these same critics often lament, as does Jean Wagner, that "The poem tells us nothing of its author, unfortunately, and has nothing specifically Negro about it."[35] Wagner is correct that there is nothing in the subject, language, or form of "Bar's Fight" that implies that it was written by a slave woman. But to call this "unfortunate" seems more an expression of personal preference than an aesthetic evaluation. Such lamentations speak more readily about the misperceptions of the reader than about any racial passivity or alienation of the writer. Yet the general tenor of the critics who labeled the eighteenth-century African American literature as "the Mockingbird School" on the grounds that these writers did not include anything "specifically Negro" is in itself more unfortunate. It implies that one's racial characteristics are not intrinsic, but must be proven by manifesting themselves through particular subjects, themes, or, perhaps, literary techniques. It implies that such manifestation, moreoever, must be overt and unmistakably "specifically Negro," when in fact one of the distinguishing characteristics of African American literature may well be that it is "masked," "two-toned," or "double-voiced."[36]

"Bar's Fight," like many other writings by blacks in the eighteenth and nineteenth centuries, focuses on experiences not directly resulting from slavery or racial prejudice. In so doing, it demonstrates a sense of empowerment and social awareness beyond that which some might ordinarily attribute to persons enslaved. Reading "Bar's Fight" in its social context offers new possibilities for interpreting the text, and the poem in turn promises to newly interpret Lucy Terry's world and the aesthetics of early African American writers. Such an approach in this case suggests that specific racial referents were not only unnecessary but antithetical to the poet's purpose. Based on the evidence of Lucy Terry's life and times, it is clear that by assuming the role of historiographer without acknowledging this as an unusual position for one of her sex, race, and class, Terry is using silence to amplify her message. The absence of racially explicit references does not so much imply misconceptions about her social status as it indicates that on this occasion, in this speech act, Lucy Terry chose to speak as significantly as possible.

The extent to which Terry's status influenced the reception of her work must be extrapolated by examining the tenor of her times. A brief summary of the historical context suggests that her racial identity was known and had considerable social importance. Though the issues would become more compelling during the Revolutionary War, the early eighteenth-century colonists were increasingly uncomfortable about the role of blacks in American society. Stirred by the "Great Awakening," some puzzled about the proper relationship between brothers and sisters in Christ who were racially distinct. Some recognized the paradox of asserting colonists' rights to traditional English liberties while denying those rights to a significant portion of the colonies' inhabitants. Others were less bothered by moral and philosophical implications than they were by the political and economic impact of the increasing percentage of black slaves within the population.

These various factors created a disease manifested by increasingly reactionary social behavior. Five years before the occasion for "Bar's Fight," arson attributed to a few blacks had stampeded New York colonists into an alarming display of racial prejudice. As during the notorious Salem witch trials, hysterical accusations by those who had themselves been accused snowballed the event beyond the power of logic. Only when several prominent white men were named as conspirators did common sense prevail. By that time the jails were packed with black people, thirty-one had been executed, and seventy had been expelled from the colony. Closer to Deerfield, in the same year the *Boston News-Letter* reported an incident in Roxbury, possibly the first recorded lynching in the country. And only a year before "Bar's Fight," Massachusetts passed a law prohibiting blacks from participating in the government lottery. White colonists were increasing the social distinctions between the races through legislation and overt racial discrimination. Obviously, black colonists, whether free or enslaved, were affected. Historian Winthrop D. Jordan concludes that what "had once been perhaps close to an actuality, that some free Negroes would think of themselves as full members of the white community," was no longer commonly assumed.[37]

There is little direct evidence of the extent to which general public sentiment was reflected in Terry's immediate situation. It could well be that her own experience of racism was less intensely hostile than those of blacks in other areas. Deerfield was a frontier settlement and, characteristically of such situations, racial and sexual discrimination tended to be less restrictive. But given the customs and practices of her own community, it is clear that she would have had "specifically Negro" experiences. According to Deerfield historian George Sheldon, slaves worked side by side with their owners and "became in measure members of the family holding them" (905). In certain years it was not unusual for the marriages and deaths of slaves to be recorded in the town book. But individuals such as town clerk Deacon Thomas French could and would unilaterally refuse services or recognition to blacks or slaves. Sheldon apparently intended to emphasize the racial tolerance of that particular community when he writes that some "semi-independent property" even had personal accounts at the local store and charged such items as jackknives, shoe buckles, and powder. These accounts were settled by cash or "foxes," and he declares, "I do not recall one [account] that is not balanced and square" (894). However, terms such as "semi-independent property" and the implication that these acts were privileges, not rights, testify to the separate and unequal conditions under which Lucy Terry lived. Moreover, Sheldon makes it clear that even in Deerfield, slaves were not treated as social equals. They ate and lived in their own corners of the family cabin or in outbuildings. Though they may have belonged to the same congregations, black members worshiped from separate pews.

Additional clues to Terry's own attitudes and responses to this situation come through the form and content of those fragments of her life with which we are familiar. At least two nineteenth-century historians verify that Lucy Terry was well known as a skilled communicator and an advocate of personal freedom. Her reputation was such and her impact was so profound that she was included in Josiah Holland's *History of Western Massachusetts*. In the section devoted to Deerfield, Holland writes, "The men of note who have originated in Deerfield have been many, but only a few can be noticed" (359). To represent Deerfield's first century, he chose two ministers, a senator, a lawyer, four military officers, and Lucy Terry. In a single paragraph, he identifies the eight men by title and contribution. To "Luce Bijah" (a combination of Lucy Terry's and her husband's, Abijah Prince, first names), Holland devotes an entire paragraph. In Holland's summary of the life of the woman he calls "one of the most noteworthy characters in the early history of Deerfield," he offers several anecdotes concerning her celebrated "wit and shrewdness," identifies her as "a poetess [who] commemorated in verse the event of the 'Bar's Fight,'" (360) and then prints the poem, thus preserving what is apparently the only extant example of Terry's poetry.

What is especially remarkable about her inclusion in the *History of Western Massachusetts* is the fact that Lucy Terry Prince moved from Deerfield sometime after her twenty-fifth birthday and lived most of her long, adventurous life in Vermont. It is possible that on the Massachusetts frontier, territorial boundaries and social attitudes were more relaxed and the possibilities for merit to outweigh racist or sexist attitudes made it easier for Terry to become a Deerfield legend in her own time. Still, as "Luce Bijah" implies, this woman was not accorded the respect that would compel the use of her surname or any title generally appended to adult women. In the mid-nineteenth century when Holland compiled his history, her designation as "a colored woman" and the identity of her former master remained a vital part of this legend. Finally, Holland's word choice, calling Terry a "noteworthy character" but calling the others of her time "men of note" is a significant diminution.

"Luce Bijah" also occupies a prominent position in *The History of Deerfield,* written by George Sheldon, descendant of early Deerfield settlers and president of the Pocumtuck Valley Memorial Association. Sheldon's account supplements Holland's by providing the genealogy of the Prince family and by offering a section on "Negro Slavery" in Deerfield. From Sheldon's account one learns that Lucy Terry was part of a visible black community and that her life with Abijah Prince was considered "a realistic romance going beyond the wildest flights of fiction" (901). According to Sheldon, Lucy Terry Prince was an established poet who may have held poetry readings at her house. He maintains that she composed at least two versions of "Bar's Fight."

As a slave girl, Lucy Terry could not have escaped knowing that her opportunities and privileges were different from those of girls who were white and free. Yet in spite of the restrictions placed upon her, she exercised what prerogatives she could. This is apparent as early as age five when during the "Great Awakening" the African child converted to Christianity. Though it was unusual for slaves to be accepted as members of New England congregations, at age fourteen Terry "was admitted into the fellowship of the church."[38] The self-esteem manifested by this woman must have impressed a number of people, including the man she married, Abijah Prince, a free black landholder from a neighboring town. How and when she was emancipated is not clear, but within a year of her marriage, her first child was born free. The Prince home became a community gathering place and the storytelling of Lucy Terry Prince was a central attraction. According to historian John Hope Franklin, she had "a seemingly limitless store of tales about Africa and other faraway places that filled many an hour with excitement and pleasure" (66).

Lucy Terry Prince's reputation for "wit and shrewdness" extended beyond the spinning of a good tale. Her linguistic facility was such that after she had argued her side of a land ownership dispute before the Supreme Court, Presiding Justice Chase declared that she had "made a better argument than he had heard from any lawyer at the Vermont bar" (Sheldon 950). When neighbors tore down her fence, Prince convinced the governor's council to insure that her family and property receive the protection accorded other citizens of the village.[39] In another celebrated instance, she addressed the Williams College board of trustees with "an earnest and eloquent speech of three hours, quoting an abundance of law and Gospel, chapter and verse," in a futile attempt to change their rejection, on the basis of race, of her son's application for admission (Sheldon 900). Lucy Terry Prince knew first hand the oppression of slavery and the burden of racial prejudice but she continued to assert her rights as a member of that community.

Reading "Bar's Fight" in context shows it to be a highly significant work. First of all, since "Bar's Fight" is, as far as we know, the earliest extant written poem by a black person in North America and one of a relatively small number of surviving texts, it seems obvious that black people, whether slave or free, did not ordinarily write commemorative verses in rhymed couplets. Moreover, we must remember that the paucity of extant literature is not peculiar to African Americans but that American literary history in general does not include many poems from the colonial period. Few colonial men and virtually no women had the education or the time to compose verse. From this perspective, "Bar's Fight" is an exceptional occasion in eighteenth-century American literature. And since few individuals, then as now, could know the origin of that poem and not be affected by its author's gender, class, and race, it is also a persuasive argument for new attitudes about slaves, blacks, and women.

Today, works such as "Bar's Fight" contradict established beliefs about the abilities and interests of early African Americans to such an extent that some scholars find it nearly impossible to accept their authenticity. Though they have little difficulty acknowledging the complexity of early black music and oral literature, they are reluctant to assume a similar level of sophistication with written language. This has led them to suggest that close textual readings are futile because there is no way of proving that the manuscripts reflect the black author's words. Since few voice similar doubts about the writings attributed to Anglo Americans, this is a suspiciously chauvinistic approach. Unless scholarship can prove that the words are not those of the author, especially when the personal and public facts support the possibility that they are the author's words, it is more logical to assume that, in general, the written version of works attributed to early African American writers are as authentic as the texts ascribed to Anglo American writers of the same era. Though biographical information does not prove that the extant version of "Bar's Fight" is exactly as Terry composed it, nonetheless, the known details of her life are strong proof that she was habitually inclined to dispute, discuss, and otherwise engage in compelling and complex discourses. And if, as Henry Louis Gates, Jr., and others have argued, the act of signifying derives in part from African culture and slaves early mastered that method of discourse, then to suggest that "Bar's Fight" ought to be read as significantly as possible is an appropriate proposition.

In Terry's poem we find no apology or other indication that she considered her poetic activity unusual. However, based upon what we know of her life, it is fair to assume that she was quite aware of racial attitudes that would consider her poetic expression surprising and that she was asserting her right to the language and to the poetic form in spite of those attitudes. It is reasonable to assume that "Bar's Fight" was written not simply in celebration of those who died but also in defiance of those who deny the creative spirit or circumscribe the range of their fellow humans.

The poem begins with apparent objectivity, stating the facts of the event; however, words such as *valient, ambush,* and *slay* in the third and fourth lines provide an interpretation of the incident. These were brave people who were entrapped by murderous Indians. The narrator's emphasis upon the elements of surprise and adventitiousness underscores the tragedy of that outcome. Eleazer Hawks couldn't fight because he was shot from ambush. Eunice Allen, though a mere girl, would have outrun her assailants had she not tripped over her petticoats.

In the fifth line, the poet begins to define the relationship between the audience and the narrator. The narrator makes a pact with the readers to be accurate and inclusive, promising not to leave out the names of those who died. The narrator is thus recognizing the claim to authority and the assumption of responsibility inherent in written history. Yet the narrator does manipulate the material and does omit one individual from this account. Caleb Allen, who also escaped, is not included in the poem. According to Holland in *The History of Western Massachusetts,* Eleazer Hawks died first, then Simeon Amsden, then Samuel Allen (175). Terry makes Allen first and Amsden "found dead" apparently by the survivors. In the published version of "Bar's Fight," the omission of the survivor increases the tragedy of the event, and in having Amsden "found dead" the focus shifts from the actions of the Indians to the actions of the townspeople.

There are many ways of explaining this breach of contract. In spite of her promises, the writer may have had inaccurate information and therefore got the sequence confused. Or the poem itself may have been longer and what exists is but a fragment of the original. Holland's version of the incident could have been muddled by time, and Terry, who lived during the event, may have been correct in her account. Equally as reasonable is to assume that the poet took license to arrange and to select according to her own purposes.

The latter interpretation seems to be supported by other elements of the poem. For example, historical accounts of this incident suggest that the Indians were looking for hostages when Eleazer Hawks, who was separated from the rest of the party, fired at an animal and startled the Indians into their attack. Terry omits this information and creates a more melodramatic situation wherein villainous "creatures" ambush valiant men and innocent women and children. In another instance, Terry develops the story of Eunice Allen more extensively than those of the other participants. The average number of lines for each individual is about two-and-a-half, with the exception of Eunice Allen. In six lines the poet gives a graphic description of Eunice Allen's encounter, including an interpretation of her intent ("Hopes to save herself by running"), prediction of her ability (had she not tripped, she'd have saved herself), and a three-line description that shows the young woman being caught, tommy-hawked, and abandoned for dead. Terry does not tell us that Eunice Allen lived (another seventy-two years). These emphases and omissions suggest that the poet is taking artistic control. By devoting six lines to a graphic description of the fate of thirteen-year-old Eunice Allen, Terry vilifies those who would so brutalize a young woman. She makes clear the shared danger of all settlers and the appropriateness of celebrating the heroic actions of women and children also.

Pronoun choices may provide some further idea of the author's persona. The statement that Oliver Amsden's death caused "*his* friends much grief and pain" (emphasis mine) reveals that the narrator was not a close friend of all the victims. Nor was the narrator a part of the discovering party, since she uses "they" to identify those who found Simeon Amsden's body. However, the narrator is certainly a member of the surviving community. Twice the narrator uses the inclusive "we" when articulating the surviving community's reactions. See, for example, line eight, where she says "His face no more shall *we* behold" (emphasis mine). When one considers the order, emphasis, and narrative stance, the poem may be seen as an autobiographical declaration.

Since both George Sheldon and Josiah Holland identified Lucy Terry Prince as a poet, it is probable that she earned this appellation on the basis of more than a few lines created when she was sixteen years old; however, no other works are extant. And it is probable that Lucy Terry also served as a model to other African American women including her daughter, Durexa, who, according to Sidney Kaplan, enjoyed a reputation as a poet in her own right.[40] Nonetheless, the record of black literary activity is silent until 1760 when Jupiter Hammon, a Long Island slave, published a broadside entitled *An Evening Thought: Salvation by Christ with Penitential Cries,* and Briton Hammon, "a Negro Man, Servant to General Winslow of Marshfield, in New England," published the fourteen-page pamphlet, *A Narrative of the Uncommon Sufferings and Surprising Deliverance of Briton Hammon.* One year after the publications by these two writers, the young girl who would become the next published black woman in the colonies was sold in Boston to John Wheatley, a merchant and prominent Boston citizen.

Some twenty years after "Bar's Fight," fourteen-year-old Phillis Wheatley published a poem, "On Messrs Hussey and Coffin," in the *Newport* (Rhode Island) *Mercury* on December 21, 1767. During the next two years, Wheatley published at least seven poems in London and New England. By 1772, she had enough material to advertise for subscriptions to a volume of poems. Though Wheatley enjoyed an international reputation as a poet and had a faithful band of local supporters, Boston was not ready to accept an African slave woman as a legitimate poet. In a letter of May 29, 1772, John Andrews apologized to a friend for not sending a promised copy, saying "The want of spirit to carry on anything of the kind here has prevented [publication]."[41] With the support of the Countess of Huntingdon, they found Britain more tolerant, and in 1773, what is apparently the first volume of literature written by a black in this country was published in London under the title *Poems on Various Subjects, Religious and Moral*.

Though slavery might be considered both a religious and a moral issue and though Phillis Wheatley was herself a slave, she did not directly address this issue in her book. Modern critics have regarded this as indifference to racial oppression, transference of hope from physical to spiritual freedom, or even worse, acquiescence to doctrines of racial inferiority. Some have suggested that Wheatley, having left Africa at age five or six and having enjoyed an unusually protected life as the personal servant of a well-to-do intellectual and relatively liberal Boston family, had little sense of enslavement. Yet close reading of the text in the context of Wheatley's personal situation and the general climate of the times makes it clear that Phillis Wheatley had deep personal concerns about slavery and freedom. The perspectives from which she explored the ideas of freedom and responsibility were both religious and secular. Her poems, especially when considered in light of her letters and the biographical facts available, are autobiographical in that they reveal her personal experiences and chronicle her resistance to socially imposed roles. Wheatley imbued her poetry with the sensitivity and passion of a slave woman as she revised traditional poetic forms and language to accommodate new messages.

During Wheatley's time, many white people were seriously debating the natural capacities for intelligence and sensibility that people of color possessed. In *White over Black: American Attitudes toward the Negro, 1550–1812* Winthrop Jordan states that both sides generally agreed that blacks were "ignorant, stupid, unteachable, barbarous, stubborn, and deficient in understanding" (187). Thus the debate among those who blamed environment for creating or exacerbating such characteristics was over the corrective stategies and their expediency. Cotton Mather, for example, believed blacks presented a special challenge: "their *Stupidity* is a *Discouragement*. It may seem, unto as little purpose, to *Teach*, as to *wash an Aethiopian*. . . . but the greater their *Stupidity*, the greater must be our *Application*" (Jordan 187). But a significant number of whites were inclined to agree with Samuel Davies's viewpoint that "Your Negroes may be ignorant and stupid as to divine Things, . . . not for Want of Capacity, but for Want of Instruction; not through their perverseness, but through your Negligence" (Jordan 188). Interestingly, this is the same sort of language and the same basic debate being carried on by eighteenth-century "progressives" about white middle-class women. By color and contour, Phillis Wheatley was caught in the midst of this controversy.

The Wheatley family, though slaveholders, were part of that religious missionary movement that advocated sufficient education of Indians and Africans to facilitate their salvation and to develop their evangelical skills. They had purchased Phillis as a domestic servant, but when she made her literary proclivities known to them, they were willing to teach her to read the Bible and to allow their daughter, Mary, to tutor her in a variety of subjects. The Wheatleys liked to astonish their friends with Phillis's progress. They encouraged visits and correspondence between what William Robinson calls this "little black genius" (24) and the leading clergy and intellectuals of their acquaintance. According to biographer Margaretta Matilda Oddell, a descendant of the John Wheatley family, Phillis willingly cooperated with her owners' attempts to exhibit her achievements.[42] Says Oddell, Wheatley "never indulged her muse in any fits of sullenness or caprice," but responded readily to the numerous requests for poems commemorating specific occasions (Oddell 435). Susanna Wheatley was extremely active in arranging publication of Phillis's poems and bringing her to the attention of an international group of luminaries. The reaction of Thomas Wooldridge, who visited the Wheatley household to personally verify Phillis's achievements, is typical. After talking with Phillis, he challenged her to write a poem about a subject he selected. She agreed. On November 24, 1772, Wooldridge described the result in a letter to Lord Dartmouth:

> she was no Impostor; I asked if she could write on any Subject; she said Yes; we had just heard of your Lordships Appointment; I gave her your name, which she was well acquainted with. She, immediately, wrote a rough Copy of the inclosed Address & Letter, which I promised to convey or deliver. I was astonished, and could hardly believe my own Eyes. I was present while she wrote, and can attest that it is her own production.[43]

The visits that astonished and entertained the whites were not without benefit to the slave girl. Phillis Wheatley met some of the most important figures in the creation of Boston as a cultural and political center. She claimed as her mentors such eminences as Joseph Sewall, Benjamin Franklin, and Samuel Hopkins. She corresponded with them and she read the books that they suggested. Wheatley studied the popular literary forms and knew well the preferences of her contemporary reading public. For her own poetry she chose forms that ranged from elegies and odes to narratives and dramatic monologues. Her language was the language of eighteenth-century neoclassical literature. Her allusions were from colonial current events, the Bible, and classical Greek and Roman literature. She sent her poems to General George Washington, the Countess of Huntingdon, the King of England, Harvard University students who might be inclined to neglect their studies or their God, "To a Lady on the Death of Three Relations," and to any one else with whom she felt inclined to communicate.

In a culture that fiercely debated the intellectual capacities of black people and, by implication, their basic humanity, the effect of regular neoclassical poetry written by a black woman was jolting. In Houston Baker's words, "When Caliban does not curse, but speaks in eloquent rational terms about his own situation, it is virtually impossible to ignore his distinctive, *human* presence."[44]

Phillis Wheatley was sensitive to these attitudes and saw her poetry as one way of disproving arguments for black intellectual inferiority. She encouraged this racial awareness by repeatedly referring to her African heritage in her poems, calling attention to her "sable race" and identifying herself as "Afric's muse." Critics such as William Robinson have noted the frequency with which she called attention to her race, but they have not always understood how integral a part of her literature such self-definition is. Robinson says "Indeed many of her self-conscious revelations of her black or African or Ethiopian identity are purely gratuitous, having little or nothing to do with the poems in which they appear"(*Her Writings* 118). Wheatley's naming of herself as black, sable, an Ethiope, and Afric's muse is, however, a deliberate assertion of authority and an intrusion into the dominant discourse concerning the innate capacities of blacks and of women. Like Lucy Terry, who dared to speak her version of history, Phyllis Wheatley not only spoke but deliberately spoke as an African. Her poetry was a political act.

At the same time, Wheatley was quite serious about aesthetics and her potential status as an artist. This created a difficult situation. Her supporters encouraged Wheatley to demonstrate her mastery of traditional literary forms, but they rigidly proscribed her subject matter. Wheatley's evangelical fervor earned applause, but her enthusiasm for classical mythology and her commitment to a literary career prompted concern and discouraging advice. Her poems were inevitably praised as exhibitions of an African genius cultivated by Christianity, yet those who praised her efforts also required that she be humble about her gifts. To them her deportment was as important as her intellect. In this, it can be said of Wheatley's supporters what Charles W. Aker said about Boston Whigs: they were "psychologically unprepared to grant actual equality to any Black or to appreciate the importance of the slave's cry for freedom."[45]

Phillis Wheatley wanted to become something more than an evangelical versifier. Though her religious ardor was real, her interests went beyond the Scriptures. Her poetry is replete with references to her desire to achieve higher levels of the art and her frustration over the hindrances to that goal. While the other Wheatleys would have been content for their prodigy to read the Bible and occasionally copy their dictated letters, Phillis's ambitions exceeded her owners' original intentions, as John Wheatley's letter in the prefatory material of *Poems on Various Subjects, Religious and Moral* makes clear: "As to her Writing her own Curiosity led her to it. . . . She has a great Inclination to learn the Latin Tongue, and has made some Progress in it" (vi).

Something of the problem that Wheatley faced may be seen from the letter of introduction that she bore from Richard Carey, one of those who signed the notice "To the Publick" which prefaced her volume. Says Carey:

This will be delivered your Ladyship by / Phillis, the Christian poetess, Whose Behaviour in England / I wish may be as exemplary, as it has been in Boston. / This appears remarkable for her Humility, and / spiritual-mindedness, hope she will continue an ornament for / the Christian name and profession, as she grows older / and has more experience, I doubt not her writings will / run more in Evangelical strain. (*Her Writings* 318)

Carey emphasizes the humility, exemplary behavior, and spiritual minded-ness of "the Christian poetess" more than her poetry. His hope that experi-ence and maturity will result in more "Evangelical" writings indicates that already there was some tension between the desires of her benefactors that she be "an ornament for the Christian name and profession" and other ideas that they detected in their protégée. Her patrons were that in both senses of the word.

Further exemplification of the patronizing that Wheatley endured comes from an exchange of letters with John Thornton, the British philanthropist for whom Thornton Hall at Dartmouth College is named. Writing upon her return from England, Phillis Wheatley expresses her great comfort in know-ing that she, like kings, prophets, and angels, can meditate upon the wonders of salvation and can aspire to join with Thornton in heaven where there would be no social distinctions. Phillis is bold enough to admonish Thornton to "disdain not to be called the Father of Humble Africans and Indians; though despis'd / on earth on account of our colour, we have this Consola-tion, if he enables us to / deserve it. 'That God dwells in the humble & contrite heart'" (201). Rather than acknowledge themselves as joint heirs, Thornton warns her against being misled by her success in London and her literary achievements. He cautions, "Many a good man is often a snare, by too openly commending his good quali- / ties, and not aware how undesign-edly he spreads a net at the feet of his friend. Your / present situation, and the kindness you meet from many good people, and the respect / that is paid to your uncommon genius, extorts this friendly hint from me" (*Her Writings* 41). Thornton's assurances that she had as yet done nothing to suggest ex-cessive pride must have been small comfort. On another occasion, Thornton seems concerned that Wheatley has too great an interest in poetics. He admonishes her thus: "When I want you to have increasing views of re-deeming Love, I did not mean, that you should be able to talk more exactly about it. . . . it is very possible to talk excellently of divine things, even so as to raise the admiration of others, and at the same time, the heart not be affected by them. . . . When I wish you to have increasing views of re-deeming Love, I would have you thrown into silent wonder and adoration of the wisdom and goodness of God."[46]

It is well known that eighteenth-century America required "decorum, formality, and dignity" in its literature. And it is hardly surprising that a young female writer would be continually cautioned as to her demeanor. Though colonial women were not yet confined to the rarefaction of the nineteenth-century Victorian pedestal, the world of letters was essentially male. Before Phillis Wheatley only one colonial American woman, Anne Bradstreet, had ever had a volume published. Wheatley well knew that her access to libraries, tutoring in the classics, and especially her publication opportunities were possible only by staying in the good graces of the men and women who were her benefactors. Moreover, as a slave who suffered bouts of ill health, Phillis Wheatley was entirely dependent upon her owners' encouragement and support.

Beyond the limitations of gender and class, Wheatley had racial problems as well. Apparently her supporters preferred that Phillis not only use her talents for evangelical purposes but that she avoid social contact with other blacks. According to Wheatley scholar William Robinson, she spent most of her days "reading or writing her 'poetic performances' before curious guests, or close beside her mistress reading and discussing the Bible, or visiting among ladies of Boston's first families, holding forth on 'feminine topics'" (*Her Writings* 25). The great-grandniece of Susanna Wheatley tells an anecdote that reveals the distance from other blacks that her owners attempted to impose upon Phillis. According to Margaretta Matilda Oddell, when Susanna saw Phillis riding beside Prince, a fellow slave, she declared, "'Do but look at the saucy varlet—if he hasn't the impudence to sit upon the same seat with *my Phillis*!' And poor Prince received a severe reprimand for forgetting the dignity thus kindly, though perhaps to him unaccountably, attached to the sable person of 'my Phillis'" (Oddell 434).

That Wheatley managed to have some black friends is clear. At least six letters are extant which Phillis wrote between 1772 and 1779 to her friend Arbour Tanner, a black woman who lived in Rhode Island. Lines such as "It gives me very great pleasure to hear of so many of *my Nation*, Seeking with eagerness the way to true felicity" (emphasis mine 190) reveal that she kept abreast of the activities of the black community. The poems addressed to Phillis Wheatley by black poets Jupiter Hammon of Long Island and Horatio of Boston verify that her poetry was read and admired by blacks also. Her marriage to John Peters and the resultant excommunication from the society of her white benefactors testifies to the cost she eventually paid for her racial pride.

It is also clear that Phillis Wheatley's artistic ambitions conflicted with the racial and sexual restrictions of her time. Any aspirations toward artistic or social liberty that she harbored were dependent upon her ability to meet the conditions set forth by the Wheatleys and those of their circle. Yet many of her priorities were significantly different from theirs. To reconcile her dilemma, Wheatley resorted to the kinds of linguistic ambiguity and diplomacy that formed the patterns for nineteenth-century African American literature. Phillis Wheatley wrote two-toned lyrics. Like Lucy Terry before her, she wrote poems which by their very existence were declarations of their claims to membership in the literary community and whose significance extended beyond the obvious.

Though Phillis Wheatley played the role of the eager scribe or versifier, there is ample evidence that Wheatley had "lofty aims" for her poetry. She regularly abandoned her domestic chores to work on her poems and so often interrupted her sleep to capture poetic thoughts that a "light was placed upon a table at her bedside, with writing materials, that if any thing occurred to her after she had retired, she might, without rising or taking cold, secure the swift-winged fancy, ere it fled" (Oddell 436). Her poems continually declare that she had "high design[s]" and that she wrote from urgings greater than those of mere humans. Consider, for example, the opening lines of "An Hymn to the Morning:"

> Attend my lays, ye ever honour'd nine,
> Assist my labours, and my strains refine;
> In smoothest numbers pour the notes along,
> For bright *Aurora* now demands my song. (73)

Though some of Wheatley's poems were created quickly in response to specific requests or events, as William Robinson points out, Wheatley "was forever rewriting her manuscripts." There are several manuscripts extant that show the care with which Wheatley revised many of her works.

Of particular interest are the differences between the manuscript versions and the poems published first for colonial readers, on the one hand, and those revised for the publication of her book in London, on the other. Some of Wheatley's militantly political poems such as "America" and "On the death of Mr. Snider Murder'd by Richardson" were omitted entirely from the British edition. Others were revised in ways that would be more appealing to a British audience. Sometimes these revisions were as slight as changing a title from the very specific "To Mrs. Leonard, On the Death of her Husband" to the more general "To a Lady on the Death of her Husband." Other times they are more obviously a result of her sensitivity to her audience's political attitudes. "To the King's Most Excellent Majesty on His Repeating the American Stamp Act" appeared as "To the King's Most Excellent Majesty. 1768." The last four lines of the manuscript version are:

> Thus every clime with equal gladness See
> When kings do Smile it sets their Subjects free
> When wars came on the proudest rebel fled
> God thunder'd fury on their guilty head. (127)

The published version omits the last two lines, ending with a sentiment less emphatic but more flattering to the king: "And may each clime with equal gladness see / A Monarch's smile can set his subjects free!" (53).[47]

Another example of Wheatley's political astuteness is found in the dedication of her volume to Selina Hastings, the Countess of Huntingdon. Perhaps her mistress, Susanna Wheatley, suggested the choice. Not only did Susanna Wheatley strongly support publication of Phillis's works, but she was acquainted with the countess and knew that she had lent her support to at least one other African writer. Nonetheless, it is equally possible that it was Phillis's idea to dedicate her book to the woman to whom she had dedicated an earlier broadside and with whom she had corresponded for several years. At any rate, Phillis knew the value of the countess's endorsement. On June 27, Phillis Wheatley told her, "I . . . am not insensible, that, under the Patronage of your Ladyship, . . . my feeble efforts will be Shielded from the Severe trials of unpitying Criticism and, being encourag'd by your Ladyship's Indulgence, I the more freely resign to the world these Juvenile productions" (194).

Even as she prepared for an unprecedented literary achievement, the publication of her collected works, Wheatley must have intended that it not be her last volume. In addition to anti-British poems, there were others that she excluded. John Andrews, an early supporter of Phillis Wheatley's poetic career, was probably not the only person who felt that Wheatley was "an artful jade" who "intends to have the benefit of another volume" (*Her Writings* 42).

Given her time and circumstances, Phillis Wheatley had need for as much artfulness as she could muster. A description of the volume that appeared in 1773 suggests the role that racial stereotypes were expected to play in the audience's response to the poetry. The first volume contained a preface that reassured readers that this slave girl was not acting out of an unseemly pride or sense of place. The preface affirms Wheatley's humility by assuring readers that "she had no Intentions ever to have published [her poems]; nor would they now have made their appearance, but at the Importunity of many of her best, and most generous friends; to whom she considers herself, as under the greatest Obligation" (45). In so doing, the preface conveniently overlooks the fact that Wheatley had published several of these poems before. Next comes the letter from "the Author's Master to the Publisher" describing the circumstances and extent of Wheatley's education, thereby assuring the audience that she had had an education that would have personally acquainted her with the literary and biblical sources of her material. The refusal of Bostonians to believe that poetry of this caliber was possible from an African sensibility made it expeditious to append a notice "To the Publick" signed by the governor, lieutenant governor, and sixteen of the "most respectable characters in Boston that none might have the least Ground for disputing their original" (48). These gentlemen assured their readers that "the poems . . . [were] written by Phillis, a young Negro Girl, who was but a few Years since, brought an uncultivated Barbarian from *Africa,* and has even since been, and now is, under the Disadvantage of serving as a Slave in a Family in this Town. She has been examined by some of the best Judges, and is thought qualified to write them" (48). Even this was apparently not enough, for upon the request of the Countess of Huntingdon, distribution of the book was postponed until Phillis's portrait could be inserted.

Once the authenticity of these poems had been established, the debate shifted to quality and the significance of the writer's achievement. The September 1773 review of *The London Magazine* is typical of contemporary response:

> These poems display no astonishing power of genius; but when we consider them as the production of the young untutored African, who wrote them after six months [*sic*] casual study of the English language and of writing, we cannot suppress our admiration of talents so vigorous and lively. We are the more surprised too, as we find her verses interspersed with the poetical names of the ancients, which she has in every instance used with strict propriety. (Mason 24)

It may have been easier to publish in London than in Boston, but the British reading public was not about to concede more than minimal talent to a black woman poet. The *Monthly Review* noted, "She has written many good lines, and now and then one of superior character has dropped from her pen," but judged her work "imitative" and without "endemial marks of solar fire or spirit" (Mason 25). Had they compared her work with that of Wheatley's predecessor, Anne Bradstreet, or even with contemporary English poets, her achievements may have been more apparent. Like Bradstreet, she was one of the best educated women in the colonies or in Britain. Both women betrayed an impressive seriousness about their writing, favored religious themes, but had some fairly progressive ideas about secular issues. They echoed the major linguistic conventions, catalogued the muses in their poems, and employed verse prologues. And perhaps most importantly, their poems are their refusals to accept an inferior status and their insistence upon recognition beyond stereotypes. Anne Bradstreet dared break the silences imposed upon women and wrote her versions and her visions. Phillis Wheatley's silence was imposed not simply by gender prescriptions but by those imposed by class and by race, yet she, too, created a place for herself in the literary tradition.

Though Phillis Wheatley achieved only a qualified acceptance as a poet, her critics did not suggest that something other than neoclassical occasional poems was expected. With her "many good lines" and some "of superior character," she did manage to convince readers such as Voltaire that "Fontenelle was wrong in saying there could never be poets among the Negroes. There is at this time a Negress who writes very good verse in English."[48] One of her earliest manuscripts demonstrates her attitude and perhaps signifies Phillis's quest when she writes: "Thy Power, O Liberty, makes strong the weak / And (wond'rous instinct) Ethiopians speak/ Sometimes by Simile, a victory's won. . . ." (135). Wheatley's literary acceptance rested upon her ability to create within the established tradition. The fact that she was able to manipulate that tradition to her own expressive needs and intents is outstanding testimony of her creativity and commitment.

Wheatley is not to be charged with excessive self-importance. Her poems and letters too often express her regret that she had not "the tongue of a

Seraphim." But it is plain that she considered herself a good enough poet to address, to admonish, and to interpret ideas and events to the more privileged classes. Phillis Wheatley wrote poetry from what she termed an "intrinsic ardor," bypassing societal approval and appealing directly to the muses for fellowship into the society of poets. One of the first indications of this comes in her introductory poem, "To Maecenas," the invocation, as it were, to the volume.

The poem begins by celebrating the power of poets to evoke a variety of emotions and experiences in their readers. After praising the achievements of Homer and Virgil, Wheatley continues:

> O could I rival thine and *Virgil's* page,
> or claim the *Muses* with the MANTUAN Sage;
> Soon the *same* beauties should my mind adorn,
> And the *same* ardors in my soul should burn:
> Then should my song in bolder notes arise,
> And all my numbers pleasingly surprize;
> But here I sit, and mourn a grov'ling mind,
> That fain would mount, and ride upon the wind.
> (emphasis mine 50)

In appealing to Maecenas, the patron of artists and specifically of Horace and Virgil, Wheatley is plainly declaring her desire to be not just a poet, but a great poet. "Could I . . . claim the *Muses* of the *Mantuan* Sage," she says, then she would create superior poetry and earn greater acclaim. The lines that follow imply that her "grov'ling mind" is not merely a result of insufficient genius. Instead, they suggest that her current artistic endeavors are influenced by racism. Not being of the same culture as Virgil, Wheatley compares her situation instead with that of Terence, an African who achieved poetic greatness in the same tradition which she now claims. Her words addressed to the muses are part question and part challenge:

> The happier *Terence* all the choir inspir'd,
> His soul replenish'd, and his bosom fir'd;
> But say, ye *Muses*, why this partial grace,
> To one alone of *Afric's* sable race; (50)

As if the latter line were not enough to identify Terence's race, Wheatley appends a footnote that says "He was an *African* by birth." Phillis Wheatley was, I believe, acutely aware that lingusitic facility, artistic impulses, a love and fascination for Latin and the Holy Scriptures were not perceived by the general reading public to be within the scope of black intelligence. But while that awareness may have hindered her literary exercise, she demonstrates her refusal to allow those attitudes to prevent or to define her poetic expression. Her citation of Terence shows that Wheatley was aware that an African could become an accomplished poet. It reminds her audience of that fact even as it declares her intentions to follow his precedent.

Wheatley continues that poem, defiantly:

> Thy virtues, great *Maecenas*! shall be sung
> In praise of him, from whom those virtues sprung;
> While blooming wreathes around thy temples spread,
> I'll snatch a laurel from thine honour'd head,
> While you indulgent smile upon the deed. (50)

Claiming authority from a higher source, "him, from whom those virtues spring," the narrator will presume to "snatch a laurel" from the patron she claims. Having asserted her determination, she then requests his blessing, saying, "Then grant, *Maecenas*, thy paternal rays / Hear me propitious, and defend my lays" (51).

Many of her lays were occasional poems written to commemorate a death, a near-death, or important community event. Although some were commissioned by their subjects, others were volunteered by Wheatley as her personal commentary. Whether commissioned or inspired, their narrative stance is significant. The poems usually address an individual, taking note of the occasion and moving quickly to an analysis or meditation upon the event in terms of its spiritual lessons. Death is projected as the end of earthly travail and the reward for virtuous living. Over and over she admonishes the grieved ones to stop their useless tears and put their own lives in order. Her tone is authoritative and her language is often forceful. For example, in "A Funeral Poem on the Death of C.E. An Infant of Twelve Months," she says

> Say, parents, why this unavailing moan?
> Why heave your pensive bosoms with the groan?
> To *Charles,* the happy subject of my song,
> A brighter world, and nobler strains belong.
> Say would you tear him from the realms above
> By thoughtless wishes, and prepost'rous love? (81)

The stance is not that of an inferior. Even when she makes reference to herself as having a "grov'ling mind" or being of a lower status, she does not shrink from admonishing her reader nor does she assume she should not voice her opinion. In "An Address to the Deist" she asks, "Must Ethiopians be employ'd for you? / Much I rejoice if any good I do" (123).

In spite of her fine manners, her attitude sometimes seems more audacious than self-deprecating. Consider, for example, the poem, "On Recollection," which she wrote after a conversation wherein several ladies marveled that they did not know any poems about recollection. Wheatley took the challenge and tried what apparently had not been tried. Her opening lines, which call upon the muses to inspire "Your vent'rous *Afric* in her great design" (76), seem to indicate her own concept of self.

Wheatley's poetry reveals her courage and self-assurance coupled with a fine sense of diplomacy and decorum. Her double-toned song is also heard in her choice of biblical and classical subjects. Her 1773 volume includes three such works, "Niobe in Distress," "Isaiah 63. 1–8," and "Goliath of Gath." Two of these are significantly longer than the other pieces in the collection and all three share a common theme of pride humbled. Such was a standard concern of religious writers of that day, but given Phillis Wheatley's position as a slave woman, her choice has a multiple significance. As an example, Wheatley's treatment of the biblical account of David and Goliath, like "Bar's Fight," is, on one level, a poem to record an event, to celebrate a life, to preserve a heritage. It begins thus:

> Ye martial pow'rs, and all ye tuneful nine,
> Inspire my song, and aid my high design.
> The dreadful scenes and toils of war I write,
> The ardent warriors, and the fields of fight:
> You best remember, and you best can sing
> The acts of heroes to the vocal string:
> Resume the lays with which your sacred lyre,
> Did then the poet and the sage inspire. (60)

In her first stanza Wheatley announces her entry into an established tradition as she petitions the muses to "aid" her "high design" and let her "resume the lays" of earlier poets. Her form, beginning with the invocation of the muses and the announcement of purpose, her mixture of both classical and biblical sources, her choice of couplets in iambic pentameter, and of course her celebration of a heroic warrior, is in keeping with established literary tradition.

Yet this poem is also a testimony beyond all this. Though titled "Goliath of Gath," the poem is actually a celebration of David. Wheatley focuses upon David as an unlikely hero, a young boy, an unskilled warrior and one who was, like herself, a servant. Like Wheatley, David was a lyricist who performed, by invitation, his own songs before royalty. Like Wheatley, the David of her poem perceived himself as having come from humble origins to a land distant from that of his birth, wherein he was privileged to distinguish himself through service to his master and his God. In taking on his task, David was accused of having aspirations beyond his place and when he received public attention, there was a clamor to verify his identity and origins.

As was traditional in recounting biblical stories, Wheatley freely embellished the original text. In contrasting the physical strength and military prowess of Goliath with the relative weakness, inexperience, but natural cleverness of David, her version echoes African American folktales. Like Brer Rabbit, David chooses the weapons with which he is most comfortable. He relies upon his familiarity of the briar patch, with, in this case, his slingshot and pebbles, and upon words.

In the biblical text, Goliath is the first to speak. He disdains David for his youth and his physical appearance, curses him and threatens his annihilation for being so presumptuous as to engage in combat with one of his stature. In Wheatley's version, David calls Goliath out, accuses him of trespassing the laws of God and declares that God's will must be done. David emphasizes the incongruity of the match saying "And thou shalt perish by a beardless boy" (64). He does not claim self-designation for this role, but pronounces himself to be following God's orders. His declarations are supported by another Wheatley innovation to this tale, an angel who proclaims that "servants their sov'reign's orders . . . perform."

A few stanzas later the narrator interrupts the tale, becoming herself a character and directing the reader to the theme of this story. Goliath had been "deaf to the divine decree" and God does not need "sword, nor spear," but will use the lowly to overcome the proud. Despite David's lack of stature or weapons, he precipitates a startlingly bloody end for Goliath. The elaborate scene in which she details the pierced skull, shattered brains and torrential blood by which Goliath's soul leaves his body betrays a less pacifistic attitude than one may expect from this quiet, frail young lady. Immediately after David defeats Goliath, Wheatley makes one of the most interesting deviations from her source. In the flush of his achievement, "th' illustrious victor" seems ready to take on the entire army, asking, "Where are your boastings now your champion's dead?" (66). He and Saul's army pursue the fleeing enemy. And at this point Wheatley jumps ahead of her biblical text to chapter 18 of 1 Samuel and alludes to the adulation awarded David for his slaying of tens of thousands compared to Saul's thousands, which begins Saul's jealous attempts to restrain his protégé.

Wheatley may be writing again from personal experience. The relationship between Phillis, the renowned poet, and the Wheatley family became increasingly ambivalent. Phillis obviously was fond of them. In a letter written after Susanna's death to her friend Arbour Tanner, Wheatley says, "I was treated by her more like her child than her Servant, no opportunity was left unimprov'd, of giving me the best of advice, but in terms how tender! how engaging!" (205). However, as the letters of introduction cited earlier imply, her patrons's concern that Phillis continue to demonstrate humility and decorum imply their uneasiness over Wheatley's increasing popularity. When Phillis traveled to England, Susanna Wheatley wrote to the countess, "I tell Phillis to / act wholly under the direction of your Ladiship" and "I have given her / money to Buy what you think most pro- / per for her. I like she should be dress'd plain" (*Her Writings* 33). These comments suggest that Phillis Wheatley may have been exhibiting increasing independence. Two subsequent letters from Phillis Wheatley mention her pleasure that the countess's endorsement will protect her from "uppity criticism" and voice "very great satisfaction" in knowing that the countess has befriended another African as a Brother. Furthermore, at least one of Phillis Wheatley's admirers suggests that Nathaniel Wheatley was jealous of the attention shown Phillis. Benjamin Franklin's account of his visit to her in London notes that "her master was there, and had sent her to me, but did not come into the room himself, and I thought was not pleased with the visit." Franklin suggests he may have offended Nathaniel Wheatley: "I should perhaps have inquired first for him; but I had heard nothing of him" (*Her Writings* 36).

Phillis Wheatley certainly was feted. She was even invited to remain until the opening of the Court of St. James for presentation to the King and Queen of England. Her patron, the Countess of Huntingdon, invited Phillis to visit her in South Wales. The countess did not repeat Franklin's slight—her invitation was to both Nathaniel and Phillis—but before that trip could be arranged, Mrs. Wheatley sent an urgent message for Phillis to return to Boston. Phillis was torn between concern for her mistress and her own desire to remain in London society, but she did return. Susanna's son, Nathaniel, did not.

Like David, Phillis Wheatley behaved herself wisely and obtained such admiration that John Wheatley bowed to British public opinion and manumitted the slave poet.

The remainder of her life is sketchy. Wheatley continued to write poetry, but after the death of John Wheatley, her marriage to a proud and ambitious black man alienated her remaining white Bostonian supporters. Perhaps it was her refusal to honor John Thornton's request that she go to Africa as a missionary or perhaps it was the approaching Revolutionary War, but her British support evaporated also. Though she occasionally published poems that were increasingly direct and self-assertive and she had a celebrated meeting with George Washington, Wheatley was unable to secure the necessary subscriptions for her proposed second volume, advertised as dedicated to Benjamin Franklin. She died in poverty, but not total obscurity. Her obituary was published in the Boston papers, and upon her death "Horatio" published his "Elegy on the Death of a Late Celebrated Poetess."

Phillis Wheatley, as well as Lucy Terry, used language to express a personal song and a communal one, to continue a tradition while developing one. Their language was always subjected to interpretations engendered by non-literary expectations. As poets and as black women they knew that the connotations of their poetry would be far more complex, complicated, and uncontrollable than other poetry, yet they refused to entertain literary bigotry, and they exercised their rights to use the language of the country within which they found themselves to contribute to and to create its literary traditions. Their poems are true autobiographical statements.

THREE

Equal Men but True Women

The Post-Revolution Literature

After Phillis Wheatley's death in 1784, there is a gap of almost fifty years before another African American woman is known to have published a complete book. On one hand, this is not so surprising. American literature in general was greatly skewed toward the publication of political pamphlets and manifestos during that busy period from the American Revolution until the rise of the Romantics in the mid-1830s. Though there are no extant books, there are enough petitions, letters, and brief writings to verify that African American women were not silent during the more than a half century between Wheatley's *Poems* in 1773 and Maria W. Stewart's *Productions* in 1835. For example, in 1783 "Belinda of Boston" petitioned the general court with an autobiographical statement that sketched her early years in Africa, her abduction and enslavement, and her eventual abandonment by her rebel master who fled during the Revolutionary War. Belinda published her life story in an attempt to hold the new government to its avowed recognition of the individual's right to life, liberty, and the pursuit of happiness. She was claiming her fair reward for her years of labor by requesting a share of her former master's estate. Belinda argued:

> The face of your Petitioner, is now marked with the furrows of time, and her frame feebly bending under the oppression of years, while she, by the Laws of the Land, is denied the enjoyment of one morsel of that immense wealth, a part whereof hath been accumulated by her own industry, and the whole augmented by her servitude. (Kaplan 215)

Belinda signed the petition with her mark. Historian Sidney Kaplan speculates that another black person, possibly Phillis Wheatley, served as amanuensis (214). Whether Belinda actually wrote the petition herself is less important than the fact that her presence and her perspective were committed to paper and thereby became a part of American literature. Though she apparently did not write the document herself, she certainly provided the information that it contained and by her mark she assumed responsibility for the document. Like Wheatley and Terry, Belinda tested the new country's ability to live up to the language by which it defined itself and she testified on her own behalf to her experiences and her expectations as a member of that society.

There are other documents from this period that reveal African American women's attempts to be heard. One such example is a March 8, 1795, letter from Judith Cocks to James Hillhouse, the man who by law owned her. Hillhouse had rented Judith Cocks to a Mrs. Woodbridge, but the two women did not get along. Though a slave by law, Judith Cocks was free enough in spirit to decide she would neither work for Woodbridge nor allow her son to remain with that woman. In her letter, Cocks informed Hillhouse that she had moved away and that she wanted him to help her obtain custody of her son, Jupiter, who Woodbridge planned to take with her to Connecticut. The feisty slave woman wrote her master, "I had much rather he wold return and Live with you as she allows all her sons to thump and beat him the same as if he was a Dog." Cocks assured Hillhouse that she did intend to return to him eventually, requested that he give her greetings to his family, and advised him not to show her letter to Mrs. Woodbridge. She concluded by assuring Hillhouse that "This is my handwriting."[49] Judith Cocks's actions demonstrate the liberty that some black women, though enslaved, claimed over their lives and the lives of their children. Her assurance that the letter was indeed written by her own hand further testifies to the authority she assumed. In writing her letter, Judith Cocks claimed the right to speak her version of the experience and to enlist the support of her master for her actions. She was testifying on her own behalf and she was testing the power of her own language to change her life and the lives of others.

The attitudes and the behavior of women such as Belinda and Judith Cocks were undoubtedly known and shared by other African American women for whom we have no written record. As literacy increased among American women and as the free African American population expanded, the number of African American women who could witness on their own behalf and on behalf of others rose. For them literacy became a means of liberty. Reading and writing became their way of changing their own lives and challenging others to change. Through education of themselves and of others, through the Word, the deeds could be manifest and justified.

Though they were indeed a minority, by 1818 there were enough educated black women with sufficient leisure to organize groups such as the Colored Female Religious and Moral Society of Salem. So strongly did they equate literacy and liberty that these women wrote into their constitution a provision to begin each weekly meeting with members "reading in some profitable book" and discussing passages from the Bible.[50] By the 1820s, societies devoted to women's "mutual improvement in literature and morals" were regularly meeting throughout the Northeast and the Mid-Atlantic to discuss contemporary issues and current publications. Within such groups, African American women found the encouragement to write and they made the contacts that allowed them to publish their writings. For example, members of The Female Literary Association of Philadelphia, including Sarah Louise

Forten, who wrote under pseudonyms such as "Ada" or "Magawisca," supplied William Lloyd Garrison with many of the poems and essays that he printed in *The Liberator* (Sterling 121).

By the 1820s it was fairly common to find poems, letters and essays by African American women in local, national, and even international periodicals. Like Phillis Wheatley, these early nineteenth-century women wrote on "various subjects, religious and moral." Generally, their writings were more obviously political, more outspokenly critical, and more evangelically fervent than Wheatley's. And this may have been one reason why few, if any, saw their collected works published in a single volume.

The next books by African American women began to appear in the mid-1830s. Among the separately published texts that appeared during this period were *Productions of Mrs. Maria W. Stewart* (Boston 1835), *The Life and Religious Experience of Jarena Lee* (Philadelphia 1836), *Essays; Including Biographies and Miscellaneous Pieces* by Ann Plato (Hartford 1841), and *Memoirs of the Life, Religious Experience, Ministerial Travels and Labours of Mrs. Zilpha Elaw* (London 1846). The fact that they were published in several different places, were concerned with different issues, and were created by women of different social classes suggest that these books did not emanate from the actions of a special coterie of well-connected individuals but that there was in fact something about the times and the circumstances of African American women's lives in general that had changed. And yet, there was a certain uniformity to these writings. Most were homiletic combinations of autobiography, poetry, and essay. Virtually all of them were informed by an evangelical enthusiasm and authority from the Bible. The authors had known themselves converted, justified, and even sanctified to the work of God on this earth and they were attempting to impress their interpretations and their concerns upon the society at large. Though Maria W. Stewart might single out "daughters of Africa" for special comments or Ann Plato might address a poem or two to school girls, in general these writers assumed the authority and the intention to instruct audiences composed of men and women of all races. Their wisdom and their motivation they assumed from God, but at the same time, each seemed compelled to defend the propriety of her engagement in public discourse.

A consideration of a few of the changes in the status of women and of blacks between the colonial period and the 1830s suggests why this was so. First of all, with the creation of the United States of America, men and women's roles were divided more distinctly and consciously. When Lucy Terry and Phillis Wheatley were writing, a woman's inclination toward the literary arts was surprising, eccentric maybe, but not "beyond her realm." During the colonial period, women often participated in economic, political, and literary affairs. Some ran businesses, some worked farms, and a few even voted and held public office. This is not to suggest that colonial America was free of sexual stereotypes or that women were not expected to focus their energies upon domestic concerns. The notion of women's basic subserviency to men had been transported along with other values and customs from the old country. But the necessities of frontier life had encouraged many pragmatic exceptions to the rule in order to insure survival and comfort in a new land. According to Alice Brown, one of the very few women historians in the nineteenth century, the early colonists were "English to the bone, though, once under these brighter skies, their outlook changed and their expression became swiftly modified by soil and climate and dramatic conditions which were absolutely strange."[51] But as the colonies became more stable, gender roles became more distinct. John Winthrop's comment about Anne Yale Hopkins helps illustrate the attitude that prevailed in the more established colonies. Winthrop wrote in his *History of New England* that Anne Hopkins was "a godly young woman, and of special parts" who suffered a mental breakdown because she had given "herself wholly to reading and writing, and had written many books. . . . if she had attended her household affairs, and such things as belong to women, and not gone out of her way and calling to meddle in such things as are proper for men, whose minds are stronger, &c. she had kept her wits and might have improved them usefully and honourably in the place God had set for her."[52] Winthrop's diagnosis assumes differences in roles and in abilities between the two sexes. Colonial American women were expected to attend to matters of the heart and hearth and to leave intellectual concerns to men. However, Winthrop's statement also shows that Puritan men did not totally deny women's cultivation of their mental facilities nor did they exclude them from the public debate. Anne Hopkins had been able to study and to write several books. Winthrop's criticism may be interpreted as opposing what he deemed Hopkins's immoderate behavior rather than her literary interests in general. Anne Hopkins had, Winthrop charges, given herself "wholly to reading and writing" and neglected her other duties. Such a way of acting during a time when every individual's labor was necessary for the survival of the community would have undoubtedly produced a fair amount of personal stress and communal consternation regardless of the colonial aesthete's gender. In the eighteenth century, successful colonization was first of all a matter of physical endurance and practical ingenuity. The fact that the New England emigrants had fled religious intolerance did not mean that they could or desired to encourage metaphysical explorations.

A factor that stems from gender divisions but manifests itself in ways most relevant to the creation of literature is the access to formal education and the decline of literacy among women relative to men. Among the first generation of New England settlers, 50 percent of the men and 33 percent of the women were able to sign their names.[53] By the end of the colonial period more than 80 percent of the men could sign their names, but only 40 to 45 percent of the women could do more than make their "mark" (Lockridge 42).

Generally, colonial leaders and some of their wives had at least a rudimentary education. But the number of colonists who had the literacy and the leisure to write for publication during colonial times was relatively small. As time passed and physical conditions became easier, more colonists could develop their intellectual and aesthetic inclinations. However, formal education was generally accessible only to the sons of the more affluent community leaders. In some cases a young woman of the privileged class was allowed a rudimentary education in order, as Cotton Mather argued, to "Enable her to do the *Man* whom she may hereafter have, *Good and not evil all the days of her Life*" (James 14). But since composition was traditionally an advanced subject, this meant that a young woman might be taught to read but not to write.

Nonetheless, colonial America was relatively hospitable to its intellectual women. According to Alice Brown, colonial women were not "encouraged in the pursuit of literature. . . . Still, when a star had really risen (especially if it took good care not to depart from its orbit; the woman poet must, . . . attend also to her household minutiae), it was hailed with acclamation" (156–57). And when compared to their European sisters, American women writers were relatively numerous. Emily Stipes Watts says in *The Poetry of American Women from 1632 to 1945*, "In the Course of Western civilization, poetry by American women is one of the first bodies of verse written by many women over an extended period."[54] Unless Watt's assertion is blatant hyperbole, our pride in the mere existence of early American women writers should be tempered only by our awareness of the profound loss to western literature that the absence of women's voices signifies. However, the literary achievements of women such as Anne Bradstreet, Mary Rowlandson, Sarah Kemble Knight, Mercy Warren, and Susanna Rowson are known to few of today's readers. And studies such as that by Emily Stipes Watts have charted the development of that literature from the apparently innocent verses that Anne Bradstreet dedicated to her family to the more assertive lays of Susanna Rowson, who in 1804 wrote:

> While Patriots on wide philosophic plan,
> Declaim upon the wondrous rights of man,
> May I presume to speak? and though uncommon,
> Stand forth the champion of the rights of woman?
> Nay, start not, gentle sirs; indeed, 'tis true,
> Poor woman has her rights as well as you;
> And if she's wise, she will assert them too. (Watts 68)

But the contributions of African American women writers were not so well promulgated then or now. The problems of gender were exacerbated by problems of race, and in some instances, of class. Yet, within the context of gender alone one can evaluate more clearly the changes between the writings and the attitudes of eighteenth-century women such as Alice, Lucy Terry, and Phillis Wheatley and those women who wrote in the nineteenth century. Even with the restrictions of race and class, the colonial black women took for granted interests and activities which by the 1830s were considered beyond the woman's sphere. Although Lucy Terry was unable to convince the trustees of Williams College to admit her son, she was able to present her petition to them personally. When her lawyer, Isaac Ticknor, seemed to need assistance in arguing her case before the Supreme Court, she joined him before the bench and demonstrated considerable rhetorical skill. By the nineteenth century, the restrictions against women's participation in public discourse would be by custom, if not by law, almost insurmountable.

Phillis Wheatley was quite outspoken about both religious and political concerns. She wrote to Harvard University students and admonished them about their academic and spiritual responsibilities. She wrote to the King of England concerning the repeal of the Stamp Act. She followed closely the events of the War of Independence and wrote to General Washington urging him to continue his good efforts but to do so only guided by virtue. And though a slave and unschooled, Phillis Wheatley's education was sufficient for her to publish a reply to a rebus that required familiarity with Hebrew, Latin, and British and American history.

Colonial women such as these whose literary creations have been preserved for this age, and, especially, those who were white and freeborn, were not prohibited by reason of gender from participating, at least verbally, in the worlds of international politics, metaphysical speculation, or social responsibility. Though women were considered subordinate to men, those who had sufficient education, enough leisure, or strong motivation to be concerned with matters beyond the hearth and home were usually able to exercise those interests.

Toward the end of the eighteenth century, however, as the forefathers began to conceive a new nation dedicated to the proposition that all men (of European origin) were created equal, they did not include women in their considerations. This did not pass unchallenged by women such as Abigail Adams. While husband John was in Philadelphia tending to government business, Abigail ran the farm, reared the children, served as a judge, and regularly kept her husband advised of the military and political situation in the Boston area. John Adams relied upon his wife's letters for their political briefings and he sometimes requested that she lobby particular civic and religious leaders toward causes they both supported. Excerpts from the correspondence between the Adamses during that period have become familiar examples of early feminist activity. In the famous segment from her letter of March 31, 1776, Abigail wrote:

> in the new code of laws which I suppose it will be necessary for you to make, I desire you would remember the ladies and be more generous and favorable to them than your ancestors. Do not put such unlimited power into the hands of the husbands. Remember, all men would be tyrants if they could. If particular care and attention is not paid to the ladies, we are determined to foment a rebellion, and will not hold ourselves bound by any laws in which we have no voice or representation.[55]

John's reply indicated his awareness that the revolutionary spirit had permeated all strata of colonial society but that he did not take seriously the declararations of independence by any but his fellow men. In his words:

> As to your extraordinary code of laws, I cannot but laugh. We have been told that our struggle has loosened the bonds of government everywhere; that children and apprentices were disobedient; that schools and colleges were grown turbulent; that Indians slighted their guardians, and negroes grew insolent to their masters. But your letter was the first intimation that another tribe, more numerous and powerful than all the rest, were grown discontented. This is rather too coarse a compliment, but you are so saucy, I won't blot it out. Depend upon it, we know better than to repeal our masculine systems. (155)

Her husband's reply shows him willing to indulge his wife's sauciness but taking her pleas no more seriously than he did the discontent of other subordinates. To John Adams and his fellow men, the democratic spirit of the times had stimulated a perceptible agitation among the lower orders that was a bit aggravating, but more amusing than threatening. Once the new rules were in place, he assumed things would settle down as before.

But Abigail, like the Indians, Negroes, students, and apprentices, was not to be so easily dissuaded. She wrote to her friend Mercy Warren:

> He is very sausy [sic] to me, in return for a List of Female Grievances which I transmitted to him. I think I will get you to join me in a petition to Congress. . . . I ventured to speak a Word in behalf of our Sex who are rather hardly Dealt with by the Laws of England which gives such unlimited power to the Husband to use his wife Ill. . . . So I have helped the Sex abundantly, but I will tell him I have only been making trial of the disinterestedness of his Virtue & when weighd [sic] in the balance have found it wanting." (Brown, 238–39)

True to her word, Abigail took up the matter again and again. In a letter of May 7, 1776, for example, she wrote:

> I cannot say that I think you are very generous to the ladies; for, whilst you are proclaiming peace and good-will to men, emancipating all nations, you insist upon retaining to men, an absolute power over wives. But you must remember that absolute power is like most other things which are very hard, very liable to be broken; and, notwithstanding all your wise laws and maxims, we have it in our power, not only to free ourselves, but to subdue our masters, and without violence, throw both your natural and legal authority at our feet. (169)

Abigail Adams was correct. The resistance to "absolute power" was more pervasive in American society than the framers of the Declaration of Independence had anticipated. Not only had the spirit of democracy permeated the masses but post-revolutionary economic and religious developments further threatened the patriarchal structure. As manufacturing and industry made the integration of life and work less complete, as the "work day" (that definable period during which one labored for the capital with which to purchase many of the things formerly created for oneself or by one's own family) became more standard, two things happened. It became clear that women, as well as men, could go outside the home for work and for reward. It became important to more men that some things, such as home and hearth, remain outside the turbulence of the rapidly changing world in which they found themselves. They wanted their homes to become castles, their secure retreats from the hustle and bustle that stimulated and frightened them. What was, as many historians have pointed out, an accepted way of life—that is, the woman being primarily in charge of the family and the home as her usual part of a shared commitment to the welfare of the family— became an ideal to which she was pressed to aspire. The notion of spheres became an ideology.

Nancy F. Cott summarizes it in this way:

> Long before publicists began to harp on woman's "separate sphere," women traditionally conducted their daily business in the household. For several mutually reinforcing reasons, . . . that domestic sphere became more conspicuous and more clearly articulated as woman's prerogative at the end of the eighteenth and beginning of the nineteenth centuries. The shift of production and exchange away from the household, and a general tightening of functional "spheres" (specialization) in the economy and society at large, made it seem "separate."[56]

The situation developed gradually, but by 1830 American society had embraced the "doctrine of domesticity." Within its tenets laws previously ignored and paternalism earlier checked by the requirements of frontier life were recognized and embraced. Gender distinctions that by circumstance were often more attitudinal than actual became prescribed practice.

The literature of the period played a vital role in reflecting these social attitudes and strengthening them. Again, I quote Nancy F. Cott:

> an emphatic sentence of domesticity was pronounced for women. Both male and female authors (the former mostly ministers) created a popular literature, consisting of advice books, sermons, novels, essays, stories, and poems, advocating and reiterating women's certain, limited role. That was to be wives and mothers, to nurture and maintain their families, to provide religious example and inspiration, and to affect the world around by exercising private moral influence. (8)

For some women, the notion created opportunities even as it eliminated some responsibilities. Barred from some arenas, women had full rein within others. Thus, within the "domestic sphere," some women were free to initiate and to manage their own activities. According to Carl N. Degler's interpretation, "Domesticity, in short, was an alternative to patriarchy, both in intention and in fact. By asserting a companionate role for women, it implicitly denied patriarchy."[57] Some feminist political scientists have challenged this interpretation of companionate marriages. They argue that while women may have been at the center of the private sphere, that sphere existed for, and was controlled by, men. Thus, they conclude that the domestic ideal was but another form of patriarchal control. While the fundamental necessity for and the manner of participation in the separate spheres is debatable, the doctrine of domesticity created, as the lives and works of many women of this period prove, the opportunity for both femininity and feminism.

We must remember, however, that our knowledge of women's attitudes toward the "doctrine of domesticity" comes primarily from material left by a relatively small group of middle-class white women in New England. Most of the journals, diaries, letters, and such that record women's points of view as well as the published literature of both male and female authors originate from and document New England society. New England shop girls and factory workers undoubtedly had a different reality from that of their middle-class sisters. Historians of Southern women's history, such as Anne Goodwyn Jones, have pointed out that the ideals and ideas of Southern white women had distinct differences from those of the North.[58] And for most indentured servants, domestics, and black slave women, the domesticity discussion was probably irrelevant. There is merit to Carl N. Degler's argument that "there is some reason to believe that middle-class family values and practices penetrated to lower social strata" (30). But it is also true that an icon of a culture does not necessarily typify it. Some women quietly and others not so quietly exercised substantial social power. Others were utterly exploited. Some publicly appeared as the dependent while in reality it was their labor that fed and clothed their husbands as well as the rest of their households. Nonetheless, the Cult of True Womanhood had a tremendous effect upon roles and words expected or tolerated by American society.

Middle-class black society was not immune to the doctrines of True Womanhood, but the circumstances of black women's lives did not allow them to fully subscribe to all its tenets. Genetics sometimes worked against the cultivation of pale complexions and eighteen-inch waists and even those whose ancestry included some of the "best white blood of the south" were quite aware of the painful circumstances that spawned their fair skins. Economics and the realities of social discrimination made probable that at least a portion of the black woman's domesticity would be realized in homes other than her own. Still, a casual comment in a letter dated March 23, 1835, from Sarah L. Forten, poet and prominent member of Philadelphia's African American community, to Elizabeth Whittier, sister of John Greenleaf Whittier, exemplifies the pervasiveness of magazine etiquette. Wrote Forten in a postscript, "I recall with feelings of shame, Hannah More's advice to young Ladies—wherein she recommends them, 'never to write a letter in a careless or slovenly manner—it is a sign of ill breeding or indifference' &c.&c. *My* excuse is haste—and one which I hope will for this time, at least, be accepted" (Sterling 122–23). Forten's was essentially a polite apology which was not meant to be taken seriously. She was an accomplished writer and so thoroughly a "lady" that she would never allow a careless or slovenly correspondence to be mailed even if, by chance, she should produce such an item. Forten's remarks indicate that though the lives and choices of some African American women may have been substantially removed from those of New England middle-class white women, middle-class black women read and considered the pronouncements of many of the same popular nineteenth-century writers as did their white counterparts. These pronouncements, centering as they often did upon morals and religion, may seem overly genteel to modern readers. When the texts are considered in context, it becomes more apparent that these writings were, as Sandra M. Gilbert and Susan Gubar assert, "covertly subversive, producing decorous surfaces that erupted to reveal indecorous, even Byronic, passions for liberty, as if many had decided to follow a dictum like Emily Dickinson's to 'tell all the truth / But tell it slant'" (*Norton* 186).

African American women writers in the first half of the nineteenth century were, almost without exception, like Sarah L. Forten, freeborn, northern, urban, and middle class. Working within or around the Cult of True Womanhood, they created a literature dedicated to moral improvement and social welfare. Their motivations and their justification for writing to the general public, even when blatantly political, were routinely articulated in religious terms. Their literary styles varied according to the current aesthetic tastes and their own interests and abilities, but overall these writers were pragmatic. They wrote literature intended to instruct and to please an audience that was more general than many of their contemporaries envisioned. These writers employed when useful the images, language, and structures common to white male literature, but they were increasingly direct and assertive in defending or correcting misconceptions about race and gender. As the abolitionist movement grew, African American women wrote more overtly on issues such as abolition, suffrage, and temperance; but during the first part of the century, their writings emphasized religious conversion, angelic living, and heavenly hopes.

The separate sphere ideology was a major consideration for African-American women writers in at least two ways. Often they addressed individual works to a female readership. For example, Ann Plato identifies her intended audience in the title and in the text of her poem "Advice to Young Ladies." The poem begins:

> Day after day I sit and write,
>   And thus the moments spend—
> The thought that occupies my mind,—
>   Compose to please my friend.
>
> And then I think I will compose,
>   And thus myself engage—
> To try to please young ladies minds,
>   Which are about my age. (93)

Secondly, their writings generally espoused the true womanhood ideology even as they reinterpreted that doctrine to support a wider sphere. Plato's "Advice to Young Ladies" admonishes them to embrace religion and to strive to live angelic lives. At the same time, she prefaces this by advising them to become educated and to develop their women's literary tradition:

> The greatest word that I can say,—
> I think to please, will be,
> To try and get your learning young,
> And write it back to me. (93)

Moreover, Plato's final stanza may be interpreted as insurgent feminism. Plato concludes her "Advice":

> Perchance that we may ne'er fulfill,
> The place of aged sires,
> But may it with God's holy will,
> Be ever our desires. (93)

In her "Lines upon Being Examined in School Studies for the Preparation of a Teacher," Plato repeats these tendencies. She expressly desires "To cultivate in every youthful mind, / Habitual grace, and sentiments refined" (94). This seems, on the surface, to be quite fitting for a young woman. "True women" were cultivated, graceful, and sensitive. As wives and mothers, they were expected to create homes and to rear children with these attributes. However, the word "every" extends the narrator's responsibilities beyond her immediate family and suggests a larger, more public role. Moreover, the occasion of this poem, the interview for a job, is unusual for a woman. "Lines, Written on Being Examined" contrasts the "mere worldly" with the "true intelligence" and concludes with the affirmation that her goals and her success are determined by God. In the final lines of this poem, Plato uses the word "sphere" twice, but the interpretation that she gives to this word is not the usual one assumed by the more conservative elements of society. The poem concludes:

> Oh, grant me active days of peace and truth,
> Strength to my heart, and wisdom to my youth,
> A sphere of usefulness—a soul to fill
> That sphere with duty, and perform thy will. (94)

The volume within which these poems appear was published in 1841 as *Essays; Including Biographies and Miscellaneous Pieces, in Prose and Poetry*. The closing poem of Plato's volume suggests that she intended to publish a sequel, but there is no record of any other work by this young woman. In fact, very little is known about Ann Plato beyond that extrapolated from her text. She was an educated young woman, probably a schoolteacher, and her literary efforts were supported by the Reverend J. W. C. Pennington, a former slave who had become the minister of the Hartford Congregational Church and was the author of several published works himself.

The number of newly rediscovered writers from the first half of the nineteenth century suggests that Ann Plato in Connecticut along with "Ada" and "Sophonisba" in Philadelphia and Maria Stewart in Boston were part of a widespread and serious group of African American women determined to do more than merely make their marks. They intended to continue Phillis Wheatley's legacy by snatching their laurels and presenting their lays. However, the particular middle-class women's literature that they represent did not become the pattern in African American women's literature until nearly a half century later. Their basic design was woven in more vivid color and detail by an African American woman of the working class who, empowered by the same evangelical urge but decidedly non–middle class, was freer to respond to her spiritual promptings. Jarena Lee's work and words reached a larger cross-section of African Americans than did those of most writers of that era.

FOUR

"Great Liberty in the Gospel"

Jarena Lee's Religious Experiences, Life, and Journal

The Life and Religious Experience of Jarena Lee, a Coloured Lady was first published in 1836 in Philadelphia.[59] It is a very small volume, about twenty pages long, which begins with Lee's birth in 1783 and ends when Lee had become a prominent evangelist. Lee's narrative describes briefly her childhood, then focuses upon her religious conversion and the process of her sanctification. Lee devotes the majority of her text to her efforts to fulfill the charge that she believed God had given to her, that she "Go, preach the Gospel" (156). At the time that *The Life and Religious Experience* was published, Jarena Lee had been actively traveling and conducting religious services for almost twenty years. Her evangelism had taken her up and down the eastern seaboard into slave states, into Canada, and as far west as Dayton, Ohio. Believing hers to be a message for all humankind, Lee preached to women and men, to free people and slaves, to African Americans and Anglo-Americans and, with the help of translators, to Indians. During one four-year period she traveled sixteen hundred miles, many of them on foot, sometimes preaching twice a day. Yet her desire was to reach even more of the "fallen sons and daughters of Adam's race" (160) and her narrative was intended as an extension of her ministry. She had been anxious to publish her life story for a long time but it was not until 1833 that she could accumulate the money necessary to finance the editing of her journal into a publishable manuscript. Even then, she was unable to afford the extensive narrative that she had desired, and *The Life and Religious Experience* ends abruptly at 1821 with a comment that it would take another two hundred pages to include all her material and with the promise that she would publish a longer work later. In 1849, Jarena Lee fulfilled this promise by publishing the *Religious Experience and Journal of Mrs. Jarena Lee.*[60] This "revised and corrected" version was "written by herself" and brought her life history up to 1842.

The *Religious Experience and Journal* was nearly three times as long as *The Life and Religious Experience*. The 1849 text was constructed primarily by inserting before the last two paragraphs of the 1836 text some seventy-five pages that detailed her ministerial efforts: the miles she traveled, the Scriptures from which she preached, the number of people converted, and the people with whom she interacted along the way. The *Religious Experience and Journal* is, as William Andrews has noted, "often tedious reading,"[61] but it does in fact give us an expanded self-portrait of Jarena Lee and of the writings of the period that her text represents. Though the first twenty pages of both versions are the same, the 1849 edition is a substantially different work. The change in title, the repetition of particular information and experiences, the postscript with which it ends all create a tone and content that require readers to understand the first pages differently. The basic effect is that the expanded version contextualizes certain experiences in the early pages, heightening their significance and accentuating the increasingly stringent limitations upon women's freedom of movement and of speech outlined in the previous chapter. *Religious Experience and Journal* shows that the sin against which Jarena Lee struggled was as much manifested by the increasing restrictions against and silencing of women and the lower classes as anything else. And while there is little information available by which we can compare the public reception of the 1849 edition with that of its predecessor, details of its publication history indicate that this second work excited more controversy. Unlike the 1836 narrative, which was tolerated and even supported by church leaders, this 1849 text stirred strong resistance and biting criticism. Yet through it all, Jarena Lee claimed essentially the same right to testify against prevailing and stronger authority as did earlier women writers. As she wrote in the 1849 journal, "I had my talent and to use it I was not ashamed" (*Journal* 76).

Emulating the techniques of reversal demonstrated by Phillis Wheatley in "On Being Brought from Africa" and "An Address to the Deist," Lee uses her alleged inferiority to emphasize the power of her message and in so doing, she, too, implies an authority superior to those whom she addresses. Implicitly calling upon the New Testament admonishment that the last shall be first, Jarena Lee presents her success as an evangelist as an example of God's ability to use even "a poor coloured female instrument" to convert sinners and to carry out His divine plan. She directly confronts the clergy who were attempting to organize and control religious expression by reminding them to avoid placing their logic and their rules above God's. "O how careful ought we to be, lest through our by-laws of church government and discipline, we bring into disrepute even the word of life," she warns, and continues "For as unseemly as it may appear now-a-days for a woman to preach, it should be remembered that nothing is impossible with God" (157–58). Lee continues this argument for a full two pages, citing numerous instances of God's using women for His work and repeatedly contrasting divine omniscience and omnipotence with human interpretation. "Is God straitened; must he take the man exclusively? May he not, did he not, and can he not inspire a female to preach the simple story of the birth, life, death, and resurrection of our Lord, and accompany it too with power to

the sinner's heart" she argues. And separating herself from those who are
not convinced, Lee claims divine empowerment: "As for me, I am fully
persuaded that the Lord called me to labour according to what I have received, in his vineyard. If he has not, how could he consistently bear testimony in favour of my poor labours, in awakening and converting sinners?"
(158).

Jarena Lee wrote and published through the authority of her religious
conviction. She had neither formal education nor social status to make it
easier for her, but nonetheless she "felt a great liberty in the gospel" and
through that she was empowered to overcome the obstacles that one of her
gender, class, and race inevitably faced in trying to speak the Word and
make it clear. Though she does not give the details of her struggle to write
and publish her life story, Lee does confess that once the bound volumes
were delivered, she lost her confidence. But then, she says, "my mind was
directed to a Presbyterian sister and on my way I met Bishop Allen's widow
who bought one, and that afternoon I sold one dollar and fifty cents' worth"
(*Journal* 77). Buoyed by their ready acceptance, she began to sell her book
at "camp-meetings, quarterly meetings, in the public streets, &c." (*Journal*
77). The Bishop Richard Allen had long been one of her supporters, but it
is important that when her resolve weakened, Lee's "mind was directed" to
his wife, that it was her sisters to whom she turned and from whom she got
not simply moral but financial support. Eventually Lee's first literary efforts,
while not applauded by everyone, were, like those of Maria W. Stewart, Ann
Plato, and Zilpha Elaw who followed her, supported by both women and
men. Finally, the narrative was so well received that when during a visit to
Cincinnati, Ohio, she had exhausted her supply, church officials encouraged
her to republish the work. Accordingly, she arranged a second edition of
one thousand copies, which were printed in Cincinnati in 1839 (*Journal* 85).

The Life and Religious Experience of Jarena Lee, a Coloured Lady is
an excellent example of literature by African American women published
during the early nineteenth century. Currently, it is believed to be the next
separately published volume by an African American woman after that by
Phillis Wheatley. The precedent for African American women to use their
experiences as literary subjects began with Lucy Terry and Phillis Wheatley,
and by the time that Lee published her work, it was not unusual for African
American women to write biographical essays and to publish lettters and
personal essays. But as the earliest extant personal narrative written and
published by an African American woman Lee's narrative represents a new
development in that literary tradition. However unique her choice of genre,
Lee does share with other African American women a design of purposeful
writing within both a women's and an African American literary tradition.

Jarena Lee's *Life* is "women's literature," for the religious evangelical
experiences that she recounts were generally those encountered by most
women who embraced the Calvinist Methodism of that period and whose
personal interpretations of their religious duties went beyond that of joining

ladies' auxiliaries or becoming ministers' wives. Like those by other women, Lee's narrative assumes a readership of both sexes but acknowledges more than male texts do the presence and the specific interests of female readers. It is "African American literature," for her experiences were colored by prevailing racial attitudes that influenced Lee to regularly identify individuals by race and often to mention peculiar burdens and opportunities imposed upon her ministry by racism. Like most early nineteenth century writing by African Americans, Lee's narrative assumes a black audience as well as a white one and incorporates elements from both cultures. Understanding Jarena Lee's narrative in particular and African American women's writings in general requires that one understand how their texts reconstruct both traditions in ways that resemble both but are unique to themselves. The discussion of Jarena Lee's *Life and Religious Experience* that follows will emphasize the influences of her multicultural literary heritage upon her narrative's form and content as an example of how this reconstruction works generally.

The most important literary strands from which Jarena Lee's accounts are constructed are American spiritual autobiography, the Christian conversion experience as recorded in the New Testament, and the particular adaptations of both of these by women and by African American writers. Nineteenth-century American spiritual autobiography continued a literary tradition that had produced Augustine's *Confessions* and Bunyan's *Grace Abounding*. The best known examples in the American colonies were the narrative journals created by Puritans and Quakers during the eighteenth century, but Americans of all persuasions believed it was their duty to record their most noble or praiseworthy achievements. Believing there is no more praiseworthy quest than that for salvation, they had produced diaries, journals, testimonies, broadsides, pamphlets, and full-length books that chronicled the religious experiences and convictions of repentant criminals and esteemed church leaders; of soldiers, sailors, ransomed captives, and freed slaves; of Puritans, Calvinists, Quakers, and Methodists; of men, women, and children from all social classes and educational levels. Spiritual autobiographies were exceedingly popular during the seventeenth and eighteenth centuries, but the Second Great Awakening revived and revised the genre.

In keeping with current evangelical theology, the nineteenth-century spiritual narratives had at least one significantly different focus from earlier narratives. Calvinist theology had presented a God of stern and unknowable aspect. He and He alone determined those whom He would choose for salvation and those He would not. Such theology inspired the Puritans to examine closely their actions and attitudes to confirm their fellowship in the elect; this preoccupation was reflected in their autobiographical works. Quaker writers were less concerned with verifying their salvation. According to Daniel Shea in *Spiritual Autobiography in Early America*, the Quakers related their long searches for Truth, searches which were inevitably founded in the Society of Friends' doctrine. The essential elements of such narratives included "the influence of pious parents, decisive or extraordinary spiritual experiences, adoption of Quaker beliefs, and the evangelizing activities, frequently involving extensive travel, which followed from his new convictions."[62]

The teachings of the evangelical revivalists, particularly those of Charles Wesley and the Methodists, presented a more benevolent God than the Puritan God. Theirs was a God that promised happiness to individuals who dedicated their lives to making a world more in accord with God's purpose. Central to Calvinist Methodist belief was the idea of salvation by Grace. That is, individuals could influence their own lives; they could, in fact, make choices that encouraged the prospect of a greater peace on earth. But first, they had to acknowledge their sinful natures, completely dedicate themselves to God's service, and "take up the cross of Jesus Christ and follow Him." Bearing witness to their choice was a central concern of their narratives.

Overall, American spiritual autobiographies were narratives of religious testimony, the spiritual and ministerial experiences of those who heeded God's call. The narratives began with an apologia for publication which was at once a denial of egotism and an assertion of special authority. God, they all maintained, prompted the author to write as witness, as a prophet to reveal His workings on earth, to stimulate converts, and to reassure the converted. In the spiritual autobiography, the writer's individuality is subordinated to the writer's instrumentality as God's servant. Language and form are highly conventional, echoing both the biblical and the English literary traditions upon which the narrative is modeled. The document is essentially a chronological, first-person account that begins with birth or childhood and continues until shortly before its publication, with only occasional digressions to argue theology or to interpret biblical passages. In spiritual autobiography, details such as family history, physical descriptions, education, occupations, the names and circumstances of siblings, spouses, or children, and even the dates and places of crucial incidents in the narrator's life are minimized. The spiritual narrator's secular or personal experiences are given as means of contrast, as points from which to identify the difference between corporeal and spiritual development, and are not allowed to obscure the primary intentions of the narrative. This reticence to present the non-religious aspects of their experiences is particularly noticeable in the cases of women narrators, many of whom, including Jarena Lee, identify themselves only by their married names.

A good example of how this worked out in African American spiritual narratives is found in *A Narrative of Some Remarkable Incidents in the Life of Solomon Bayley* (1825). The first words of the narrative are "Solomon Bayley, unto all people, and nations, and languages, grace be unto you, and peace from God our Father, and from the Lord Jesus Christ."[63] After a paragraph that asserts his intention to leave his personal testimony to God's kindness and mercy, Bayley then begins, "I was born a slave in the state of

Delaware, and was one of those slaves that were carried out of Delaware into the state of Virginia" (591). He then describes his attempts to become legally free, a process which was symbolic of and, in some ways, a result of, his attempt to become spiritually free. Although he mentions his wife, family, and various individuals with whom he interacted, Bayley rarely identifies them by name. His focus is upon his spiritual strivings.

Jarena Lee was one of many who kept a religious journal which later provided the details for her publications. Both of Lee's books are chronological accounts written with a mixture of biblical rhetoric and plain language. *The Life and Religious Experience* and the beginning of *Religious Experience and Journal* appear very similar to other spiritual narratives of the time, particularly those by the "holiness" segment within Calvinist Methodism. They espoused a spiritual progression of three phases. First there is a sudden and traumatic conviction of sin; the sinner repents and begins to strive for grace or a sign of redemption. During this time the penitent experiences a series of temptations and struggles with overwhelming guilt, often including suicidal urges or physical illness. Then comes a personal conviction of salvation and, eventually, sanctification. Finally, the narrator relates the experiences of this sanctified life as that of an evangelist who suffers, and succeeds, along lines similar to those of Jesus Christ and His early disciples.

The narratives of sanctification are a form of spiritual autobiography but they modify the earlier works to such an extent that they are sometimes subcategorized as conversion narratives. They go beyond the actual conversion, however, and cover an extended period of the author's life or examine in minute detail the daily activities and thoughts that define the quality of her or his election. They are declarations of sanctification, of the writer's election to serve as an example of God's power, as a guide to conversion for sinners, as a model of determination and strength to converts, as a manifestation of the saving power of Grace.

The sanctified narrator's description and analysis of her or his conversion is a central part of the work; however, the conversion occurs fairly early in the narrative and the emphasis is upon the process from repentance and justification by faith to the development of conviction and sanctification. The story is told in two parts, first the conversion experience or the testimonies of the penitent's awakening to a sinful state, the struggle with the fear and guilt which that discovery induced, and the circumstances under which the convert is ultimately convinced of personal salvation. Then follows the evangelical process, of which the narrative is in fact a part. The sanctified individual struggles to bring the good news to others and by those efforts to help bring about God's plan. The narrator presents life before conversion as an existence in slavery to sin, the life afterwards as a progression toward salvation. Such progress is presented, most often, as a journey, beset by trials and dangers, from imperfection to perfection, from bondage to freedom. It is not unusual for the narrator to indicate that she or he had been unusually inclined toward or interested in social things, the "ways of the flesh," that she or he had, in fact, persecuted or ridiculed those perceived to be Christians.

The Holiness theology provides the basic pattern for narratives such as that by Jarena Lee, but the narrators found their archetypal model in the New Testament account of the transformation of Saul. During a journey to Damascus, Saul, the persecutor of Christians, is metamorphosed into Paul, the principal founder of Christian theology. The change is all the more miraculous because Saul was not an obscure or intellectual disbeliever. Saul had acquired a reputation as an activist and a major threat to the emerging Christian church. At the beginning of the persecution against the church in Jerusalem, Saul had held the coats of those who stoned Stephen. His zealousness had increased to the point that he requested and received warrants to ferret out and to persecute Christians wherever he might find them. Saul was on just such a mission when he was confronted by God. Though traveling with a large entourage, all of whom heard the judging question: "why persecutest thou me?" Saul alone saw the "blinding light." From this experience Saul temporarily lost his sight, his authority, and his direction only to emerge with a new vision, a new name, and a new mission. His new life was as adventurous as his former one. His service was neither easy nor safe. But by his strength, his courage, and his testimony, Paul became an example of God's power and of a sanctified life. Like others, Jarena Lee believed herself to be a part of this tradition. She likened herself to Jonah and other prophets, quoted Scripture, and, most important, she not only described a conversion experience strikingly similar in both incident and language to Saul's but also made direct comparisons between her life and his.

Jarena Lee was not born a Christian. "My parents being wholly ignorant of the knowledge of God, had not therefore instructed me in any degree in this great matter," she wrote (148). Yet, she suddenly realized her blindness when after having lied to her mistress about the completion of a task, "the spirit of God moved in power through my conscience, and told me I was a wretched sinner" (148). Shaken with guilt, she vowed to reform but did not. Like most conversion narrators, Lee persisted in her sinfulness with occasional twinges of conscience until one fateful day. For Lee, it came in 1804 when attending a religious revival: she was confronted with an overwhelming realization of worthlessness and guilt. She was so distraught that she decided to kill herself but was prevented by an unaccountable change of emotion which she later came to know as "the unseen arm of God" (149). Lee's mental turmoil was such, however, that she became deathly ill for three months. Upon regaining her strength, she spent much time searching Scripture, visiting churches, and praying. Yet she was unable to find solace until she encountered a particular messenger from God, whereupon Jarena Lee began the next phase of conversion.

In the biblical account, Saul realized his guilt and was physically incapacitated. Blind, unable to eat or drink, sorely troubled, he prayed for relief. Then God sent Ananias and, "At once something like fish scales fell from Saul's eyes." In Jarena Lee's case, she heard the words of Richard Allen, a Methodist minister and the founder of the African Methodist Episcopal Church, and she says:

> That instant it appeared to me as if a garment, which had entirely enveloped my whole person, even to my fingers' ends, split at the crown of my head, and was stripped away from me, passing like a shadow from my sight; when the glory of God seemed to cover me in its stead. (150)

Her progress was not without its detours and pitfalls. She describes her experiences according to Holiness theology through the words of William Scott who, like Ananias to Paul, appears to help the penitent Jarena. He advises her that "the progress of the soul from a state of darkness, or of nature, was threefold; or consisted of three degrees, as follows: First, conviction for sin. Second, justification from sin. Third, the entire sanctification of the soul to God" (155).

After due searching and suffering, Lee one day heard a voice, followed its instruction, prayed, and felt "as if lightening had darted through me." She recalled that a "spirit said, 'Bow down for the witness—I received it— *thou art sanctified!'* The first I knew of myself after that," she says, "I was standing in the yard with my hands spread out, and looking with my face toward heaven" (156). After her sanctification, Jarena Lee was called to preach. As it had been with Saul, many Christians were at first suspicious of her and she was subject to the hostility of unbelievers, to their verbal abuse and life threats, as well as to the physical hardships of the itinerant preacher.

Like other religious autobiographers, Jarena Lee wrote her story as a continuation of her ministry. She was certain of the significance of her existence. She knew herself to be a prophet and an exemplar not by her own efforts but through God's grace and for His plan. Said Lee, "For the satisfaction of such as may follow after me, when I am no more, I have recorded how the Lord called me to his work, and how he has kept me from falling from grace, as I feared I should" (168). In all essential features, *The Life and Religious Experience of Jarena Lee* and the beginning of *Religious Experience and Journal* conform to the basic patterns of American spiritual autobiography as derived from the New Testament example of Saul of Tarsus.

Equally as important as the New Testament influences are the African American influences. To begin with, there was an African tradition of praise songs which can at least account for the African Americans' openness to the autobiographical tradition. Though African culture may have placed less emphasis upon the individual and significantly differed in its religious beliefs from the Christian concepts that underlay American spiritual narratives, praise songs were statements of self-identity as well as historical accounts of ancestral lives and times. These oral narratives may well explain certain stylistic features recognizable in early African American texts such as the petition mentioned earlier by Belinda of Boston and in Olaudah Equiano's *Interesting Life*.

Secondly, although spiritual autobiographies by African Americans were, at first, quite similar to those by other colonial Americans, there were subtle differences. One of the earliest African American autobiographies, *A Narrative of the Lord's Wonderful Dealings with John Marrant, a Black* (1788) is an example of both conventionality and difference.[64] Using the basic conversion narrative formula, Marrant briefly summarizes his early life. He was born in New York, and he lived in Florida and Georgia before arriving in Charleston, South Carolina. At age eleven, Marrant refused to learn a trade, insisted upon becoming a musician, and soon mastered the violin and French horn. His musical talent and his dancing opened "a large door of vanity and vice," and Marrant confesses that by the time he was thirteen, he was "devoted to pleasure, and drinking in iniquity like water; a slave to every vice suited to my nature and to my years" (181). His early movements suggest his rootlessness and contribute to his "Everyman" characterization. His popularity as an entertainer demonstrates his leadership in activities generally understood by Calvinist Methodists as sinful.

Like Saul of Tarsus, Marrant was also on an anti-Christian mission when he was converted. En route to a dance, he chanced upon a revival meeting and agreed to disrupt that service by blowing his horn during the sermon. But just as he was about to blow, the minister pointed in Marrant's direction and announced the test by saying, "Prepare to meet thy God, O Israel." Marrant continues, "The Lord accompanied the word with such power, that I was struck to the ground, and lay both speechless and senseless" (182). Marrant's companions, like Saul's, witnessed the effects of his encounter with God but did not experience it themselves. When he had recovered his senses, Marrant was beset with anxiety and guilt and could neither eat nor sleep. On the third day of his travail, he was relieved by the intercession of a Christian model who, like Ananias, had been sent as a mentor. Once converted, John Marrant began a series of trials. His family and friends decided he was mad. Marrant became suicidal, but was saved by fasting and prayer. He fled the hostility of his family and neighbors, wandered through the wilderness, and avoided harm and hunger by what he understood as God's providence. Eventually, Marrant met an Indian who became his companion and guide. Marrant's first evangelical efforts were with the Indians. Later, he was sent to Nova Scotia where his ministry was directed at both blacks and Indians.

Marrant's narrative, emphasizing his conversion and missionary experiences, was well received. Published first in London, it went through five editions in its first year. His narrative appeared in several countries and was translated into Welsh. As late as 1820 new editions of the revised and en-larged version were still being published in the United States.

Though essentially a conversion narrative, John Marrant's work com-bined elements of several popular genres; some of the narrative's success may be attributed to its combination of adventure, piety, and a shrewd narra-tive strategy. It has elements of the Indian Captivity narrative. Like John Smith, Marrant encountered hostile Indians and was saved from execution by the chief's daughter. It is a war story. Marrant was pressed into service by the British during the Revolutionary War, during which time he endured great storms at sea, fought courageously, and was wounded. And it has certain romantic elements: for example, he was the lost son who survived wilderness experiences and returned from presumed death.

This literary experimentation was not accidental, for there is sufficient textual evidence to indicate that the narrative was written with a knowledge of generic conventions and reader expectations. We are told that Marrant related his story to William Aldridge, who retained Marrant's ideas though not always his language and who made "no more alterations . . . than were thought necessary" (180); thus, there is no reason to believe that the narra-tor's voice is not that of John Marrant. Marrant assumed that his life and his experiences had significance and he published them, he stated, "in hopes they may be useful to others, to encourage the fearful, to confirm the waver-ing, and to refresh the hearts of true believers" (180). At one point Marrant says, "The following particulars, . . . are less interesting; and yet, perhaps, some readers would not forgive their omission" (195). In another place he presents an account of the conversion of a young girl, "in hopes the Lord may make it useful and profitable to my young readers" (197).

In intent, structure, and subject matter, *A Narrative of the Lord's Won-derful Dealings with John Marrant, a Black* is basically a conversion narra-tive. John Marrant recounts the same kinds of experiences, espouses the same religious beliefs, and engages in the same publication ministry as white conversion narrators; however, the title page proclaims a distinctive factor. The protagonist is a black man. Marrant's narrative shares this peculiarity with works by other African American writers. From the earliest examples of *Briton Hammon, Negro Man* (1760) to *Olaudah Equiano, or Gustavus Vassa, the Africa* (1789) to *Solomon Bayley, Formerly a Slave* (1825), *A Colored Female of Philadelphia* (1832), and *Jarena Lee, a Coloured Lady* (1836), the names of African American authors were regularly identified by race. Obviously, such insertions manifest the assumption of a crucial difference. And, the very significance of that difference becomes apparent when one considers the rarity of white writers who identify themselves by race and of male writers who include the fact of their sex. The writings of blacks, and women, were the unusual, the Other, and were so identified even when their form and content were virtually indistinguishable from those of white men.

When considered from this perspective, other details become more important. For example, John Marrant's narrative was first published in London, where it enjoyed enormous success. Probably most of its initial readers were white. Though his narrative was similar to many other best-selling works of that time, the preface by his editor William Aldridge, the vocation of Marrant's patron, the Countess of Huntingdon, and the appendices from his former employer suggest that someone had determined that John Marrant had a greater than usual need to establish his authority and that the endorsement of these individuals would accomplish that aim. Critics such as Robert Stepto have demonstrated that the use of such "authenticating devices" was characteristic of nineteenth-century slave narratives.[65] These devices, however, began with early black writers such as John Marrant.

It is not unimportant, then, that Jarena Lee's title identifies her as "A Coloured Lady." In so doing her narrative follows a tradition of African American literature, a tradition which on one hand appears to acknowledge a difference important enough to mention specifically but which on the other implies an equality of experiences and the legitimacy of erecting an African American life as an example. In the specific instance of Jarena Lee, this duality includes a challenge to and an extension of the concept of a "lady." The tenets of "True Womanhood" assumed physical as well as social attributes that African American women did not generally possess. The concept of a "Coloured Lady" would startle many readers, for it contrasts greatly with the portrait of the pale, modestly—even elegantly—costumed, genteel woman most often imagined. Many of her readers would find Jarena Lee's claim to the title especially surprising since she was a dark-skinned, poor widow who placed her child in the homes of others and pursued the unusual and dangerous life of an itinerant evangelist of a radical fundamentalist religion. There are many other examples of small modifications in African American literature. Such changes alone may seem accidental or trivial until their aggregate in many works by black or female writers or their regular absence in works by white men calls attention to their significance.

Modern readers are also apt to overlook or to devalue references to specific experiences with racial connotations with which the writers' contemporaries were much more familiar. John Marrant, for example, published his work to be "useful to others" (180). The others in the late eighteenth century were explicitly recognized as people of color, for while he was examined and ordained in London, John Marrant was officially commissioned to preach to the Indians and blacks of Nova Scotia. In general, *The Life and Religious Experience of Jarena Lee, a Coloured Lady,* like Marrant's narrative, subordinates racial considerations to spiritual ones. Yet, when Jarena Lee wrote her narrative, the antebellum period was dawning and racial discrimination was increasing in the United States. Her readers would recognize some obstacles in her spiritual journey as precipitated by racism and that furthermore, Jarena Lee's frequent identification of individuals as "a coloured physician," "an aged slaveholder," or "a coloured friend" were not gratuitous. This "Coloured Lady," like Marrant, wrote her narrative "for the satisfaction of such as may follow after me, when I am no more" (168). The stated intention of her work is religious, and those who "may follow" her were most certainly those who would accept the religious doctrines which her life and her narrative espoused. As an evangelist Lee did not restrict her efforts to a particular denomination, class, or race. Her ministry, like her autobiography, was addressed to what in the nineteenth century was often termed "a promiscuous audience," that is, an audience of males and females from various backgrounds. Jarena Lee emphasized that, during her ministry, she preached to whites and blacks, free people and slaves, Southerners and Northerners without distinction. Contemporary readers would recognize, however, the conditions under which Lee ministered to her various audiences. For example, like Amanda Smith and Zilpha Elaw, two other African American evangelists who wrote accounts of their spiritual labors, Jarena Lee spent considerable time at camp meetings. In general, such meetings were integrated and preachers of both races addressed mixed congregations. Yet even camp meetings carefully adhered to certain protcol. For example, physical accommodations were usually racially segregated and certain activities or services were dominated by whites and others by blacks.

Social and political issues do not dominate Lee's *Life and Religious Experience* because it was axiomatic that every individual, regardless of social condition, ultimately faced the same basic choice between heaven and hell. At the same time, religion was a social commitment that allowed the pleasure of fellowship with saints and the duty of proselytizing sinners. Though the spiritual quest was expected to be a sojourn apart, Jarena Lee's autobiography makes clear that slavery and racism make the quest of even the most spiritually minded individuals more isolated than it would otherwise be. Moreover, Jarena Lee makes it clear that spiritual progress was complicated by the fact that she was a black woman. There are several instances wherein Jarena Lee interrupts the narrative flow to comment on the impact of race or to include occurrences that illustrate the effects of racism. Perhaps the most significant example concerns her search for a church home. Jarena Lee was awakened to her own sinfulness by the preaching of the British evangelist Joseph Pilmore and by a Presbyterian missionary. For a while she worshiped with Pilmore's largely white congregation, but as she noted, "it appeared that there was a wall between me and a communion with that people, which was higher than I could possibly see over, and seemed to make this impression upon my mind, *this is not the people for you*" (150). Lee does not tell how she came to attend the English church where she worshipped for three months, but she does clearly indicate that "a wall" made her consult another domestic servant; with that individual's help she discovered the congregation where Richard Allen preached. Her first visit convinced her that "this is the people to which my heart unites" (150). Readers of her time would recognize immediately the racial implications of Lee's affiliation. They would know that during the time Lee joined Allen's congregation, it was known as the Free African Society and was in the process of becoming the African Methodist Episcopal church. They also knew that the African Methodist Episcopal separation from the Methodist Episcopal church was not from matters of theological principle but because of the attitudes of intransigent white racists and the resulting determination by black Christians to establish a congregation wherein they would be respected.

Another of the ways in which the unique experiences of African Americans informed their texts is seen in the Solomon Bayley narrative cited earlier as an example of biblical language and the conversion narrative form. Bayley's narrative, like those of many African American slaves, established a concomitant process of freedom from sin and freedom from slavery. Those narratives pose "slavery" as "evil" and give "freedom" both a physical and spiritual dimension. Lee's 1849 text is more explicit in this than the one with which we are primarily concerned here. But when the *Religious Experience and Journal* is read against the 1836 narrative, the subtleties of the earlier text are highlighted.

It is not my contention that Jarena Lee was consciously evoking the African praise song tradition nor that she had read John Marrant's narrative, or even that she made a belated response to Solomon Bayley's call. I am suggesting, however, that when Jarena Lee was writing her *Life,* African Americans had developed a discernible narrative tradition. Among the early religious narratives that helped shape this literature and with which Jarena Lee may have been familiar are *A Narrative of the Uncommon Sufferings, and Surprizing Deliverance of Briton Hammon, Negro Man* (1760), *A Narrative of the Lord's Wonderful Dealings with John Marrant, a Black* (1785), and *A Narrative of Some Remarkable Incidents in the Life of Solomon Bayley, Formerly a Slave* (1925).

Beyond the general influence of African American literary tradition, there are more specific possible models for Jarena Lee's narrative. First, Richard Allen was Jarena Lee's pastor, friend, and mentor. Allen had been the amanuensis for John Joyce's narrative, and Allen's own work, *The Life Experience and Gospel Labors of the Rt. Rev. Richard Allen* had been published in 1833, only three years before Lee's. There is, moreover, direct evidence that Jarena Lee was familiar with at least one other contemporary African American religious narrative. In her 1849 text, she mentions a work called "the Essence of John Steward, a coloured man" which she says told of "his miraculous call to the ministry" and his success in "Christianizing the Methodist Indians in Sandusky" (*Journal* 48). A Methodist preacher in Albany, New York, introduced her to Steward's work. From this we can also surmise more about the impact of African American literature upon less read or illiterate people, for Lee's comments concerning the Steward text reveal that books such as these were discussed in church services. In this instance, John Steward's book had greatly enhanced a revival at the Albany church by encouraging them to hold a fast (*Journal* 48).

Clearly, Jarena Lee knew herself to be part of a literary tradition. As had American autobiographers from Puritan days on, Jarena Lee had kept a journal. On her final pages, Lee reveals that her journal furnished the material for her narrative and that it contained material enough for a book almost ten times as large as the narrative which she was then writing. Apparently this journal was quite extensive and the product of many years of recording her experiences, and while Jarena Lee did not claim special literary skills, she clearly believed that her life was exemplary, her words were valid, and her written testimony merited publication. Her assertion of authority begins on the title page, which informs the reader that this publication had been "revised and corrected from the original manuscript, Written by herself." The strands from which Jarena Lee wove her narrative were patterned after the American spiritual autobiography: they were colored by the particular variations of her African American cultural heritage, but they were shaped by her condition as a woman of the early nineteenth century. Women writers of that time, even when their techniques and subject matter were basically the same as male writers, shared cultural contexts that shaped their thematic emphases. Those emphases were generally formed by the convergence of the doctrine of domesticity with the religious revival that swept the United States during the turn of the century. The Second Great Awakening and its offspring, the Holiness movement, were not limited to a particular denomination; they were characterized by unprecedented demonstrations of interdenominational and interracial cooperation. Nonetheless, the Wesleyan Methodist movement had a major impact upon the Second Great Awakening in general and upon Jarena Lee's work in particular.

In retrospect, it is easy to understand why militant Wesleyan Evangelicalism particularly inspired women and people of color. First of all, John Wesley was himself more liberal toward women than most religious leaders. He encouraged them to speak publicly and to assume positions of leadership and responsibility. While Wesley's attitudes toward women were not always shared by other Methodist ministers, his sanctions did establish precedents. Moreover, the teachings of the Methodists with their declaration of justification by faith, their promise of redemption, and their corresponding threat of ultimate punishment for those who sinned against others had particular appeal to individuals who felt oppressed or impotent. And perhaps most important was the concept of conversion and sanctification that the Second Great Awakening proclaimed. There was a great democracy in the assertion that all humans were sinners but that the gift of salvation was free to all who would believe. It put men and women of all races on essentially the same plane. They were brothers and sisters in Christ. In addition, the ideas of conversion and sanctification made some people feel more powerful because the decision to surrender to God was actually an act of will, a decision made for and over one's own life. For some individuals, whether victims of racism or sexism or simply those floundering in the sea of social changes that urbanization and industrialization had created, the only power they believed was spiritual.

The upsurgence of militant Protestantism was the source of practically every other significant social movement of the nineteenth century, and women constituted the bulk of these Christian soldiers. This was especially noticeable in the Southern states where at the end of the eighteenth century white women constituted as much as 60 percent of the membership of the evangelical churches even though men were the numerical majority in the South. At first, this was not perceived as a catalyst for social change. The organizations that the women formed were auxiliaries to those headed by men, and as with the traditional family the women who headed these groups were subject to the authority of the men. The women's roles as teachers, nurses, missionaries, and other servers were perceived as mere extensions of the domestic sphere.

Women may have begun their organizing as helpmeets inspired by the religious flames of their fiery-tongued ministers. But as Abigail Adams prophesied to her husband, the women began to realize that "wise laws and maxims" notwithstanding, they themselves possessed the power to effect change. They had discovered that power through the doctrines of domesticity, conversion, and sanctification. Nancy F. Cott explains that "The submission required of those who were to be saved was consistent with female socialization, but this submission was also an act of initiation and assertion of strength by female converts. Conversion set up a direct relation to God's authority that allowed female converts to denigrate or bypass men's authority—to defy men—for God."[66]

Cott and others agree that religious conversion signaled a "new birth" into an extended family of "sisters" and "brethren." This church family often replaced the biological family in providing a sense of security, a sense of purpose, and a model for living. The support of other female converts and the religious duty to become a worker for Christ strengthened female bonding and encouraged the formation of women's groups. Since the doctrine of domesticity identified women as "naturally moral and benevolent," few objections were raised. This convergence led, for many, to the idea that "the world is only a large home" (Degler 298). Thus, "woman's sphere" expanded and that expansion created for wives and mothers, in particular, the psychological and social space in which to develop their ideas of self and to realize their greater power. Carl N. Degler points out that "for many married women religious activities opened up new horizons without calling into question their domestic duties or outlook. . . . The moral character of these early benevolent societies and concerns encouraged women who worked in them to slip over into activities with a strong aura of social reform about them" (302). Nowhere was this more evident than in the emergence of female evangelists. In her article "She Hath Done What She Could,"

Barbara Welter explains that women who pursued a divine calling, the missionaries abroad or at home, were distinguishing themselves outside the home and hearth of a mere man:

> the itinerant preacher who spoke until midnight and was off in her jinrikisha at dawn, felt herself necessary and important. Unlike many American women she defined herself in terms other than those of her husband and children. The historian of the religious experience must always consider that, however much religion involved the working out of social, political, and economic necessities, it was also a matter of individual will and conscience. For the nineteenth-century American woman, on the foreign mission field her life had meaning and joy and was infused by a sense of privilege at being the special recipient of God's grace. As they said on their gravestones, "She hath done what she could."[67]

Most women did not wander far from their hearths, but those who did quite often wrote about their experiences and their testimonies were published and read and vicariously experienced by many others. These publications signaled a change in women's self-identity. To write of one's religious conversion or one's evangelistic experiences was to write of oneself as an individual of worth and of significance. And to write of these experiences as a woman was to change the genre. Jarena Lee's narrative demonstrates several of those changes common to women's conversion narratives.

Sexism was a reality in Jarena Lee's life which had to be accommodated in the narrative form. The description of the actual conversion was not particularly different from other narratives. Lee could and did recognize her sinfulness through direct confrontation with the Holy Spirit. She was instructed in the process of sanctification by one who had been sent to help her. She knew herself to be sanctified and she accepted her responsibility to proclaim the gospel to others. It was here, in her efforts to follow a ministry to which she believed herself called by God, that the conflict for Jarena Lee, as for other women, appeared. After his conversion, Saul "went straight to the synagogues and began to preach about Jesus" (Acts 9:20). Those who heard him were amazed at his conversion—but that was an aid to his purpose, for he was then proof of God's power to change lives. When Richard Allen, Lee's mentor, received his call to preach, he not only went freely about the countryside but he was helped in his efforts by a series of established church leaders. With Jarena Lee, the church authorities and religious community had no problem accepting the validity of her sanctification; they balked, however, at the notion that a woman may be called to minister. Richard Allen explained to her that he knew of an instance wherein a woman had verbal license to exhort and that she apparently had "done much good. . . . But as to women preaching, . . . our Discipline knew nothing at all about it—that it did not call for women preachers" (157).

Lee tried to reconcile the inner voice she heard with the words of those among whom she lived. At first, she did the conventional thing. She married a minister and tried to find fulfillment as his helper. She could not. Her frustration took the form of debilitating illness. She became an invalid, but she did not die because the one thing that bound her to the earth was "that I had not as yet preached the gospel to the fallen sons and daughters of Adam's race, to the satisfaction of my mind. I wished to go from one end of the earth to the other, crying, Behold, behold the Lamb!" (160–61). Then Lee had a dream that the sun rose, became obscured by a cloud, then shone more brightly than ever. She accepted this as God's sign to her that her light was only temporarily obscured and that she would one day preach.

For Jarena Lee, as for many other women evangelists, gender expectations made their lives more difficult. After Lee finally received permission from church leaders to exhort and to hold prayer meetings, she still faced problems of public acceptance. Not only was she often denied the use of the church buildings by men who could not condone women speaking publicly, she herself was at first intimidated and preferred to work in private homes with friends and neighbors. Another problem was travel. Early nineteenth-century roads, transportation, the semi-wilderness condition of rural areas, the distances between settlements, and hostile weather made travel difficult and dangerous for any one, but especially for women.

One particular subject that concerned female narrators but not their male counterparts was marriage. Though evangelists generally shared a variety of obstacles and frustrations, the conflict between marital roles and one's Christian responsibilities was more common to women writers. This problem is addressed more directly in books published later in the century, when women's rights was a more defined issue. But Jarena Lee's narrative gives some attention to her domestic arrangements. Problems of childcare, absent from the discussions of male narrators, appear frequently in women's literature. Jarena Lee devotes an entire section of her narrative to her marriage, which she depicts as another test of her religious commitment, another occasion from which to learn humility and trust in God's will. Such attitudes were also characteristic of her contemporaries, such as Zilpha Elaw and Rebecca Cox Jackson.

The problems of gender expectations and domestic responsibilities were also addressed in ways other than the relation of actual experiences. Indeed, the cross of sexism often seemed to loom over every technical decision the writer made. For example, it was common to preface the narrative with a scripture that established the theme. Jarena Lee chose as her epigraph a selection that linked her with the line of prophets from the Old Testament on, but one that specifically includes women in that tradition. And Lee emphasized that connection by italicizing the reference to women. Both *The Life and Religious Experience* and *Religious Experience and Journal* begin with the following quotation from Joel (2:28): "And it shall come to pass . . . that I will pour out my Spirit upon all flesh; and your sons, and your *daughters* shall prophecy" (emphasis hers).

Another feature of women's spiritual autobiography is the citation of arguments for women's ministries, arguments which by their very repetition become almost characteristic of this literature. Consider for example the words of Mary Bosanquet Fletcher, the British evangelist whose narrative was "must reading in nineteenth-century American Holiness circles":

> No, I do not apprehend Mary could in the least be accused of immodesty when she carried the joyful news of her Lord's resurrection, and in that sense taught the teachers of mankind. Neither was the woman of Samaria to be accused of immodesty when she invited the whole city to come to Christ. . . . Neither do I suppose Deborah did wrong in publicly declaring the message of the Lord.[68]

Maria W. Stewart, whose *Productions* preceded Jarena Lee's narrative by three years followed the same basic argument. Wrote Stewart:

> What if I am a woman; is not the God of ancient times the God of these modern days? Did he not raise up Deborah, to be a mother, and a judge in Israel? Did not queen Esther save the lives of the Jews? And Mary Magdalene first declare the resurrection of Christ from the dead? Come, said the woman of Samaria, and see a man that hath told me all things that ever I did, is not this the Christ? St. Paul declared that it was a shame for a woman to speak in public, yet our great High Priest and Advocate did not condemn the woman for a more notorious offence than this; neither will he condemn this worthless worm. (68)

Jarena Lee's adherence to women's narrative conventions is clear then when she writes: "And why should it be thought impossible, heterodox, or improper for a woman to preach, seeing the Saviour died for the woman as well as the man? . . . Did not Mary *first* preach the risen Saviour, and is not the doctrine of the resurrection the very climax of Christianity . . . ? Then did not Mary, a woman, preach the gospel? For she preached the resurrection of the crucified Son of God" (158). Occasionally Jarena Lee framed her arguments of the validity of black and of female preachers as reiterations of other debates, but more often, as in the instance quoted above, she interrupts her narrative to sermonize upon this point, suggesting thereby that this issue continued to be a major concern for her. Unlike Richard Allen and other literary progenitors, Jarena Lee was able to use the incongruity of her call to minister as proof of God's omnipotence. She valiantly argued that by the instrumentality of a "poor coloured female" God was revealing the power of his gifts in the same manner as when he chose illiterate fishermen as disciples (158–59).

In the final paragraphs of Lee's work, she addressed the scoffers and skeptics thusly:

> It is known that the blind have the sense of hearing in a manner much more acute than those who can see: also their sense of feeling is exceedingly fine, and is found to detect any roughness on the smoothest surface, where those who can see can find none. So it may be with such as I am, who has never had more than three months schooling; and wishing to know much of the way and law of God, have therefore watched the more closely the operations of the

Spirit, and have in consequence been led thereby. But let it be remarked that I have never found that Spirit to lead me contrary to the Scriptures of truth, as I understand them. "For as many as are led by the *Spirit* of God are the sons of God." (168–69)

In her concluding paragraphs, Jarena Lee demonstrates a strong conviction of her own authority. Citing her minimal formal education, she suggests that her observations may be more accurate because they were not derived from the teachings of theologians. Rather than obscure her reliance upon intuition, dreams, and "uncommon impressions," Lee proposes that these may well be gifts of the Spirit which more than compensate for any assumed inferiority of logic, reason, or research. Statements such as this, when considered with others that sprinkle her document, challenge her readers to accept a woman's right to public discourse.

Less obvious to modern readers but certainly clear to her contemporaries is the feminist foundation of Jarena Lee's declared intentions for the dissemination of her work. In writing "for the satisfaction of such as may follow after me," Jarena Lee was testifying to her belief that her life and her experiences had meaning not only to her family and friends but to the public at large and especially to coming generations. Hers was a consciously political act, directly defying conventions of female self-effacement and modesty which made many women writers apologize for publishing, avoid the personal narrative form, or assume pseudonyms.

Jarena Lee's literary aspirations, like her other goals, were in direct conflict with the attitudes and intentions of many with whom she tried to work. The politics of publishing are even more discernable when one considers the struggle over publication of Jarena Lee's second book. The African Methodist Episcopal church had recently directed its Book Concern "to publish religious tracts and pamphlets as was deemed best for the interests of the Connection."[69] Jarena Lee was a longtime member of the A.M.E. church in Philadelphia, the widow of an A.M.E. minister, the protégée of A.M.E. Bishop Richard Allen, and the author of a best-selling narrative. The A.M.E. Book Concern was not only involved in an effort to publish inspirational autobiographies and journals but was having some difficulty establishing a financial base from which to operate. Although it had committed in 1842 to publish the autobiography of Richard Allen and the journal of Joseph M. Corr it had not yet sufficient funds or subscriptions to make this feasible.[70] Jarena Lee's *Life and Religious Experience* was a proven seller; however, her efforts to convince the A.M.E. press to publish her narrative were futile. Lee does not herself record the negotiations, but in an unusual action, the 1844 New York Conference had authorized the Book Concern "to examine and publish the biographical document of Jarena Lee, 'if they should approve of it and think it proper to do so'" (Payne 178). The next year George Hogarth writing for the Book Concern reported that "The manuscript of Sister Jarena Lee has been written in such a manner that it is impossible to decipher much of the meaning contained in it. We shall have to apply to Sister Lee to favor us with an explanation of such portions of the manuscript as are not understood by us" (Payne 190).

The consensus of the gentlemen of the Book Concern is informative. They found it "impossible to decipher much of the meaning." The thousands of readers who had purchased Lee's first book had apparently understood her meaning. It is logical to assume that at least some of those who introduced and carried the motion to nominate its sequel for publication had read it and considered the book appropriate for A.M.E. sponsorship. And Lee's second book, like her first, essentially followed the established literary tradition for spiritual autobiography. So what was it that made Jarena Lee's narrative so difficult to understand? What was it that the committee wanted Sister Lee to explain? A likely answer is that they had been tested for their ability to accept the testimony of an African American woman and been found wanting. As we have seen before, such reactions were neither unexpected nor insurmountable. African American women's responses to and anticipation of that resistance became part of their literature and Jarena Lee was no exception. Given that context, the pride and determination in the final words of Jarena Lee's 1849 text are clearer:

> P.S. Please to pardon errors, and excuse all imperfections, as I have been deprived of the advantages of education (which I hope all will appreciate) as I am measurably a self-taught person. I hope the contents of this work may be instrumental in leaving a lasting impression upon the minds of the impenitent; may it prove to be encouraging to the justified soul, and a comfort to the sanctified.
>
> Though much opposed, it is certainly essential in life, as Mr. Wesley wisely observes. Thus ends the Narrative of JARENA LEE, the first female preacher of the First African Methodist Episcopal Church. (97)

Jarena Lee's purpose, audience, form, and general content remained essentially those of the religious narrator. Her work is similar to that of Maria W. Stewart, Zilpha Elaw, Rebecca Cox Jackson, and Nancy Prince, who were her contemporaries and who also embraced a Christianity that moved them to literary activity. Jarena Lee's persistence in joining the public discourse is a political resistance similar to that of Lucy Terry and Phillis Wheatley before her and of Harriet Jacobs and Frances E. W. Harper who came afterwards. In a direct and faithful way Jarena Lee rendered the experiences and vision of a people, but it is an experience colored and shaped by her race and sex, and one which thereby enables us to create a fuller, more vivid understanding of our literary and social past.

FIVE

Gendered Writing for Promiscuous Audiences

African American Women's Literature in the Antebellum Period

Jarena Lee was one of many women whose spiritual conversions led them to act and to record their actions in ways that challenged the established order and led to new models of literary expression. Angelina Grimke was another. As a white woman from a prominent family of Southern slaveholders, Grimke represented a culture almost completely opposite that of Jarena Lee. But in 1836, the same year that *The Life and Religious Experience of Jarena Lee, a Coloured Woman* first appeared, Grimke published *An Appeal to the Christian Women of the South,* a text very similar in thought and impact to Jarena Lee's work. Both publications defied the social convention that women should not discuss theology and politics. Their breaches of propriety were based on a shared belief that when spiritual and social decrees conflicted, one's religious obligations had precedence. Preaching the "doctrine of obeying God, rather than man," Grimke and Lee not only disobeyed the edicts of church and political leaders, but they urged others to do likewise.

In language that echoes Lee's reply to the elders who tried to restrict women's evangelism to prayer meetings and exhortations in their front parlors, Angelina Grimke posed a series of rhetorical questions including: who defied the pharaoh? who served as prophetess to backsliding people? who proclaimed the coming of the Christ child? and who labored in the gospel fields? Answering each with the phrase "It was a woman," Grimke urged her sisters to break their bonds of silence and to enter the public discourse because it was their duty as Christians and because their failure to help the oppressed among them could directly increase their own oppression. Quoting Esther (4:13–16), Grimke italicized particular words to emphasize the essence of her warning:

> Think not within thyself, that *thou* shalt escape in the king's house more than all the Jews, for *if thou altogether holdest thy peace at this time,* then shall

there enlargement and deliverance arise to the Jews from another place: but *thou and thy father's house shall be destroyed.*[71]

Angelina Grimke and Jarena Lee exemplify the symbiotic relationship between the religious revivals of the Second Great Awakening and the social reform movements that emerged from it. The Great Awakening's emphasis upon the eradication of sin in oneself evolved into a fervent belief in the moral duty to eradicate sin in this world. Definitions of the domestic sphere and religious obligations expanded to include the community, the city, and the nation. The imperatives of sanctification led the converted to challenge traditional beliefs and practices. They created a gospel of social reform that included a more secular feminism and the claiming of authority for civil disobedience. Just as Lee came to believe that sanctification made her responsible to a higher authority than that of the male clergy and that her call to preach required that she not limit her preaching to people of her own race or sex, so too did other women, such as Angelina Grimke, Zilpha Elaw, Rebecca Cox Jackson, Lucretia Mott, Nancy Prince, and Harriet Beecher Stowe, decide that they must read, pray, speak, and act publicly. Their understanding of their evangelical missions increasingly required them to confront practitioners of evil and, when necessary, to lead the Christian soldiers into battle.

Despite their similarities in origin, references, and intent, the examples of Jarena Lee and Angelina Grimke also serve to illustrate the crossroads where paths for African American and Anglo-American women writers abruptly diverged. Those black women who published between 1836 and 1861 generally wrote, like Jarena Lee, to promiscuous audiences. White women, on the other hand, increasingly followed Angelina Grimke's model of addressing their texts to a female readership.

This division was not a matter of African American women's lack of interest in gender issues or Anglo-American women's preoccupation with sexism. Though Jarena Lee's main concern was to continue her evangelical work by recording her conversion, her calling, and her ministerial experiences, Jarena Lee had concerns as well that were more common to women than to men. She regularly experienced the effects of sexism in her life and upon her authorial aspirations. She did not omit these concerns from her narrative; instead, she deliberately identified instances of sexist behavior and clearly confronted gender issues. Likewise, Angelina Grimke was not the only white woman who understood the common sources of the oppression of slaves and the repression of women. Part of her mission was to help others understand that abolition was not a concern more important to men than to women. Grimke's earliest publications were sponsored by anti-slavery groups, and when she addressed her audiences in person, it was as usual for her as it was for Jarena Lee to see men interspersed in her audiences. However, during the antebellum period white women generally followed Angelina Grimke's lead and framed their arguments for, aimed their rebuttals at, and chose their references to appeal to women because their works, whether about purely domestic issues or not, were increasingly identified as "woman's literature." Black women's writings were not.[72]

This does not mean that African American women did not write literature by, for, and about women. On the contrary, the existence and the records of African American women's groups such as the Female Literary Association in Philadelphia, the Ladies Literary Society of New York, and the Afric American Female Intelligence Society in Boston show they regularly wrote, read, and discussed literature by, about, and for women. African American women, like other mid-nineteenth century women, responded to the forces that compelled and circumscribed their participation in the literary discourse. They too were highly concerned about religion, temperance, education, suffrage, and other such issues. They too had opinions about women's roles, duties, and privileges. And they too wanted to convey their ideas in writing to female audiences. The problem is that white women cared little about and accepted even less of what black women thought and, consequently, black women could not get their writings published as readily as white women could.

To recognize that antebellum African American women had trouble finding publishers is not to suggest that they were the only ones shut out of print. Texts by women of color and by women of the newly literate, the immigrant and the working classes, were missing as well. Nor is it to say that men, specifically African American men, found it easy to be published. Though economic growth and technological innovations were combining with the increased literacy and leisure to create an unprecedented demand for and production of reading material, publishers continued to rely primarily upon white Anglo men of the urban Northeast to fill their lists. The newly developing markets diminished the influence of particular factions and marked the introduction of a greater diversity of subjects and politics, making, for example, the censoring of abolitionist views more a matter of politics than economics; nonetheless, any and all writers who deviated from the standard configuration of geography, race, class, and gender had a difficult time being printed.

Woman's literature was, in part, an acknowledgment of men's lack of interest in or respect for women's words. It was a compromise to literary conservatism. And it was a genre that did not offer white women writers unfettered freedom. Mary E. Bryan's essay "How Should Women Write?" shows that in 1860, at the height of women writers' popularity, their very existence was still controversial and their writings had not obtained the respect and latitude that women desired. Bryan summarizes the situation this way:

Men, after much demur and hesitation, have given women liberty to write; but they cannot yet consent to allow them full freedom. They may flutter out of the cage, but it must be with clipped wings; they may hop about the smooth-shaven lawn, but must, on no account, fly. With metaphysics they have nothing to do; it is too deep a sea for their lead to sound; nor must they grapple with those great social and moral problems with which every strong soul is now wrestling. They must not go beyond the surface of life, lest they should stir the impure sediment that lurks beneath.[73]

Though she probably did not intend to transgress the boundaries that Bryan describes, Harriet Beecher Stowe exemplifies the perils of mid-nineteenth-century women who presumed to "grapple with those great social and moral problems."[74] In both form and content Stowe's *Uncle Tom's Cabin* conforms to the domestic fiction genre generally reserved for women writers. The book is in tone and theme decidedly sentimentalized Christianity. Stowe's implied audience is, as Jean Fagan Yellin has pointed out, "repeatedly addressed as 'mother'" (85). However, the book also reveals slavery as an evil threatening the individual and the nation and posits a reformed governmental ethic. And, most damagingly, it had been published first in *The National Era,* an anti-slavery paper read by both men and women. Such factors made the political implications of *Uncle Tom's Cabin* too obvious to be ignored or excused. The book was vehemently attacked, and much of the assault was in terms of gender. Many readers who shared her sentiments were disturbed nonetheless by the fact that a woman had expressed them. Even the fabled response of President Lincoln that she was the little lady who started the great big war implies that Stowe, like Pandora, had caused a lot of trouble for her superiors when she ignored the sanctions that insured order and the proper progression of events. The outraged allegations that Stowe had exceeded her authority and had "unsexed herself" buttress Mary Bryan's claim that the acceptance of women's writing, especially as it concerned metaphysics and problems of moral and social concern, was only within carefully defined parameters. The vituperation with which Stowe's writings were received certainly persuaded many women that their most expedient route was through a more gender-specific literature.

The point of noting that African American women had problems being published is not to make them seem more put upon than other writers who were not Anglo, urban, erudite males. Nor is the evocation of woman's literature as a compromise that restricted itself generally to Anglo-American women writers meant to suggest that Anglo-American women had it easy. But what the record shows is that at the moment when woman's literature was emerging as a discrete and popular genre, the color line was as much, if not more, of a barrier between women than gender distinctions were between white men and white women. The irony is that during the period when abolition and woman's rights were the most striking topics of public discourse and when woman's literature emerged as a discrete genre, the voices of those who embodied the merger of both were the least heard. Anti-slavery papers occasionally included poems, letters, or essays by African American women, but among the multitude of pamphlets and books that the abolitionist press distributed, African American women's writings are virtually non-existent. As woman's literature expanded to the point that it supported its own magazines, and publishers competed to contract some manuscripts long before they were even written, one searches in vain the pages of those periodicals and the spines of those books for the contributions by African American women that their abilities and interest would have produced.

The plain fact appears to be that racism was more of an obstacle for African American women who chose to write for women's audiences than it was for those who wrote to promiscuous audiences, that a good amount of black women's problems in getting published stemmed from white women's general lack of interest in what their sable sisters had to say. However, scholars have been slow to analyze the particular impact of race upon the women's movement. Most ignore it, and those few who donate a few paragraphs to the concept generally have accepted at face value the rhetoric of sisterhood. One of the early exceptions is historian Rosalyn Terborg-Penn, who in 1978 advised us that "Discrimination against Afro-American women reformers was the rule rather than the exception within the woman's rights movement from the 1830s to 1920 . . . , antebellum reformers who were involved in women's abolitionist groups as well as woman's rights organizations actively discriminated against blacks," that the disfavor was obviously returned because some African American women preferred to form their own organizations rather than join racially integrated groups, and "that white women accepted black men more readily than black women in their reform circles."[75]

More recently, scholars such as Hazel Carby, Minrose Gwin, and Jean Fagan Yellin have begun to analyze seriously the influence of racism upon American women's lives and literature. Some of the findings of a recent symposium entitled "Sex, Race, and the Role of Women in the South," for example, that "race both defined southern women's identity and tended to divide those women," while based upon data concerning southern women, can be applied in essence to American women outside those geographical lines.[76] For example, Jean E. Friedman's conclusion that "Families determined settlement, church structure and social relationships in the Old South. Slavery simply reinforced family status, and family status determined relationships including female relationships in the pre-war South" (10–11) is particularly applicable to New England, where family connections also determined one's associates.

The literary apartheid that marked woman's literature in antebellum America was not total. African American women generally subscribed to the same journals and read the same novels as did other American women. As Charlotte Forten's journals reveal, they appreciated and applauded the literary productions of some of their white sisters. Frances Harper's immediate literary response to Harriet Stowe's publication of *Uncle Tom's Cabin* with "To Mrs. Stowe," "Eliza Harris," and "The Slave Mother" demonstrates the cross-fertilization that continued between the two developing literatures. And while it is less easily documented, it is logical to think that the same kinds of networks and curiosity that brought Phillis Wheatley or Ann Plato to the attention of white readers would have continued, though perhaps on a smaller scale, to attract some readers. Certainly, on an individual level the friendships of some women helped obviate the color line. For example, writing under her pseudonym "Ada," Sarah Forten wrote "Lines Suggested on Reading 'An Appeal to Christian Women of the South,' by A. E. Grimke," and Angelina Grimke reciprocated her friend's gesture by using one of Sarah Forten's verses as an epigraph for *An Appeal to the Women of the Nominally Free States.*

However, as the century progressed and as the religious impetus for social reform issues gave way to more secular concerns, the camp meetings, revivals, and church services that had served as common sites for religious women of all races during the major part of Jarena Lee's ministry became increasingly segregated. Nor did women come together through their social welfare activities, for on the whole, these efforts began and continued as racially restricted endeavors. During the antebellum period, the anti-slavery movement was about the only area in which white women and black women came into contact on anything near a level of equality.[77]

In a rather peculiar way, the anti-slavery movement may have been the one place where black women writers may have found it easier to be published than white women abolitionists did. Social mythology in the United States presented white women with a nearly insolvable conundrum that black women did not have. White women were already stretching their boundaries by writing in public. They had to be quite careful not to appear indecorous or unfeminine, to speak or to even know about aspects of slavery not fit for ladies. That left little or nothing for them to write about beyond platitudes and generalities. Black women, on the other hand, were not expected to be refined, chaste, or ladylike so they could speak more freely. Moreover, the very facts of their literacy and their poetic aspirations could be used to assure whites that freed slaves were able to achieve similar levels of education. Abolitionists could speculate about the untold number of black bards, rendered silent and impotent in the prison house of slavery, who could be trained to become as articulate as these black females. Simply because American racism was such that it consistently identified blacks with slavery and made little distinction between middle-class, Northern daughters of free birth and the most oppressed and brutalized slaves in the rural South, it allowed, even imposed upon, virtually every African American woman writer the authority of slave experience. For example, Frances Ellen Watkins Harper was a free-born, middle-class, black woman whose tenure at the Watkins Academy had provided her with a more thorough formal education than most nineteenth-century Americans, black or white, male or female. Yet William Lloyd Garrison began his introduction to her *Poems on Miscellaneous Subjects* by talking about slavery and declaring that slaves did not know the meaning of the word "literature." While he does not attempt to pass Harper off as a slave woman, Garrison makes much of her having once resided in a slave state. That geographical proximity plus the fact that she was "identified in complexion and destiny with a depressed and outcast race" made it inevitable that her collection of poems—though only about one-third of them directly dealt with chattel slavery—would "deepen the interest already so extensively felt in the liberation and enfranchisement of the entire colored race."

Such racial myopia was an important problem for black women, a problem shared in some aspects with their male counterparts. While white abolitionists were eager to privilege the authenticity of black writers' descriptions of slavery, it was only insofar as their descriptions confirmed what white readers had already accepted as true. In those cases, white readers tended to regard the discussions of slavery by blacks with greater interest, believing that they were writing from direct experience.

Perhaps more galling to the black abolitionists than the restrictions upon their descriptive summaries was the prohibition upon their analysis or interpretation of slavery or the society in which it flourished. The case of Frederick Douglass, wherein he was repeatedly required to narrate some of his own history as a slave but admonished to leave the philosophy and interpretations to the (white) orators who preceded and followed him, was only one of many instances that prove this point. Douglass by dogged resistance that lost him several important sponsors was able to break his verbal bonds. Despite the preferences of abolitionist leaders and the potentially high cost of estranged mentors, a few others also refused to restrict their comments or their involvement to the narrow issues of slavery and used their prominence in the abolition movement to gain access to white readers outside that movement. Frances E. W. Harper and Sojourner Truth were two women who were very passionate and articulate about equal rights in general and women's rights particularly and who had some success in sharing their opinions on these subjects with whites. Still, as the controversy over Sojourner Truth's addressing the Akron convention illustrates, many of their feminist colleagues vehemently objected to having their movement connected with "abolitionists and niggers." And while Frances Harper's letters describe sharing the podium with white abolitionists, they do not suggest that her Anglo sisters supported her efforts to desegregate the Philadelphia streetcars. In general, during the era of the most fervent social reform, an era that saw the end of slavery and the rise of women's liberation, the color line divided African and Anglo-American women, restricting their occasional cooperation to anti-slavery issues and causing woman's literature with its more diverse interests to develop along separate paths.

These paths were often parallel. The writings of both groups were frequently peopled by protagonists who were "Byronic heroines," that is, each was a "brooding outcast who reject[ed] any cultural commandments that fail[ed] to meet the needs of . . . her own soul."[78] The fiction and the autobiographies of both African and Anglo-American women included what Sandra Gilbert and Susan Gubar describe as "the one plot that seems to be concealed in most of the nineteenth-century literature by women . . . a story of the woman's quest for self-definition" (*Madwoman* 76). And both were "concerned with assaulting and revising, deconstructing and reconstructing those images of women inherited from male literature" (*Madwoman* 76).

There are two major divergences, however. Many of the inherited images against which African American women wrote were created or perpetuated in the literature of Anglo women. And, in a distinction which is crucial to Nina Baym's definition of women's fiction and to virtually all of those who have elaborated upon her work, African American women writers could not assume a readership composed primarily or exclusively of women like themselves.

The most prominent African American writers of the antebellum period are Jarena Lee, Zilpha Elaw, Nancy Prince, Harriet E. Wilson, Frances E. W. Harper, and Harriet Jacobs. Of these only Harriet Jacobs explicitly directed her writing to women. In targeting a woman's audience, Jacobs was not ignoring men. She wrote generally in the tradition of abolitionist literature with the intention of convincing "the people of the Free States what Slavery is."[79] The "abler pens" to which she wished to add her testimony was a coalition of writers from several literary traditions, including the slave narrative and the anti-slavery novel. Overall, Harriet Jacobs intended to reach a diverse audience, one not limited by gender, race, politics, or literary preferences. But she directly identified "the women of the North," a group that included women of color but one that implies especially white middle-class women who had not yet committed themselves to the anti-slavery struggle, as her intended audience. Her text includes elements of several traditions, most especially that of the African American women writers, but it also crosses the color line and, in so doing, it significantly alters its root tradition. Jacobs's aim required new strategies of authorship. It complicated issues of authority and authenticity. We will examine Jacobs's *Incidents* in depth in the following chapter. But in order to understand how Harriet Jacobs's text is both a critical change in and a continuation of mid-nineteenth-century literature, it is important to consider what other antebellum African American women were doing in autobiography and in fiction.

Zilpha Elaw's *Memoirs of the Life, Religious Experience, Ministerial Travels and Labours of Mrs. Zilpha Elaw, an American Female of Colour* (1846) and Nancy Prince's *Narrative of the Life and Travels, of Mrs. Nancy Prince* (1850) are important as autobiographical precedents. Like Harriet Jacobs, Harriet E. Wilson chose to combine elements of autobiography and of fiction. Wilson created an autobiographical novel that she called *Our Nig; or, Sketches from the Life of a Free Black* (1859), while Jacobs used novelistic techniques in her autobiography, *Linda; or, Incidents in the Life of a*

Slave Girl. Frances E. W. Harper contributed numerous poems and essays that could also be examined in this discussion, but her 1859 short story, "The Two Offers," is the most relevant example.

Zilpha Elaw wrote her *Memoirs* as a token of "esteem and Love" for the British Christian community with whom she had spent the past five years.[80] Like Jarena Lee, Zilpha Elaw intended her autobiography as an extension of her evangelical efforts. Like Lee and other religious women, she declared the priority of God's law over men's customs. And again like Lee, Elaw did not restrict her missionary efforts but traveled throughout the United States, preaching to blacks and whites, women and men, bound and free.

Zilpha Elaw's book was to serve as the record of the gospel message that she preached, but her dedication implies that it was also intended as a literary contribution. Elaw was writing in opposition to literature that she judged detrimental to Christianity and to good race relations. In her dedication, she stresses the importance of selecting and reading the right material, saying, "Take heed what you read: as a tree of knowledge, both of good and evil, is the press; . . . Above all, shun an infidel, obscene or disloyal newspaper press" (52). Instead, Elaw advises her readers to "Give your cordial preference" to the Bible and to "Cautiously, diligently, and habitually observe and obey the directions and statutes of Christ and his apostles, that your foundation may be built not upon the sand of current traditions and prejudices, but upon the prophets and apostles, Christ Jesus being the chief cornerstone" (52). Her own writing was intended to counter the bad literature of her time and to exemplify right writing.

Zilpha Elaw claims the authority of a dual heritage and it extends itself into secular issues and personal behavior. Her autobiographical "portrait" illustrates, she says, "as did the bride of Solomon, comeliness with blackness; and, as did the apostle Paul, riches with poverty, and power in weakness" (51). Authorization of herself as being in the tradition of an Ethiopian queen and of a converted Gentile whose status authorized them to teach, to interpret, to correct, and to lead redefines her marginality to move her from the fringes to the front. Such a genealogy invites wide interpretation. For example, her warning to build "not upon the sand of current traditions and prejudices" would recall the reluctance of early Christians to accept Paul's authority, would allude to racism and sexism, and certainly could imply that any of her Anglo sisters (and brothers) who resisted hearing her words was going against the dictates of the God who appointed her as His spokesperson. Her injunction to "take heed what you read," an injunction that specifically identifies the "obscene or disloyal newspaper press," applies to more than matters of biblical interpretation. Zilpha Elaw carefully constructs herself as a comely black woman whose economic poverty and political weakness has endowed her with a wealth of spiritual insight and moral power. Elaw's narrative demonstrates an important feature of African American woman's literature by asserting the importance of race and gender to definitions and experiences even when neither of these is the focus of the work. In other words, the point of the writing is not to explain to whites, to men, or to women what it means to be black or a woman, but both gender and race are assumed signifiers throughout the writing.

As the personal narrative of a black woman who claims authority from her specific racial experiences by which to instruct and to encourage white readers concerning their personal lives, Zilpha Elaw's *Memoirs* anticipated Harriet Jacobs's *Incidents*. And it provided a precedent among white readers for the stance that Harriet Jacobs was to take in her narrative.

Though Nancy Prince was also a religious woman who justified her unusual choices and attributed her insights to "divine aid," hers was more than a spiritual autobiography. It was also a travel narrative, an adventure tale, and an expository essay. In fact, Prince had published the first part of her book in 1841 as a brief pamphlet entitled *The West Indies: Being a Description of the Islands, Progress of Christianity, Education, and Liberty among the Colored Population Generally.*[81]

Though she was a religious woman who claimed God's authority for her independence and visibility, Nancy Prince claimed more secular and pragmatic reasons for publishing her text. She desired to support herself in her old age. As a secularized autobiography that incorporated elements of several genres, it suggests a number of comparisons with Jacobs's *Incidents in the Life of a Slave Girl*, which will be the object of our extended discussion later. One particular aspect of Nancy Prince's text bears examination at this point because it presages a theme of Jacobs's book. As implied by her self-designation as "Mrs. Nancy Prince," Nancy Prince was very careful to establish herself as a respectable woman. She eschewed publicity and wrote, she says, not in a "vain desire to appear before the public" but because circumstances compelled her to sacrifice her normal reticence for a more pressing need.[82] Knowing that her frequent and often solitary travels might allow her readers to be sufficiently skeptical about her sense of decorum and to distance themselves from her, Prince emphasizes her personal morality and discretion by frequently asserting that she associated with only the most "respectable colored families" or "religious people." She demonstrates the lengths to which she would go to avoid even the appearance of evil with the story of how she refused two consecutive invitations to stop and rest and endured frostbite to her "feet, hands and ears" rather than stay at houses that she merely suspected were "not good" (13). In Russia, though she visited the court of the czar and reported on the fashions and entertainments of that society, she makes it clear that she did not gamble or dance or participate in activities which would have been unacceptable in New England polite society. Most of her stay in Russia, Prince writes, "was taken up in domestic affairs" and in attending Protestant services "twice every Sabbath, and evening prayer meeting, also a female society, so that I was occupied at all times" (39).

Yet, while she so carefully documents her ladylike ways, Nancy Prince frankly admits more intimate knowledge of the sexual perils of womanhood than white women writers generally did. She volunteers that her own sister had been "deluded away" into prostitution. Rather than suffer silently her embarrassment or passively assume this to be a fait accompli, when she learned of her sister's misfortune Nancy Prince went to Boston, enlisted the aid of a friend, marched into the brothel, and wrestled her sister away from the "mother of harlots" who tried to keep her there. Nancy Prince reports that her repentant sister "often said she was not fit to live, nor fit to die" (15). However, Prince concludes that her sister was too hard upon herself, that she was the victim, and that the true culprit was the corrupt woman who entrapped and violently restrained the naive young woman. Quoting the biblical verse that the "lips of a strange woman drop as an honey comb" (14), Prince reverses the conventional portrayals in novels of seduction in two ways. The seducer is not a smooth-talking unscrupulous man who lures the young nursemaid into a life of degradation. Nor does the honey-voiced woman seduce an unsuspecting man. In this incident the evil one is a woman, a "*mother* of harlots" (emphasis mine 14) who deliberately creates a perverse family.

By her own example, Nancy Prince suggests that respectable, Christian women such as herself and her readers should adhere to the most stringent moral standards, but they should neither abandon nor condemn their weaker or less fortunate sisters. She writes that "Even now, I cannot refrain my feelings, although death has long separated us; but her soul is precious; she was very dear to me" (15). In her exoneration of the fallen woman, in suggesting that her soul remained "precious" and that her love for her sister continued, Nancy Prince advocates greater tolerance and more forgiveness among women, an argument that is also central to Harriet Jacobs's work.

Had Harriet Jacobs's publishers not gone bankrupt before printing her book, it would have been issued in the same city in the same year as was Harriet E. Wilson's. One can only speculate about the effect that might have had upon literary history. Certainly the complementary elements of these texts would not have escaped the reviewers. One was autobiographical fiction concerning the life and experiences of a free mulatto woman born and reared in the North. The other was a fictionalized autobiography of a mulatto woman born and reared in the slave South. Both commented upon racial relations in the North and both were clearly concerned with gender issues, politics, and economics. Both were written in opposition to social and literary conventions. Both show clear debts to African American literary tradition, especially the slave narrative, and to the Anglo-American literary tradition, especially woman's fiction.

The striking similarity of Harriet E. Wilson's *Our Nig; or, Sketches from the Life of a Free Black* to the "overplot" of woman's fiction has been amply demonstrated by Henry Louis Gates, Jr., in his introduction to the 1983 reprint of that novel.[83] Wilson's heroine, Frado, is an orphan who is oppressed by her paired opposite, Mrs. Bellmont. Bereft of the protections offered by family or money, she endures a series of trials, but through perseverance and improvement she claims her rightful place. In Frado's case, she becomes an accomplished seamstress, she begins to read good books, and by applying "every leisure moment . . . to self-improvement, and a devout and Christian exterior," she gains self-respect, friends, a husband and a child.[84]

The precedent for mulatto characters in sentimental fiction had been established by earlier writers such as Mattie Griffiths and Harriet Beecher Stowe. But Harriet E. Wilson modifies them in a striking way. Mulatto women characters generally were the offspring of illicit relationships between white men and black slave women in the South. Frado's mother, Mag, was a white woman who had been seduced and abandoned. Mag's mistake caused her rejection by white society. She was rescued by "a kind-hearted African" who in exchange for her sewing his clothes would provide her fuel to heat her home and later offered to marry her. Frado was the child of this union. This was an important difference in the literary depiction of the mulatto and it was an unusual coda to the plot of the seduction novel.

Race is a more complex signifier in Wilson's text. It is not simply that Harriet E. Wilson had Frado experience or witness numerous instances of discrimination and oppression. It is more a matter of Wilson's tone, the nature of the incidents, and their importance in the overall context. For example, Frado made an unfortunate marriage. In woman's literature, more than one young heroine discovers that her husband is not what he appeared to be when he was her suitor. However, in Frado's case, her husband's fraud not only increased her personal sufferings but it had racial implications as well. Frado married a man who she had believed to be a fugitive slave and who had often left her alone and unprovided for while he went to "lecture." Emphasis upon the desperate straits that his disappearances created for Frado makes it clear that her husband failed to protect and to support his family, increases the necessity for Frado's continued self-reliance, and fits within established concepts of woman's fiction. But her eventual discovery that he "had never seen the South, and that his illiterate harangues were humbugs for hungry abolitionists" (128) is a striking political statement. In one incredibly powerful sentence, Harriet E. Wilson exposes a weakness of white abolitionism and invites a more racial reading of the first words of her title and her own chosen pseudonym, "Our Nig."

Since *Our Nig* resembles the popular literature of its day so closely, it is not surprising that Herbert Ross Brown included it in his *Sentimental Novel in America, 1789–1860*. What is curious is that Brown attributes authorship of the text to a white male and that he describes the book as "daring to treat with sympathetic understanding the marriage of Jim, a black, to a white woman who had been seduced and deserted."[85] The blurring of gender distinctions in anti-slavery novels is discussed in depth in the analysis of *Incidents in the Life of a Slave Girl*, to follow. For now, it is sufficient to note that in this genre mistakes about the author's gender were not uncommon. What concerns us more at this point is Brown's conclusion that Wilson's treatment of the marriage is "sympathetic." The author clearly states that Jim married Mag because he pitied her and "Pity and love know little severance. One attends the other" (10). Mag married Jim, we are told, because she believed she had only two options, marrying him or begging in the streets. Wilson shows that Mag's decision was compelled by self-interest and desperation and that as Jim's wife Mag enjoyed "a more comfortable dwelling, diet, and apparel" (14) than ever before in her life. Jim's action was first stirred by a "finer principle," but the narrator candidly asserts that he also was "proud of his treasure,—a white wife" (14). The description of this union subverts the tradition of interracial relationships common to literature by whites. Far from being sympathetic, this depiction bears the fine flavor of cynicism.

Had Brown read more carefully, he might also have discerned a higher level of irony and even anger toward prejudice than that which marked even the most passionate of white abolitionists. Consider the following passage when Frado is casting about for some way to earn a living:

> She learned that in some towns in Massachusetts, girls make straw bonnets—that it was easy and profitable. But how should *she,* black, feeble and poor, find any one to teach her. But God prepares the way, when human agencies see no path. Here was found a plain, poor, simple woman, who could see merit beneath a dark skin; and when the invalid mulatto told her sorrows, she opened her door and her heart, and took the stranger in. (124)

As expressed, the concern was not whether Frado was constitutionally able to learn. The problem was whether racial and class prejudice would prevent her finding someone who would teach her. The solution is provided by divine intervention. "God prepares the way, when human agencies see no path" can be interpreted to mean that despite the absence of any equal opportunity reform efforts, with God's help one can find a "plain, poor, simple" individual who is willing to follow her conscience and not social convention.

Even if tone differences such as these might escape notice, Wilson's depiction of a white mother is startling. While it was a literary commonplace to describe black women as so brutalized that they had lost all intrinsic social and maternal sensibilities, it is almost without precedent in Anglo-American woman's literature to speak of a white woman, especially a mother, in this manner. Yet the narrator of *Our Nig* says that Mag, who after Jim's death had returned to her hovel and begun living with a ne'er-do-well white man, "had no longings for a purer heart, a better life. . . . She asked not the rite of civilization or Christianity" (16). And when her lover proposed that they give the children away and seek their fortunes elsewhere, Mag's reply was "Who'll take the black devils?" (16).

The fourth significant publication by an African American woman that preceded Jacobs's *Incident* was Frances Ellen Watkins Harper's short story, "The Two Offers," which was published in the same year as *Our Nig*. Both are among the earliest examples of fiction by African Americans and both exemplify many of the characteristics of mid-nineteenth-century woman's fiction as defined by Nina Baym. Both tell "the single tale" of that genre: "the story of a young girl who is deprived of the supports she had rightly or wrongly depended on to sustain her throughout life and is faced with the necessity of winning her own way in the world" (Baym 11). Both are about the psychology of women, especially as it concerns the development of self-esteem:

> At the outset she takes herself very lightly—has no ego, or a damaged one, and looks to the world to coddle and protect her. . . . To some extent, her expectations are reasonable—she thinks that her guardians will nurture her, for example. . . . But the failure of the world to satisfy either reasonable or unreasonable expectations awakens the heroine to inner possibilities. By the novel's end she has developed a strong conviction of her own worth as a result of which she does ask much of herself. She can meet her own demands and, inevitably, the change in herself has changed the world's attitude toward her, so that much that was formerly denied her now comes to her unsought. (Baym 19)

Wilson and Harper both tell "the single tale," but from decidedly different perspectives. Frado was from a despised union, bound out to a harsh and exploitative mistress, and dependent upon the casual protection of Mrs. Bellmont's sons. Harper's Janette had a family network upon which she could depend, options and opportunities for advancement that were, in this telling of her story, unmarked by racial discrimination.[86] Frado struggled to survive, while Janette searched for independence and the opportunity to make the world better for others. Though both become writers, Frado's was a decidedly pragmatic decision; she needed the royalties to support herself and her child. Janette, on the other hand, chose that profession because it enabled her to participate in political and moral reform. In focusing upon the trials and triumphs of its heroine in a realistic setting that provides insight into the broad characteristics of the region within which Frado lived, *Our Nig* is more typical of woman's fiction. "The Two Offers" is what Nina Baym calls a "generic variant" of that genre. It is a "moral fable" that

> arranges events in an order that displays the ineluctable operations of a principle; although settings may be real, they are rather implied than represented. Action and character are schematized according to the principle that is being illustrated. Generally, this principle is illuminated in two contrasting characters, one showing right and the other wrong behavior. For each of these characters, good and bad results flow inevitably and without impediment from good and bad actions. (33–34)

The contrasting characters in "The Two Offers" are Janette Alston and her cousin Laura Lagrange. Laura is the traditional angelic heroine. The beloved daughter of "rich and indulgent" parents, she had grown into an "accomplished lady," one who was beautiful, pious, pure, submissive, domestic, and educated enough to make someone a perfect wife. Janette's parents had been "rich only in goodness and affection." When they died, she had been determined not to rely upon the charity of her relations and after years of struggle and some setbacks, including an "all-absorbing love" that was not to be, Janette became a famous writer and a woman of "calmness and strength."

Harper uses an omniscient narrator to emphasize the principle which the contrasting behaviors of the two heroines represent. Janette and Laura appear together in only two scenes. When the story begins, the two women have interrupted their letter writing and knitting to discuss Laura's dilemma. The sharing of an important problem establishes their intimate relationship, but the actual dialogue is abstract and philosophical, revealing their contrasting views. Laura, believing that spinsterhood was something to be avoided at all costs, was trying to decide between two marriage offers but knew that neither man satisfied her expectations. She was afraid to refuse them both because the "risk of being an old maid" was "not to be thought of" (*Brighter* 106). Janette shared Laura's belief in "the deep necessity of woman's heart for loving," (*Brighter* 106) but she was not convinced that a bad marriage was preferable to none. "Is there not more intense wretchedness in an ill-assorted marriage—more utter loneliness in a loveless home, than in the lot of an old maid who accepts her earthly mission as a gift from God, and strives to walk the path of life with earnest and unfaltering steps?" (*Brighter* 106)

The second scene takes place ten years later. Laura had accepted one of her two offers and married a man with "flashing eyes" and "pleasing address" but of little moral fortitude or personal discipline. As scripted for good women, she had "learned" to love her husband with "deep and undying devotion," but when he became a gambler, a reveler, and a drunkard, Laura could not cope with her disappointment. Their only child died, and Laura's devastation was complete. Meanwhile, Janette had spent her years working on behalf of the poor and the oppressed—women, children, and most especially the enslaved blacks. She had learned the difference between espousing unpopular causes and espousing unrighteous ones, and she knew that "true happiness" resulted from the right combination of independence and service. The cousins meet again as Laura lies dying from a broken heart. The death leaves Janette a "sadder and wiser woman" with a renewed resolve to "make the world better by her example" (*Brighter* 114).

The contrasting characters in moral fables by women writers bear a surface resemblance to the two female types that regularly appeared in literature by men. Laura is similar to the beautiful, sensitive, accepting, and nurturing angel of the house. Janette, by her unwillingness to compromise her ideals, her refusal to accept marriage as a woman's only legitimate role, and her willingness to enter the public sphere would then correspond to the aberrant female. However, in woman's literature, there are important differences. As Sandra M. Gilbert and Susan Gubar explain in *Madwoman in the Attic,* even the most superficial woman writer had to confront "all those patriarchal definitions that intervened between herself and herself" in order to write anything that resembled her own reality. She had to "examine, assimilate, and transcend the extreme images of 'angel' and 'monster' which male authors have generated for her (17).

Frances Watkins Harper was not a superficial writer. Her moral fable moved beyond the either/or to critique three roles that women might assume. Janette is the heroine against which two other women's roles are measured. Laura, the character who most closely resembles the "angel," is like most passive women in woman's fiction, "an anachronism from an earlier time" (Baym 28). The narrator makes it clear that Laura's inability to cope with the changes that life offered caused her death and that the inadequate development of Laura's "whole nature" caused that inability. The second foil is Laura's mother-in-law, a character who is known in this text only through the behavior of her son. His weakness, we are told, came about because he never learned to distinguish between the appearances of refinement and the truly cultivated life. He had not learned to value common sense over sensibility or high morals over high living. "His father had been too much engrossed in making money, and his mother in spending it, in striving to maintain a fashionable position in society, and shining in the eyes of the world, to give the proper direction to the character of their wayward and impulsive son" (*Brighter* 110). Harper does not blame this materialistic woman entirely for the weaknesses of her son. Both the father and the mother are indicted for failing to provide the proper upbringing to a son who was by nature "wayward and impulsive."

The irresponsible mother had been a "belle," the character most often excoriated by women writers. Like Frances Watkins Harper, most women writers denounced the "belle," but they, as did Harper, generally excused the belle as being "not entirely to blame; behind her behavior lay a sadly defective system of woman's education that encouraged her feelings at the expense of her reason, gave her mind no objects worthy of its own powers, and accustomed her to the sense of her own trivial and superficial nature" (Baym 28–29).[87]

Frances Watkins Harper joins her sister writers with this explicit critique of traditional literary depictions:

> You may paint her in poetry or fiction, as a frail vine, clinging to her brother man for support, and dying when deprived of it; and all this may sound well enough to please the imaginations of school-girls, or love-lorn maidens. But woman—the true woman—if you would render her happy, it needs more than the mere development of her affectional nature. Her conscience should be enlightened, her faith in the true and right established, and scope given to her Heaven-endowed and God-given faculties. (109)

Frances Watkins Harper also writes in accord with white woman's literature when she reveals the "good and bad actions" that precipitated good and bad results as the response to a tripartite problem. First, society offered

very restricted roles for women: they could marry and be considered successful or they could remain single and be known as failures. Second, society
sanctioned only the development of women's "affectional natures," causing
them to trust the "whole wealth of a woman's nature on the frail bark of
human love" (*Brighter* 109) and leaving them unprepared for adversity and
imperfect human conduct. And third, when the inevitable occurred (death,
desertion, or other reversal of family fortune), the community condemned
those women who could not transcend their training and invent socially
acceptable alternatives.

However, Frances Watkins Harper's fiction differs markedly from that
of Anglo-American women in several ways: in details of characterization,
specific issues that claim attention, and the audience for whom she wrote.
In Anglo-American woman's fiction, the heroine may have to support herself
and sometimes her dependents, but she is rarely a professional woman by
choice. Her professional achievements are subordinated to or substituted
for the traditional roles she should have assumed. She supports herself by
writing or by teaching, but her true reward is the self-esteem brought by her
marriage, motherhood, and happy home. This was not the case in "The Two
Offers," in *Our Nig,* in *Incidents in the Life of a Slave Girl,* or in most
African American woman's literature. African American heroines generally
concluded, as did Janette Alston, that they had "a high and holy mission
on the battle-field of existence," that their families and their commitments
extended beyond the four walls within which they resided.

"The Two Offers" aspires beyond the question of the proper cultivation
of individual natures. It examines the opportunities, choices, and consequences offered in a rapidly changing society, confirms traditional values,
postulates new women's roles within those values, and introduces anti-slavery activity as a valid expression for women. Marriage remains an institution
"fraught with good for humanity" and woman's role is still to serve and to
nurture. But in this story, Harper advocates the necessity of educating
women in ways that would help them survive in an imperfect and changing
world. "The true aim of female education should be, not a development of
one or two, but all the faculties of the human soul, because no perfect
womanhood is developed by imperfect culture" (*Brighter* 109).

"The Two Offers" is colored by details which may be attributed to Harper's personal reality, a reality influenced not only by temperament and
gender but also by race. The manner in which Janette chose to reform the
world is significant. She was a writer in whom "the down-trodden slave
found an earnest advocate," and at the same time "the flying fugitive remembered her kindness. . . . Little children learned to name her with affection,
the poor called her blessed, as she broke her bread to the pale lips of hunger"
(*Brighter* 114). The implication here is that Janette did more than write. She
followed words with action. She aided the fugitive. She fed the hungry. She
acted out principles of Christian sisterhood. In linking anti-slavery rhetoric
with pragmatic religious action in ways that identify women's work to in-

clude the superintending of children's welfare and feeding the poor, Harper extends the definition of woman's sphere beyond that advocated by most white feminist-abolitionists who tended to speak fervently of the enslaved but avoided any direct contact with them or their kindred.

More than once Frances Watkins Harper had explicitly rejected the notion of writing on one topic (as white abolitionists advised black writers to do) or to one segment of an audience (which was characteristic of woman's literature as practiced by white women). In her words and through her deeds, she associated herself with causes and workers who understood the interaction of past, present, and future and who addressed the diversity of concerns that African American women embraced. "If our talents are to be recognized," she stated, "we must write less of issues that are particular and more of feelings that are general. We are blessed with hearts and brains that compass more than ourselves in our present plight. . . . We must look to the future which, God willing, will be better than the present or the past and delve into the heart of the world."[88]

Frances Watkins Harper did not write primarily to women. "The Two Offers" was published in the *Anglo-African Magazine,* a periodical created by black people for black people and, as its masthead proclaimed, "devoted to Literature, Science, Statistics, and the Advancement of the Cause of Human Freedom." Some women contributed regularly to its pages, but the *Anglo-African Magazine* was not a woman's journal. In the same period in which Harper's story appeared, Martin Delaney's *Blake; or, The Huts of America,* commonly considered the most militant and nationalist of nineteenth-century black fiction, also appeared.

Each of the African American women writers discussed thus far adapted literary and social conventions to fit their own concerns. In so doing they reaffirmed certain social and aesthetic values while confirming larger definitions of each. The words of Albert E. Stone are applicable to their works, for they exhibit their "belief not only in individualism as a common cultural value but also in *identity* as a vital personal achievement."[89] During a period when black individuality was being ignored and women's identities were being redefined, these women inserted themselves into the public discourse as individuals and as representatives. In so doing, they invoked their prerogatives as artists to appropriate literary forms as their needs and desires directed.

Some of their methods appear to us as more subtle acts of resistance and redirection than they actually were at that time. For example, most included in the titles of their narratives the words "Written by Herself," immediately asserting their authorship. Of the five mentioned in this discussion, only Frances Harper did not. This may be the exception that proves the rule, for Harper's text was the only one published under circumstances that assumed a predominantly black readership.

These writers were also scrupulous about naming themselves and claiming their titles of respect. Jarena Lee, Zilpha Elaw, and Nancy Prince were all widows whose marriages had presented obstacles to their free expression. However, each one chose to be identified by the title of "Mrs." This was not an uncommon practice among American women writers, especially given the skepticism about the propriety of professional women writers. But African American women had a particular imperative. "Mrs." was a title of respect and achievement. During the antebellum period, racial etiquette did not extend the basic gestures of dignity and authority to African Americans generally. The designation of self on the title page as "Mrs." lay claim to the authority and respect that as matrons they felt entitled, a claim at least partly asserted in defiance of whites who tended to omit such deferential titles in referring to black women.

Within this context, Jarena Lee's identification of herself as "a Coloured Lady" is revealed as an aggressive declaration, for it immediately asserts— again in opposition to prevailing white attitudes—the compatibility of those terms. And it claims thereby the right of women of color to don the cape of ladyhood when they so desired. Moreover, while Jarena Lee's immediate proclamation of her racial heritage continues a practice established even before Phillis Wheatley's publication, the context of Lee's publication suggests that hers was more a statement of affirmation and defiance than it was for Wheatley. In the antebellum period, the practice became the rule. Some, such as Zilpha Elaw and Harriet E. Wilson, state their race in their titles. Others, such as Nancy Prince, make it an early subject of discussion. Prince devotes her first pages to discussing her ancestry, and throughout her text she describes racist encounters, condemns racial prejudice, and chronicles her own assaults against that social disease.

Each of the texts discussed above provides many examples of the ways in which the antebellum writings by Anglo-American and African American women parallel, diverge, and intersect. During the emergence of woman's literature, many black women developed and used techniques and themes common to that genre. However, because racism and sexism were inextricably linked in their worlds, they did not address their writings primarily to women and their concern with "woman's place" was defined more inclusively. In general, Toni Morrison's statement about the difference between black and white women writers seems as true for the antebellum period as it is for the twentieth-century writers that appear to be her more immediate referents:

> I think women probably do write out of a different place. There's some difference in the ways they approach conflict, dominion, and power. . . . But I do think black women write differently from white women. . . . Aggression is not as new to black women as it is to white women. Black women seem able to combine the nest and the adventure. They don't see conflicts in certain areas as do white women.[90]

SIX

Writing across the Color Line

Harriet Jacobs and *Incidents in the Life of a Slave Girl*

Linda; or, Incidents in the Life of a Slave Girl (1861) by Harriet Jacobs clearly demonstrates Morrison's assertion, with which we concluded the last chapter. It is an antebellum slave narrative; that is, a personal account of life in bondage and the struggle to be free. Like most slave narrators, Jacobs relates examples from her own experience to represent the kinds of physical abuse and sufferings inherent in slave life. But male slave narrators tended to tell this story as humanity lost, then regained. They depict themselves as conditioned into accepting themselves as chattel then as awakening to their humanity and the possibilities of living self-defined lives. They claim their humanity by separating themselves from other slaves and fleeing to the free northern states. Jacobs, on the other hand, depicts herself as the young and feisty Linda Brent, a slave girl who knows herself to be an individual of value and who is decidedly aggressive in defending her right to self-determination against those who claimed otherwise. Harriet Jacobs's treatment of conflict, dominion, and power is more complex and varied than that of male narrators. As in most narratives, the resisting protagonist does flee to the North, but in Harriet Jacobs's version flight is neither the first nor the only available option for resistance. Jacob's text reinforces the images of slavery as fundamentally dehumanizing and oppressive and of slave women as particularly vulnerable to its depravities. But she also counters the prevalent literary construct of slave women as completely helpless victims. In her narrative, a young woman successfully deflects a master's sexual advances and a slave mother does not allow her children to be sold away from her. Harriet Jacobs writes an account of slavery that does not excuse the evil inherent in that institution but does reveal it as a condition within which some are able to develop strong family ties, develop bonds of affection and loyalty among women, and unite themselves into a viable and resourceful community of resisters. Through the grandmother and others who remained in the South, and who sometimes remained enslaved, but who nonetheless successfully defended themselves against slavery's unrelenting assault upon self-esteem and intellectual independence, Jacobs suggests a variety of loopholes through which slaves might retreat.

Harriet Jacobs's text represents a development in woman's literature that is parallel to those of the religious narrators who became empowered through spiritual transcendence. In Harriet Jacobs's text as in those of many women writing at the time, spiritual transcendence is of less value than intellectual, moral, and personal empowerment. Her emphasis was upon the natural rights of women and others to personal autonomy and self-expression. Writing in the first person, Jacobs recounts incidents in her life as a naive slave girl but the narrative voice is clearly that of a free, informed woman. She not only intends to demonstrate the evils of slavery but to show her female readers the similarities to their situations and to convince them that as long as there are slave girls such as Linda Brent, no woman's freedom is secure. While hers is a true account, Harriet Jacobs uses many techniques common to women's fiction. She renames herself Linda Brent and she constructs her account to revolve around lost loves, perilous situations, and obstacles overcome. *Linda; or, Incidents in the Life of a Slave Girl* is the combination of "the nest and the adventure" that Morrison identifies. It resembles in many important ways the writings of other antebellum women, but it is a testimony that could only have been written by a black woman enslaved in the United States. And Harriet Jacobs sets out to do what women of her race and class did not generally do. She identifies white women as a significant portion of her readership (1) and attempts to write across the color line, to mediate between the races and if not to resuscitate their former coalition then at least to establish that they did have mutual concerns. She sought to "arouse" the women of the North to knowledge and to action, to have them understand themselves as contemporary equivalents of those "women that are at ease," those "careless daughters" to whom the prophet Isaiah had so eloquently explained the connection between their own freedom and the freedom of the children of Israel.

Harriet Jacobs represents the incidents in her life as being at the same time unique and typical, unusual and commonplace. She asserts a common sisterhood, but at the same time Jacobs warns against conflating the situations of enslaved black women and free white ones, asserting that the former suffered perils that provided subsequent prerogatives for the latter. In tone, theme, and content *Incidents* is both a jubilation and a jeremiad, an act of pride and of humility. In the tension of such conflicting elements, issues of authority and authenticity assumed critical importance.

Consensus over who speaks of what to whom on what basis and in what manner are not requirements unique to African American women writers nor, as previous chapters illustrate, to the mid-nineteenth century. But for African American women writing just before the Civil War, the particular configurations of racism and sexism made such consensus more difficult to gain. To understand the labyrinthine intricacies such writers had to negotiate, it is helpful to return to contextualize Jacob's work.

Crucial to the understanding of *Incidents* is an examination of the generic conventions during the antebellum period and the manner in which Harriet Jacobs modifies literary techniques familiar to her anticipated audience and invents new ones in order to accommodate her testimony as she tests her readers' abilities to accept and to act upon that testimony. Several scholars have discussed the techniques common to slave narratives and to sentimental fiction that she appropriated for her text. However, discussions of generic influences generally have ignored or glossed over the impact of the religious narrative tradition and of the anti-slavery novel.

Her debts to writers such as Jarena Lee and Angelina Grimke are fairly obvious. The secular reformism from which she wrote was, as mentioned earlier, a parallel strand in antebellum literature, and both are derived from the models of spiritual autobiography. They had preached a gospel of social reform which included the assumption that certain circumstances can require civil disobedience and modification of mores and morals. They had advocated women's public intervention into issues commonly deemed political and, ipso facto, male. They had believed that communities of women could and should disregard race and class to work for the higher good.

Less obvious, but equally important are two other texts, published in 1836, the same year as those of Lee and Grimke, but by two men: Richard Hildreth's *The Slave; or, Memoirs of Archy Moore* and *Slavery in the United States: A Narrative of the Life and Adventures of Charles Ball,* edited by Mr. Fisher.[91] Both of these books incited controversies and provided models that profoundly affected the design and reception of antebellum works by African American women writers in general and of *Incidents in the Life of a Slave Girl* in particular.

In 1836 women writers were still a novelty in the United States. A few had gained some reputation as poets. And prose fiction, with its emphasis upon the cultivation of the imagination, the appeal to the emotions, and the conveyance of appropriate moral concepts, was grudgingly accommodating some of the more intrepid women. But the prose of fact—the essay, the sermon, the autobiography—was still a male domain. In the serious business of philosophy, politics, and economics—the terms under which slavery was generally discussed—the prose of fact was generally assumed to be the only appropriate genre. With the publication of Charles Ball's *Slavery in the United States,* a slave narrative that made unprecedented use of fictive techniques, and of Richard Hildreth's *The Slave,* a novel written in the manner of the slave narrative and published anonymously, abolitionist literature suffered a crisis.

Slavery in the United States: A Narrative of the Life and Adventures of Charles Ball, a Black Man was issued by abolitionists in Lewistown, Pennsylvania, to provide a slave's testimony of slavery. However, the authority of this text was severely compromised by its prefatory materials. It begins with a signed statement by W. P. Elliott, a justice of the peace and editor of the Lewistown *Gazette,* and David W. Holings, a lawyer and former congressman. Both men verify the overall authenticity of the text by saying that they knew Charles Ball and had heard him relate "the principal matters" in the book. The introduction identifies the author as a "Mr. Fisher," and Fisher admits that he has substantially modified the narrative, privileging his voice over that of his informant. He has "omitted or carefully suppressed" many of Ball's opinions in order "to render the narrative as simple, and the style of the story as plain, as the laws of the language would permit" (xi). His argument that "if the copy does not retain the identical words of the original, the sense and import, at least, are faithfully preserved," does not completely compensate for his acknowledged deviation from fact. The introductory material also states, "Many of the anecdotes in the book illustrative of southern society, were not obtained from Ball, but from other and creditable sources," and as for the question of how true this personal narrative is, "each reader must, of course, decide for himself" (ii). Thus, the text presents itself as a collaborative construct of a slave narrative and an essay on slavery.

Slavery in the United States opened a debate in which aesthetics or literary conventions were clearly entangled with pragmatic politics. Abolitionist leaders had mixed reactions. They agreed that the book's descriptions of slavery as an institution and of Ball's experiences as a slave basically were compelling indictments that corresponded in essence with factual accounts. But some argued that editorial embellishments compromised the usefulness of the text. Issues as important as slavery, they declared, must be presented only by carefully documented facts and articulated logic. Others believed that if the swaying of emotions via the rendering of the essence of truth would enlist the sympathies for their cause, then fictive embellishments were welcome weapons in the anti-slavery arsenal. They were both right. The response of the pro-slavery partisans to admitted embellishments and essentialized narrative was to label the book as fiction and therefore "untrue." But the book also proved enormously popular with other readers.[92]

Several months later, Richard Hildreth fueled the debate with his publication of *The Slave*. In his review in the April 8, 1837, *Plaindealer,* William Leggett welcomed fiction into the anti-slavery discourse saying:

> Fiction never performs a nobler office than when she acts as the handmaid of truth. . . . The story is written in the style of an autobiography, and with such an air of verisimilitude, that the reader cannot avoid the impression that the task of fiction has been merely to arrange the materials supplied by truth. (xv)[93]

But others emphatically rejected it. The controversy over Hildreth's form broke fairly neatly along the lines of ideological divisions between the two major abolitionist groups. In New York, Theodore Weld, Lewis Tappan, and other leaders of the American Anti-Slavery Society refused to allow it to be sold in their bookstore. However, through the enthusiastic support of the Boston abolitionists, the first edition was quickly sold out.

The record does not show whether "Mr. Fisher" or "Charles Ball" were concerned about the discussion or whether either one continued to experiment with the genre. Additional details about identities were not disclosed and neither published a second narrative. On the other hand, Richard Hildreth soon made himself known as the author of *The Slave*. And taking advantage of the success of *Uncle Tom's Cabin,* he published a longer version, *Archy Moore, the White Slave; or, Memoirs of a Fugitive,* in 1856. In the "new historical introduction," Hildreth describes the origins of his earlier novel and the public responses to it. Proclaiming himself the inventor of the abolitionist novel, he asserted that "the success of others, who have adopted this invention, . . . are, in a certain sense, his; he has in them the natural pride of paternity; but, while fully admitting their merits, he claims, at the same time, the respect and honor due to the father of all of them" (xxi–xxii).

Slavery in the United States and *The Slave* effectively blurred the distinctions between nonfiction and fiction. By obscuring their author's identity, they substituted sentimental and aesthetic appeal for the authority of social standing and erudition. And in so doing, they also contributed to the "feminization" of anti-slavery literature. Since women writers generally used pseudonyms or published anonymously, when *The Slave* appeared as an anonymous work of fiction, many had speculated that the actual writer was Lydia Maria Child, Harriet Martineau, or another of the intrepid women who had chosen that method of intruding further into public discourse. Child disavowed authorship, and in her denial, she implies a distinction between male and female writers. Child concluded a most enthusiastic review of the book by saying, "*If I were a man,* I would rather be the author of that work, than of anything ever published in America" (emphasis mine xiv). The reviewer for the *Boston Atlas* is not clear what gender signifiers he was detecting, but he too asserts subtle differences that may have escaped less astute readers:

> The book appears anonymously. Were it not for a few passages which we could hardly attribute to a female pen, we might suppose it the production of a lady, most favorably known as a novelist, and distinguished for her zealous exertions in the cause of abolition. But it appears to be the work of a man—and a man of singular strength and power of mind. (xi)

Exactly which passages made this a man's book rather than a woman's book are not specified, but most likely scenes such as Colonel Moore's attempted rape of Cassy or Thomas's very calculated shooting of his former overseer tilted the balance toward the masculine.

The issues of genre and authorship that greeted the emergence of the anti-slavery novel had a significance beyond the obvious. It is neither uncommon nor untoward for readers to want to know an author's identity, credentials, and intentions, and to a certain extent establishing authority and authenticity are basic concerns for every writer. However, when the writer is or is assumed to be different from most, to be, for example, a member of a group that by class, gender, or race is considered inferior, the concerns of readers go beyond aesthetics and logic. Readers resist extending to the Other the same authority and authenticity they immediately accede to white, literate, male writers. Abolitionists recognized that to genderize anti-slavery literature, to link it with "scribbling women" could weaken its political impact. Since they were already risking a great deal by admitting the arguments of black males into the debate, many firmly rejected what they believed would be additional compromises. Others assumed that the more fronts they could cover, the better. For them the anti-slavery novel was a weapon of great potential and if women could wield it, then as "unseemly" as their advent into public discourse may have been considered, the benefits would outweigh the losses.

In addition to gender and genre, race was a decided factor in the heightened debate about the form and content of anti-slavery literature. Interestingly enough, the discourse on slavery had only begun to include the testimony of African American men and the participation of those who were black or had been enslaved was sensitive and was carefully monitored. It was not just the pro-slavery faction that deprecated the integrity and intelligence of blacks. Whites generally, whether male or female, Northerners or Southerners, abolitionist or not, believed that blacks were innately inferior. A review of *Slavery in the United States* published in the *Liberator* on April 28, 1856, discloses the racism of some abolitionists by praising the editor (assumed white) for his obvious literary innovations but assuming that the black narrator would have been unable to recite accurately the facts of his experience. "It is natural," wrote the reviewer, "to suppose that Charles, in relating his adventures, would give them in glowing style, and it is evident that while the Editor declares, that in all the statements relative to the Slave himself, he faithfully adheres to the facts as stated by him, he has, nevertheless, exerted a very high degree of skill, in the introduction of such illustrations as the varied scenery of the southern and middle states would be likely to furnish."[94] Given the usual elaborate formality of this period, the designation of the subject/narrator by his given name is also telling. To refer to the slave subject as "Charles" is to diminish his status as an adult and his authority as a narrator. When coupled with the assumptions that the informant would "naturally" want to elaborate upon his own heroism but that descriptions of scenery would be the invention of the editor, as if the black man's creative facility were adequate to embroider upon his acts but not to describe the settings within which he acted, the biases of even this sympathetic reader become more apparent.

Comments concerning Hildreth's work were even more explicitly racist. Hildreth, in modeling his text upon the slave narrative genre, used the first-person point of view. However, one reviewer found this a technical flaw, for he firmly believed that no black could speak with as much sophistication as did the narrator of *The Slave:*

The book before us, written with a great deal of talent, we understand is a fiction. . . . As a fiction, it would have answered its end far better, had the author adopted a simpler style, especially as it professes to be the autobiography of a slave. In its present form it is in this respect a constant violation of probability. We read, in what professes to be the language of a slave, that which we feel a slave could not have written. (xvii)

Our discussion of Harriet Jacobs's narrative is enhanced by attention to the development of the anti-slavery novel because the emergence of that genre extended the boundaries of abolitionist literature, of women's literature, and of African American literature. The anti-slavery novel complicated the writer's task of establishing authenticity and authority, but it also connected African American and Anglo-American writing. In mediating between genders and races, the anti-slavery novel served as a conduit through which African American women could reach their Anglo sisters. Abolitionist literature now offered a continuum between the prose of fact and prose fiction on which the innovative writer could situate herself or himself. Of course, that also meant that the writer must be able to negotiate with the readers for the appropriate authority and authenticity.

While she was not a published writer, Harriet Jacobs was not unsophisticated about literature and its conventions. She had a better than average understanding of genre, of reader response, and of literature's political potential. Jacobs lived in the household of Nathaniel Willis, brother to the best-selling novelist Fanny Fern and a prominent editor and author in his own right. The Willis home was a gathering place of the New York literati and while she probably did not participate in the salon conversations, as a silent servant Jacobs had ample opportunity to absorb the critical questions and details of literary production. Jacobs was familiar with the white literary establishment, and she moved in the circles of the best abolitionist writers. During her residence in Rochester, for example, she worked in her brother's abolitionist reading room. There she must have become familiar with anti-slavery writers such as William Wells Brown, William Nell, and Frances E. W. Harper. John S. Jacobs's reading room was located above Frederick Douglass's printing shop. Even if she did not know Douglass personally, she could not have failed to have heard about the unpleasant consequences of his decisions to publish his narrative and to establish his own newspaper. When Harriet Jacobs decided to make her personal history a matter of public record, she knew the literary precedents and she knew how readers had responded to them.

When Harriet Jacobs decided in 1852 to tell her story, slave narratives by males were essential abolitionist tools. *Uncle Tom's Cabin* was a literary sensation and the efficacy of the anti-slavery novel by white writers had been firmly established. A few months before Jacobs began writing her narrative, Frederick Douglass's *The Heroic Slave* (1853) was published. While she was writing, William Wells Brown's *Clotel* (1853), Frank Webb's *The*

Garies and Their Friends (1857), Harriet E. Wilson's *Our Nig* (1859), and Frances E. W. Harper's "The Two Offers" (1859) had appeared. The generic and racial boundaries within anti-slavery literature had become so indistinct that readers could not rely upon subject matter, style, or structure to determine whether a writer were white or black or if a text were fiction or nonfiction. For these and other reasons, when Harriet Jacobs finally decided, as she says in her preface, to "add my testimony to that of abler pens," she had many options for constructing it.

Briefly summarized, *Incidents* recounts portions of Linda Brent's life as a slave and her attempts to become free.[95] Linda's was in some ways the story of a privileged slave. She lived with or near her family from her birth until her escape to the North. Her mistress was "kind" and her duties were light. Until she was about twelve years old, her childhood, she says, was "happy." But when her mistress died, Linda discovered that she had not been freed as expected but had instead been bequeathed to a five-year-old child. With her new owners, the Flints, Linda was assigned domestic duties, and though she was sometimes ill-clothed and hungry, she was not sent to work in the fields. She was never whipped or chained or raped; but she was, for years, harassed by her licentious owner, Dr. Flint, and by his jealous wife. She was able to avoid submitting to his base proposals, but Linda could manage this only by trading sexual favors for the protection of another white man, Mr. Sands. And this made her vulnerable in other ways. For example, Sands fathered her two children. Then, while serving as a congressman in Washington, he married a white woman and, upon their return, took his black daughter to be the nursemaid of their white child.

At his best, Sands had been able to provide only limited protection for Linda. Jacobs makes it clear that other factors, including her free grandmother's reputation for honesty and courage and her owner's professional and social status in the small town where they all lived, helped her deflect Dr. Flint's passions. But when he began making arrangements to move her and her children to his plantation, she knew those protections would be useless in that isolated place. She became a fugitive. Brent first hid in the home of a sympathetic white woman. When she could no longer remain there, she holed up in a snake-infested swamp and finally returned to her grandmother's home, where she retreated into an attic crawl space three feet high, nine feet long and seven feet wide. It was an uncomfortable, lonely, and dangerous place but she could, at least, remain close to her children and loved ones. From what Jacobs terms a "loophole of retreat" (114), Brent read, sewed, and peeped out upon the world. She also sought revenge upon Dr. Flint by writing letters that were smuggled to and mailed by her friends in the North and that misled and frustrated the man incessantly. Thus she survived for six years and eleven months, until a near discovery compelled her to hazard the trip North. Arriving in New York, Linda Brent, now crippled by her long confinement, did not live happily ever after. Her fugitive status made it difficult to obtain employment and dangerous to remain in one place for any length of time. Though she and her children were reunited in the North, as an unmarried black woman she was barely able to support her family. Flint's death brought her no peace, for then his heirs considered her part of his estate and continued to pursue her. Finally, despite Linda's strong protests that she was not an object to be bought and sold—Mrs. Bruce, her employer, purchased Linda and made her legally free.

Incidents in the Life of a Slave Girl is a slave narrative, but Harriet Jacobs incorporated several techniques associated with woman's fiction. She adopted the pseudonym of Linda Brent and gave fictitious names to the people of whom she wrote. Edenton, North Carolina, is rendered as a vaguely Southern landscape populated with tableaus. She privileged the elaborate diction of the sentimental novel but interrupted it with pseudo-slave dialect for characterization and effect. She omitted unique and personal details and interposed among the incidents of the central narrative the experiences of other slaves that compared or contrasted with hers. *Incidents* reads like a story of pursuit and evasion, one full of heroes and villains, of bright young men claiming the freedom to seek their fortunes and of desperate maidens trying to preserve their virtue, of mothers trying to protect their children and of the hardworking poor trying to survive the greed and exploitation of the powerful and wealthy.

Why then did *Incidents* evoke questions of authorship and genre that have persisted to the present time? It was not that Jacobs's description of slavery and her use of a heroic fugitive protagonist were unusual. By 1861 when her book was published, Northern readers were accustomed to slave narratives offering, as did Jacobs's text, an insider's account of slavery designed to correct myths about slavery and to convince readers of its horrible wrongfulness. Like Frederick Douglass, William Wells Brown, Richard Allen, Olaudah Equiano, and others, Jacobs described a power struggle between herself and those who tried to dispossess her of that self-hood. Like other slave narrators, Jacobs demonstrated her efforts to refute her master's claim that she was his "property" and "must be subject to his will in all things" (27) and in so doing served notice of her determination to maintain control of her own essential self. Jacobs revealed, as did other narrators, that this was a battle fought less on the physical level than on intellectual, emotional, and spiritual planes. Or, in her words, "My master had power and law on his side; I had a determined will. There is might in each" (85).

It was not the fact that Jacobs wrote about sexual exploitation that made her readers uneasy with her text. Seduction and betrayal were the substance from which many a nineteenth-century plot was woven, and they were also the unspoken reason for much of middle-class white society's restrictive etiquette. But Jacobs's treatment of this subject was different from that of the seduction novel. Hers was not a tale of a naive or headstrong maiden who falls victim to the wiles of an unscrupulous man, then dies. But it could appear as a variation upon the "single tale" of woman's fiction (Baym 11).

For Linda Brent, too, was deprived of the supports she had assumed would sustain her throughout life and she had, therefore, to win her own way in the world.

The conclusion of Jacobs's narrative suggests that this is an intentional disruption of literary expectations. Says Jacobs, "Reader, my story ends with freedom; not in the usual way, with marriage. I and my children are now free! We are as free from the power of slaveholders as are the white people of the north; and though that, according to my ideas, is not saying a great deal, it is a vast improvement in *my* condition" (201). There is a deliberate contrast between the happy-ever-after implications of domestic fiction and the moment of closure of this narrative. Her grandmother and uncle are dead. Her brother and son are gone to California. Her daughter is in boarding school. She is legally free because her employer has disregarded Brent's wishes and purchased her freedom; thus "God has so ordered circumstances" as to leave her bound by "love, duty, gratitude" to her mistress's side (201). Jacobs's ending is not a conclusion to a story but the scene with which she leaves her reader. Her declaration that she and her children are now as free from the slaveholders's power as Northern white people are—at that antebellum moment—is stasis but not stability. It is an ending that directly links her with her readers and it conveys the subtext to Jacobs's entire narrative: that Northern whites are not themselves finally free.

It is this subtext, specifically as it is applied to the position of women, that made Jacobs's narrative so unusual and her task as a writer so delicate. When Harriet Jacobs, a woman, a black, and a former slave, represented herself as a mediator between "the [white] women of the North" and "two millions of [black] women at the South, still in bondage, suffering what I suffered, and most of them far worse" (1), she was deviating significantly from the patterns of slave narratives and of woman's literature. When she chose to write not simply about slavery in the South but also about racism in the North and in addition about the inherent racism in the prevailing conceptions of womanhood and women's rights, she was cutting new cloth. And when she presumed, as she did, to advocate a definition of womanhood that displaced piety, submissiveness, purity, and domesticity as the length and breadth of a woman's constitution it was as revolutionary as replacing the bustle with bloomers. To make her creation attractive, Jacobs had to be cautious and yet didactic, to inform and to reform without alienating those who would best fit her designs. She would not present her version of slavery with simple pleas for pity and advocacy of abolition. Jacobs refused to reflect constructs of color that obscured gender and class similarities and allowed Northern white women to sympathize against, to rationalize about, and at the same time to ignore their own complicity in or dependence upon the oppression of female slaves. Jacobs was holding up a new mirror which did not show white women as essentially different from black women. It did not allow them to identify or to differentiate themselves as the fairest of them all. The significance of Jacobs's reconstruction is clarified by a statement of

Minrose C. Gwin in *Black and White Women of the Old South:* "white women—fictional or actual, writers or subjects—rarely perceive or acknowledge, . . . the humanity of their black sisters. Most of these white women in life and literature see black women as a color, as servants, as children, as adjuncts, as sexual competition, as dark sides of their own sexual selves—as black Other."[96]

As a black woman and an ex-slave, Harriet Jacobs knew that many of her readers would find it difficult to imagine that she would, or should, aspire to the same kinds of roles and the same level of respect accorded free white women. She knew that many of her readers' ideas of "reality" would clash with the one that she portrayed and that readers almost instinctively questioned the authority and authenticity of any writer who proffered a reality different from their own. In presenting an exposition of slavery designed to augment the record by focusing specifically upon a slave woman's life, to correct misinterpretations by demonstrating the "depth of degradation" involved in the word "slavery," and to move her audience to work unceasingly to exorcise it, Harriet Jacobs was challenging at least three closely held convictions. First, her depiction of herself and of other slave women contradicted the image of slave women as ultimate victims that was a stock element of narratives by male slaves. Second, she attributed to African American women cultural attitudes and attributes that they were not expected to have. For example, she was literate and well read, but "literate" women were middle-class and "middle-class" women were white. And third, she addressed her female readers as "women and sisters" during a time when the question articulated by Sojourner Truth—"Ain't I a woman?"—was not a rhetorical one for those to whom she spoke. Black women did not routinely claim such a relationship with white women, at least not in public and without apology.

When Harriet Jacobs wrote *Incidents in the Life of a Slave Girl,* she was doing more than recounting her victory over Dr. Flint. Jacobs's text was her way of continuing the struggle against the institution of slavery and against those individuals who were products of that institution, individuals who in divers ways had attempted to dispossess her and all slave women of their inalienable rights to life, liberty, and the pursuit of happiness. *Incidents* was another battle in a continuing war to keep herself her own property. Her antagonists include not only the noxious Dr. Flint and his hysterical wife who claimed her as their property, but also Linda's lover, Mr. Sands, who made her his mistress but not his wife; her grandmother, Aunt Martha, who urged her to watch and to pray but not to put her personal needs above the claims of her family; her Northern employer and benefactor, Mrs. Bruce, who tried to give Linda freedom by buying her; and the middle-class white women of the North who assumed female slaves would ingenuously advertise the most sordid details of their lives in order to gain truly womanly pity.

During the nine years between conception and publication, Jacobs struggled like any autobiographer to reconstruct her life truthfully but pleasingly.

It was especially difficult for her to find the words that would make clear both her embarrassment about parts of her life and her pride in her overall accomplishments, for like many African American women of her class and circumstances, she esteemed decorum and virtue even as she knew that life often required compromises in those ideals. She was so certain of her importance as example and exemplar that she struck out against Harriet Beecher Stowe, arguably the most powerful literary figure of the day, because Stowe wanted to whittle Jacobs's life into her *Key to Uncle Tom's Cabin.*[97] On more than one occasion, Jacobs had to confront her editor, Lydia Maria Child, in order to retain control over the form, the emphasis, and even the proofreading of her text. Because her foes were so big and so powerful, some literary critics have assumed that Jacobs could not have won. They interpret textual ambiguity or narrative ambivalence as signs of failure or imperfect acquiescence. But it is more logical to recognize the ambiguity that does exist as deliberate more often than not, and to understand the incorporation of various generic characteristics as part of a creative strategy to guide her readers' interpretations and to achieve conflicting goals. For Harriet Jacobs, as for other writers who were abolitionist, African American, or female, a most important problem was one that was most difficult to solve: how to evangelize with unfamiliar and unwelcome information to those whose images of ministers and evangelists were monolithic and monochromatic. It was from her own embodiment of the intersection of gender, creed, and race that Harriet Jacobs constructed *Linda; or, Incidents in the Life of a Slave Girl.*

The evidence for this is biographical, intertextual, and textual. Harriet Jacobs's letters reveal that from the beginning she had clear ideas about the form and the effect she wished her narrative to have. In 1852, she wrote to Amy Post that she envisioned a two-volume work: "I should want the History of my childhood and the first five years in one volume," Jacobs wrote, "and the next three and my home in the northern states in the second" (233). Had this structure been followed, volume one would have adhered quite closely to the traditional slave narrative form. And volume two would have preempted Harriet E. Wilson's disclosure summarized some seven years later in the subtitle to *Our Nig* as *Sketches in the Life of a Free Black, in a Two Story White House, North: Showing That Slavery's Shadows Fall Even There.*

Jacobs prepared for the formidable task of her autobiography by practicing with shorter pieces which she submitted to abolitionist papers under the pseudonym of "The Fugitive." In so doing, she developed an alchemy of personal and technical elements that transformed tales whispered into a friend's ear into a narrative accessible and acceptable to less friendly eyes. Jacobs did not aspire to literary greatness but she was determined to render a truthful account. "I must write just what I have lived and witnessed for myself. . . . You shall have truth but not talent," she warned her friend Amy Post in a letter of October 9, 1853. But at the same time Jacobs was experimenting with fictional techniques, for in that same letter she acknowledged that her recent *New York Tribune* publication in which she describes the sexual abuse of slave sisters and their mother's inability to protect them "was true in all its statement accept [*sic*] to being my Mother and sister but we grew up together" (236).

As a personal account of life in bondage and the struggle to escape it, *Incidents* clearly fits the slave narrative genre. Like the prototypical slave narrator, Linda Brent was abruptly snatched from the pastoral innocence of childhood into the persecution and perils of adult slavery. She chronicles tales of wanton abuse and brutality. She describes the experiences and ideas that led to her decision to flee. And while her flight from the slave South to the free North did not end her trials, at the conclusion of her narrative Jacobs declares that she and her children are "as free from the power of slaveholders as are the white people of the north; and though that, according to my ideas, is not saying a great deal, it is a vast improvement in *my* condition" (201).

What is even more interesting than her debt to the slave narrative form, however, is the way in which Harriet Jacobs adopted another African American literary strategy, the discursive mode that Robert B. Stepto has termed a "Discourse of Distrust." In "Distrust of the Reader in Afro-American Narratives," Stepto posits "distrust of the American reader and of American acts of reading [as] a primary and pervasive motivation for Afro-American writing."[98] This "distrust is not so much a subject as a basis for specific narrative plottings and rhetorical strategies . . . the texts are fully 'about' the communicative prospects of Afro-Americans writing for American readers, black and white, given the race rituals which color reading and/or listening." (305).

I interpret Stepto's discussion to mean that especially in situations wherein they intend to present original, individual, or revisionary ideas, African American writers begin with the assumption that some readers are likely to be unable or unwilling to concede that they legitimately could or would act, think, and write in ways contrary to the ideas with which the readers approach that text. African American writers cannot trust Anglo-American readers to respond to their texts as peers. These distrustful writers therefore develop literary strategies that initiate "creative communication" by getting readers "told" or "told off" in such a way that the readers do not stop reading but do begin to "hear" what the author is saying. Calling on the same resourcefulness, courage, defiance, and deviousness that resulted in her earlier triumphs, the same capacity and propensity for "getting told" those who would deny what she considered her legitimate authority, Jacobs initiated a creative communicative construct that forced the reader not only to read the narrative but to accept the reliability of the author and her text over their own resistive impulses. The discourse of distrust is evidenced throughout *Incidents,* but Jacobs's strategies can be represented by a close review of her prefatory material and a brief discussion of her use of characterization. Her claim to authorship begins with the front matter of the book, the title page and the author's preface. That aspect of "authority" with its implicit claims to accuracy and reliability is then supplemented by her characterizations and the community that she constructs.

Harriet Jacobs's book was published in Boston in 1861 as *Linda; or, Incidents in the Life of a Slave Girl.*[99] In calling the text *Linda,* the focus is upon a distinct individual. In identifying "Linda" as "a Slave Girl," the emphasis is upon a group or a class. But "Linda" does not appear on the title page. The title page proclaims the signifiers, *Incidents in the Life of a Slave Girl: Written by Herself.* The two titles produce a dynamic tension between subject, object, and voice. The narrator assumes the authority to create "Linda" as the subject who renders experiences, representative of other enslaved women, to readers who, as the epigraphs immediately following the title show, are themselves as much the objects of her discourse as the slave women that she represents. Moreover, the subtitle establishes the book as a black woman's text, and her authority is not easily disputed since it is *her* life of which she writes. It is not the mere reporting of her life history, but it is a narrative of *incidents* in that life. Its narrator serves as a mediator, a participant/observer now more experienced, yet still sympathetic, who looks back upon her girlhood and selects those experiences that she deems most appropriate for her audience and her literary intentions. The fact that the narrative exists testifies to someone's assumption of the subject's self-worth, of meaning and interest in this individual slave girl's experiences that exceed the specific or the personal. Reading the words "Written by Herself" that follow the subtitle and the words "Published for the author" that come at the bottom of the page, the reader confronts not only the exercise of the authorial prerogative to claim responsibility for the text's selection and arrangement, but also an assertion of the ownership of its content and the assumed power of its distribution.

The author's preface follows the title page. As is expected in the discourse of distrust, the author's first words attempt to "tell off" the reader in ways that she or he must "hear." Jacobs's preface makes clear what her title page suggests. The first sentence does more than immediately acknowledge that a reader would probably doubt the authenticity of her story. "Reader, be assured this narrative is no fiction" is neither apology nor petition. It is a reassurance and a polite command, soothingly stated but nonetheless an imperative. The next sentence neither explains nor defends. "I am aware that some of my adventures may seem incredible; but they are, nevertheless, strictly true." Instead of elaborating upon her claim to authenticity, she requires an even higher level of trust, for she advises her readers that she has not told all that she knows. She has exercised a personal prerogative to be kind and considerate to those of whom she writes by concealing certain information from those to whom she was writing. "I have not exaggerated the wrongs inflicted by Slavery; on the contrary, my descriptions fall far short of the facts," she writes. Thus, the author sets the rules.

The reader is not privy to all the facts; the writer's interpretations and decisions are to be privileged over any contrary ideas that the reader may have.

Jacobs continues to build her case for authority by describing the conditions under which she wrote and her reasons for writing. She mentions that many years ago "Bishop Paine" had urged her to write her life history but she had refused because she did not then believe she was competent to do so. In relating this, Jacobs is demonstrating not only that other people had already affirmed her ability to author a text but she is also implying the support of ecclesiastical authority. And for those of her readers who knew that Daniel Payne was head of the African Methodist Episcopal Church, one of the largest and most influential black institutions in the United States, it attributes to her an authority backed by the most influential elements of the African American community. By the same token, by her earlier rejection of the bishop's suggestion as premature and now, having "improved [her] mind somewhat since that time," having decided that this was the appropriate time to present a narrative written by herself, Jacobs confirms her authority to determine the time and circumstances under which she would enter the literary world.

The "Preface by the Author" is followed by the "Introduction by the Editor" to distinguish the roles and to establish their relationship. In stating that Jacobs decided what and how much was appropriate to relate, L. Maria Child verifies Jacobs as the author and addresses the reader's most immediate resistance by explaining how "a woman reared in Slavery should be able to write so well" (3) and what Child's role as editor actually entailed. Equally important, Child conveys her support of Jacobs's literary decisions and acknowledges Jacobs (and other black women) as her "sisters in bondage" (4). Child's introduction explicitly confirms what Jacobs's preface, tone, and text implicitly assert: that slave women have the same claim to selfhood as other women. Amy Post's statement at the narrative's conclusion reinforces Child's acknowledgment of sisterhood with repeated references to Jacobs as "my highly-esteemed friend," "a beloved inmate of our family," and a woman of "sensitive spirit" who is "naturally virtuous and refined" (203). Testimonies from white women such as Child and Post, women who were personally eminent and members of respectable families, serve to confirm that status which the black woman has already asserted.

An essential element in the success of Jacobs's strategy was her appropriation of what Karlyn Kohrs Campbell has termed a "feminine" rhetoric. Such discourse, Campbell says, is

usually grounded in personal experience. In most instances, personal experience is tested against the pronouncements of male authorities (who can be used for making accusations and indictments that would be impermissible from a woman). . . . [It] may appeal to biblical authority. . . . The tone tends to be personal and somewhat tentative, rather than objective or authoritative . . .

tends to plead, to appeal to the sentiments of the audience, to "court" the audience by being "seductive." . . . [to invite] female audiences to act, to draw their own conclusions and make their own decisions, in contrast to a traditionally "Masculine" style that approaches the audience as inferiors to be told what is right or to be led.[100]

Harriet Jacobs adopted conventions, such as reliance upon personal experience and appeals to biblical authority, most suited to her purposes, and she found it convenient to ignore others such as the seductive speaker, the tentative tone, and laissez faire lecturer. Though she was a woman writing primarily to other women, she was also a black woman writing to white women. Race created distrust. Those "feminine" rhetorical strategies that Jacobs does adopt are adapted to project images in line with her purposes as a writer and her status as a black woman.

Jacobs's shaping and coloring begins with her selection and acknowledgment of authoritative references. Consider, for example, the ways in which she uses verification, or the process of using quotations from others, to state her more accusatory or unflattering conclusions. As Campbell noted, women writers characteristically used pronouncements by men, especially to state directly the accusations or indictments that the women writers were implying, and references from Scripture to validate their claims. Jacobs has two quotations on her title page. The first declares that "Northerners know nothing at all about Slavery. . . . They have no conception of the depth of *degradation* involved . . . if they had, they would never cease their efforts until so horrible a system was overthrown." This statement is unmistakably accusatory or indicting if not actually patronizing. However, Harriet Jacobs does not attribute these words to a man, but cites, instead, an anonymous "woman of North Carolina." Given the assumed inferiority of blacks to whites, this modification would be acceptable to most readers for they could assume that a black woman's appeal to authority by citing a white woman was comparable to a white woman's seeking verification from a white man. Given the racism of that time, they would undoubtedly assume that the speaker of such a frank indictment was white, and since she at least had the good sense not to reveal her name, they could excuse the indelicacy of expression as they accepted the implied greater authority attributed to this anonymous white woman.

But this quote may be more subtly manipulative. For the woman's race is not stated, and while there are at least two white women in *Incidents* who surreptitiously work against slavery, none is as outspokenly anti-slavery as the black women in the narrative, and since Harriet Jacobs was a "woman of North Carolina," it is quite likely that Jacobs's is "quoting" her own self. For a reader to suspect that the speaker was Jacobs (or a woman of color), that reader would have to have transcended racist attitudes that would find it inconceivable that a black would speak so condescendingly to or about a white. On the other hand, if the anonymous woman of North Carolina were assumed to be white, the quotation shows that despite the color difference, an anti-slavery consensus can be reached.

Jacobs's second quotation is biblical, but it too may be another way of claiming personal authority. The words come from Isaiah 32:6, which reads: "Rise up, ye women that are at ease! Hear my voice, ye careless daughters! Give ear unto my speech." The relation between this statement and the theme of *Incidents* is fairly obvious. But the quotation does more than cite a precedent for women becoming politically active. This quotation comes from the section of Isaiah that warns directly against alliances with Egypt, a land synonymous with slavery. And in this chapter, Isaiah's prophecy is actually a warning. The women "that are at ease," the "careless daughters" who fail to rise up and support the rights of the poor and the oppressed will find themselves enslaved. Again, Jacobs has revised the feminine rhetorical convention, for this citation is more instructive and didactic than it is seductive or suggestive.

In 1857, Harriet Jacobs wrote to Amy Post about the manuscript that she had completed:

> I have My dear friend—Striven faithfully to give a true and just account of my own life in Slavery—God knows that I have tried to do it in a Christian spirit—there are some things that I might have made plainer I know—Woman can whisper—her cruel wrongs into the ear of a very dear friend—much easier than she can record them for the world to read—I have left nothing out but what I thought—the world might believe that a Slave Woman was too willing to put out . . . I have placed myself before you to be judged as a woman whether I deserve your pity or contempt—I have another object in view—it is to come to you just as I am a poor Slave Mother. . . . (242)

The passage is important for several reasons. Jacobs admits that she was deliberately ambiguous, that she omitted information that would support racist stereotypes, and that she intended to emphasize her bondage and her maternity. The passage acknowledges her understanding of audience and expectations and it states her refusal to pander to either. She has told a "true and just account" in as "Christian" a spirit as she could. But she has also argued her case before a jury that is not exactly one of her peers, and she asks to be judged on her own terms, "as a woman" and as a "poor Slave Mother." (The adjective "poor" in the context that it is used does not suggest any sense of inferiority, deprivation, or inadequacy. A better reading of the word would be as a term for the state of "lacking means to obtain the comforts of life," as "humble," or even "unfortunate.")

Several critics have identified characterization as central to Jacobs's successful attempt to, as William Andrews says, "appeal (in both senses of the word) to a woman-identified reader."[101] None is more eloquent than Jean Fagan Yellin, who summarizes the ways that Jacobs "transforms the conventions of literature" with these words:

In Jacobs's hand, the passive female of the captivity narrative acts to save herself; in her hand, the slave narrative is changed from the story of a hero who singlehandedly seeks freedom and literacy to the story of a hero tightly bound to family and community who seeks freedom and a home for her children. In her hand, the pathetic seduced "tragic mulatto" of white fiction is metamorphosed from a victim of white male deception and fickleness into an inexperienced girl making desperate choices in her struggle for autonomy; the"mammy" of white fiction becomes not the white babies' nurse but the nurturer and liberator of her own children. In her hand, the madwoman in the attic sanely plots for her freedom; instead of studying self-control within a domestic setting, the young woman learns to engage in political action. (xxxiv)

What can be added to that discussion is an assessment of how Jacobs uses secondary characters to support and to complement the heroic ideal that Linda Brent represents. An analysis of characters such as Aunt Nancy, Aunt Martha, Mrs. Flint, and Miss Emily shows that Harriet Jacobs had resolved the tension between the prevailing ideals of womanhood with the facts of her own life. One can argue, for example, that while Jacobs does leave "her reader with only hard questions" (Andrews 262), she has also provided for that reader some very plausible answers.

Jacobs's characterizations critique the two major and contrasting ideals of womanhood then vying for popular acceptance. One was that which has by now become almost a cliché, the ideal of True Womanhood, a concept that privileged the "pale, delicate, invalided maiden" and promulgated the four female principles as domesticity, piety, submissiveness, and purity. This is an ideal found in much of the woman's literature of that time (including some by women of color); it is an ideal that Jacobs does not support. In "Adding Color and Contour to Early American Self-Portraitures,"[102] I examined some of the inherent problems that this definition of womanhood held for black women in general and for slave women specifically. Suffice it to say that though Harriet Jacobs's complexion may have been pale enough and her manner sufficiently refined and elegant, the fact that her two children were from a white man, not her husband; that she survived a seven-year imprisonment; and that she had managed to support herself and her children by working as a domestic servant eliminated any serious claim to "true womanhood."

The other, competing ideology of that era is the one that Frances Cogan has termed "the Ideal of Real Womanhood."[103] Real Womanhood was not, Cogan explains, simply opposite to True Womanhood. That place was claimed by radicals such as Elizabeth Cady Stanton and Amelia Bloomer, women whom Cogan's publicist terms "alienated, steely proto-feminists who rule their worlds with a rigid back." Fortunately, Cogan is not as polemical in her description of the radical feminists as her publicist, and her definition of "Real Womanhood" bears scrutiny. Real Womanhood, Cogan argues, was a moderate approach, one that assumed, for example, that women did have a separate sphere, but a sphere that was in a far different relationship to the male domain than the advocates of True Womanhood or androgyny would concede. "The Real Womanhood ideal" says Cogan, "offered American women a vision of themselves as biologically equal (rationally as well as emotionally) and in many cases markedly superior in intellect to what passed for male business sense, scholarship, and theological understanding. . . . [It] demanded that the woman's duty to herself and her loved ones was not, . . . to die, but rather to live; not to sacrifice herself, but to survive" (5). This concept has much in common with the thinking of abolitionist women who, like Jacobs, argued for acceptance of African American women as "women and sisters." For as Yellin argues in *Women and Sisters,* while the "dominant patriarchal culture endorsed the pattern of purity, piety, domesticity, and obedience" identified by Barbara Welter, "the antebellum period produced multiple and conflicting definitions of 'true womanhood'" (*Sisters* xiv).

The women that Jacobs presents as most admirable are closer to the ideal of the Real Woman as delineated by Frances Cogan than to either of the extremes. Obviously, Linda Brent was a Real Woman. But, in keeping with the reforming motivations for her book, Jacobs populates her text with an entire community of Real Women. Aunt Martha, Linda's grandmother, is one example. Aunt Martha was so skilled in the domestic sciences that she baked both her and her son's way out of slavery and into her own home. She understood the economics of her acquisition, for she frequently used her home equity to supplement the good will of her white neighbors and friends. As a Real Woman Aunt Martha was both self-sufficient and maternal. In her house, she nurtured and sheltered her children, grandchildren, friends, and relatives. And her house was not the mean abode of the working poor, but a real home with books and silver spoons and linens, and cupboards of jams and jellies.

As Real Women do, Aunt Martha possessed real emotions. Jacobs writes that "She was usually very quiet in her demeanor; but if her indignation was once roused, it was not very easily quelled," that she had in fact "once chased a white gentleman with a loaded pistol, because he insulted one of her daughters" (29). In conflict with the major antagonist, Dr. Flint, Aunt Martha was not submissive and she was certainly his intellectual and moral superior. Although she preferred that Linda remain with her children, she did not believe that Linda should sacrifice her life for theirs.

Jacobs develops the case for Real Womanhood as superior to the concepts of True Womanhood by various methods of contrast. Sometimes it is an explicit exposé of the ways in which some women assume the trappings of True Womanhood to hide their hypocrisy and moral weaknesses. For example:

Mrs. Flint, like many southern women, was totally deficient in energy. She had not strength to superintend her household affairs; but her nerves were so strong, that she could sit in her easy chair and see a woman whipped, till the blood trickled from every stroke of the lash. She was a member of the church;

but partaking of the Lord's supper did not seem to put her in a Christian frame of mind. If dinner was not served at the exact time on that particular Sunday, . . . [after it was dished] she would . . . spit in all the kettles and pans . . . to prevent the cook and her children from eking out their meager fare with the remains of the gravy and other scrapings. (12)

And in another incident, she recounts the time that the squeaking of Linda's new shoes grated harshly upon the "refined nerves" (19) of her mistress. Mrs. Flint reacted by ordering Linda to remove the shoes and threatening to throw them into the fire if she ever wore them again. She then sent the barefoot child on an errand that required her to walk a long distance through several inches of snow. Linda's resulting illness accentuates the hypocrisy of her mistress's refinement.

One of the most extensive and telling critiques is that developed by a series of scenes involving Linda's grandmother (Aunt Martha) and her grandmother's mistress's sister, Miss Fanny. Over the forty years of their acquaintance, these two women had established a mutually supportive relationship, one that exemplified the possibilities of the mutual support Jacobs envisioned between the free white women to whom she wrote and their enslaved sisters. Miss Fanny is by all social conventions a True Woman. Linda's grandmother has earned the highest level of respect that a former slave can earn. She is called "Aunt" Martha. Miss Fanny exemplifies the best of the True Women and Aunt Martha is a (rather conservative) Real Woman.

Miss Fanny first appears as the means by which Aunt Martha finally gets her freedom. Rather than emancipate her as Aunt Martha's mistress had promised, as executor of her estate Dr. Flint had decided to discreetly sell her. The grandmother, "a very spirited woman," understood his hypocrisy and insisted upon being sold at public auction. At that auction, when the better element of the townspeople were deploring but doing nothing about the shamefulness of Flint's selling the old family retainer, Miss Fanny, who the narrator describes as a "feeble . . . maiden lady" (11) quietly but firmly defied her nephew by purchasing her friend for fifty dollars and then setting her free. The full implications of Miss Fanny's actions and her grandmother's debt to her are understood only when compared with the later incident that it foreshadows, Mrs. Bruce's purchase and release of Linda. Miss Fanny's action is one possible answer to the question that Harriet Stowe poses in *Uncle Tom's Cabin,* "what can one individual do?" Miss Fanny has neither husband nor wealth. She cannot even read or write, but she does have a "big heart overflowing with human kindness" (12) and sufficient capital to purchase and to liberate one slave. Her demeanor is mild. Her action is less a rebellion than a gentle rebuke or quiet demonstration of compassion.

In a later scene, Miss Fanny again shows what one woman can do without damaging her own social status. When Linda has been banished to the Flints' plantation, Miss Fanny, in quiet defiance, visits her there. Jacobs uses this incident to contrast the satisfaction that accrues to women and sisters against that which comes to those who would disrupt this bond. Despite their differences, Jacobs reports that "My grandmother loved this old lady, whom we all called Miss Fanny" and paints an idyllic scene of sisterhood:

> She often came to take tea with us. On such occasions the table was spread with a snow-white cloth, and the china cups and silver spoons were taken from the old-fashioned buffet. There were hot muffins, tea rusks, and delicious sweetmeats. My grandmother kept two cows, and the fresh cream was Miss Fanny's delight. She invariably declared that it was the best in town. The old ladies had cosey times together. They would work and chat, and sometimes, while talking over old times, their spectacles would get dim with tears, and would have to be taken off and wiped. When Miss Fanny bade us good by, her bag was filled with grandmother's best cakes, and she was urged to come again soon. (88-89)

Jacobs then contrasts this relationship with the one that developed between her grandmother and Mrs. Flint. As an infant, Mrs. Flint had nursed from the black woman's breast. When she became a woman and a mother, Mrs. Flint had continued to come to her to "have a feast of 'Aunt Marthy's' nice cooking," and as readers would recognize for emotional support and guidance. But when Dr. Flint began to harass Linda, rather than unite in defense with her, Mrs. Flint became jealous of Linda and she stopped visiting Aunt Martha. Throughout the book, Mrs. Flint is shown to be insecure, isolated, and victimized by her own unwomanly and self-destructive actions. Mrs. Flint's situation as a hypocritical True Woman compares most unfavorably with the sisterly satisfactions enjoyed by Miss Fanny.

This incident carries a second and more subtle message. In making Miss Fanny the beneficiary of Aunt Martha's kindness and in showing the hurt that Mrs. Flint causes Aunt Martha, Jacobs implies Aunt Martha's superiority to both kinds of True Women. The discussion between Linda and Miss Fanny that directly follows their reminiscences over tea supports this reading of the subtext. In answer to Miss Fanny's question as to whether she could help Linda in any way, Linda replied that she could not. Accepting her statement, Miss Fanny, in truly passive "womanly" fashion, told Linda that she wished her and all her family "at rest in their graves" for only then would she "feel any peace" about them. The response that Linda hid from her but not from the reader is a clear contrast: "the good old soul did not dream that I was planning to bestow peace upon her, with regard to myself and my children; not by death, but by securing our freedom" (89).

Further discussion of these and other female characters, particularly the African American women, would show more of the nuances and modifications of this overall pattern. Through characters such as Aunt Martha, Miss Fanny, Mrs. Flint, and Linda, Harriet Jacobs offers various examples of women's responses to their social situation. Through their words and deeds, she shows the possibilities and pitfalls of developing a supportive network of women who could have significant effect upon the lives of "the two millions of women in the South, still in bondage" (I), a bondage that degrades all the women associated with slave holders. Jacobs discloses both the positive and negative interactions and mutual dependencies that slavery creates for women. In exposing the facade that masked some who were considered True Women, Jacobs moves beyond the conventional abolitionist pronouncements and interrupts the discourse on equal rights.

In these and other ways, Harriet Jacobs reveals herself to be an individual of interest, a social critic of perspective, and a writer of daring and skill. As a slave, Linda Brent was dispossessed of some very real privileges and rights. But in bondage and in freedom, she struggled to maintain her right to be and to think as her imagination and experience determined. She was without many desired facilities— she didn't have a room of her own in which to write—nor could she afford to sign her own name to what she had written. But Jacobs possessed—what African American autobiographers in general have shown themselves to have—a story to tell and the ability to tell it. Despite all efforts to silence her or to ignore her contributions, she succeeded in adding her testimony to those of other pens. *Incidents in the Life of a Slave Girl* appeared at the same time that the Civil War began. Harriet Jacobs and her daughter Louisa joined the many African American and Anglo-American women who went into the war-torn south to establish schools and hospitals, working out their ideas of women's roles and sisterhood. Jacobs took her pen with her and wrote eloquent and persuasive letters to Northern newspapers, reporting on the progress of Reconstruction and rousing men and women of the North to support financially and politically the institutions that they were building.

Incidents in the Life of a Slave Girl is a forerunner of the postbellum literature by African American women, literature which, with the elimination of legal slavery and other women's increasing recognition of women's joint concerns, including suffrage, temperance, and the Reconstruction of the country, makes possible once again a conversation between women across the color line. In the Reconstruction period that follows, other writers, such as Charlotte Forten, Frances Harper, and Elizabeth Keckley, found audiences for their concerns on a variety of issues. Though their difficulties with authority and authenticity were by no means ended, their work shows that many of the strategies invented by Harriet Jacobs were adopted and adapted by her sister writers to great effect.

SEVEN

Romance and Scandal in a Postbellum Slave Narrative

Elizabeth Keckley's *Behind the Scenes*

Had circumstances been different, perhaps *Incidents in the Life of a Slave Girl* would have achieved the classic status of *Uncle Tom's Cabin* or *Narrative of the Life of Frederick Douglass, an American Slave*. As it happened, however, less than four months after *Incidents* was published, shots were fired at Fort Sumter. For the anti-slavery reader, the plight of the poor slave became more than a philosophical, sociological, or evangelical concern. And even the most careless daughters and sons had to confront the reality of secession and its implications for their personal security. Though many realized that the war was not being fought to free the slaves, everyone knew that the outcome of the war would settle the question of slavery. And as the body count increased, as draft laws were enacted, as black volunteers were rejected, it was no longer possible to pretend that racism flourished only in the swamps and fields south of the Mason Dixon line. Brought up short by the convergence of there and here, them and us, the readership for slave narratives decreased sharply. From this perspective, the fact that *Incidents in the Life of a Slave Girl* garnered attention sufficient to justify a British edition in 1862, that it excited a flurry of media attention, and that it strengthened Harriet Jacobs's influence with an even greater number of influential and respectable people suggest that had the manuscript been published in 1858 when it was finished, its author might have been granted an audience with President Lincoln also. Perhaps he might have announced her as another "little lady who started this great big war." But the reality is that the publication of *Incidents* was eclipsed by the commencement of the Civil War. Its author and the rest of the nation turned from anti-slavery to pro-Union concerns.

Traditional accounts of the war between the states have focused upon the bloody battles and the men who fought and died in them. But not all the soldiers who joined that massive mobilization were male, nor were bullets and sabers their only weapons. Hundreds and thousands of women warriors enlisted in the struggle. According to historian Sara M. Evans, two weeks after the war began, women had mobilized over twenty thousand aid societies to supply the military with food, clothing, medical supplies, and money.[104] While most remained away from the fronts and worked through women's auxiliaries, hundreds of women fanned out over the Southern landscape, braving bullets, repelling guerilla terrorism, and fighting to death or exhaustion. As had been the case in the American Revolution, some women disguised themselves and fought as men. Others, like Harriet Tubman, donned bloomer dresses and led as many as 800 soldiers in military sorties. More often, women joined the army as nurses, cooks, and laundresses.

But for the vast majority of the women warriors, the male troops, the rifle and sword, the taking of territory were not the first priority. Northern women, many no longer at ease because they'd read Jacobs's book, left their hearths and homes to help their sisters in the South establish hospitals, schools, and shelters for the displaced and devastated civilians caught between the two armies. Waging war with blankets and books, pen and paper, they found hopelessness, illiteracy, ignorance, poverty, and pain. Harriet Jacobs and her daughter Louisa were among the first to enlist in this part of the war effort. The authority that Jacobs had established with *Incidents* now translated to her other writings. She had become known among abolitionists as "Linda Jacobs" and it was as "Linda" that she often signed her letters describing the work being done and enlisting support for the struggle.

Among Jacobs's soldier sisters in Washington, D.C., was Elizabeth Keckley. Keckley, the founder of the Contraband Relief Association, was also a former slave. Like Harriet Jacobs, she had succeeded in freeing herself, in establishing herself as a woman of refinement and integrity, and in winning the confidence and support of prominent white women. Like Jacobs, Keckley had long resisted the importunities of friends to write the story of her bondage and freedom. She too had suffered indignities and been forced to make choices that she might whisper into the ear of a dear friend but did not wish to promulgate. But as with Harriet Jacobs, public events stirred her to sacrifice her privacy and write her personal history, not to gain sympathy for herself but for the good it could do for other, less fortunate women.

Unlike Jacobs, however, Elizabeth Keckley wrote her narrative after the Civil War. Emancipation had made an anti-slavery focus unnecessary and undesirable. In general, readers in the reunited states were more interested in healing wounds and moving toward a harmonious future than in rehearsing past wrongs that had divided and devastated their nation. Like other postbellum narrators, then, Keckley modified the tone and the interpretation of her story of life in bondage. She, as they, chronicled the atrocities and deprivations engendered by that system, but reinterpreted this suffering and degradation as a historical moment necessitated by the brief reign of evil in a land that was intended for better purposes. Like other postbellum slave narrators, Keckley justified the slaves' suffering as God's way of instructing His people. This did not mean that these writers neglected to catalog examples of the cruelty, capriciousness, and dehumanization of that institution or that they did not emphasize the contagion that deformed or destroyed everyone who came near it. But after the war, the South was less often depicted as a prison house or a contemporary Egypt from which a Moses must arise and lead his people to freedom. Slavery was reinterpreted as a wilderness experience and the chosen people were all those of the United States, whose sins of doubt and indecision that had allowed the evil forces to gain control had to be punished by this woeful period. Slavery, national division, the war itself were all necessary for the instruction and correction of the nation. Job replaced Moses as a dominant symbol. Slavery had hurt everyone, but the slaves had suffered most, and by biblical example they knew that more pain meant more gain for those who had kept the faith. In Elizabeth Keckley's words, "A wrong was inflicted," but slavery was also the "fire of the crucible" and "the fire may inflict unjust punishment, but then it purifies and renders stronger the principle."[105] She can "afford to be charitable," she says, because "I was a feeble instrument in His hands, and through me and the enslaved millions of my race, one of the problems was solved that belongs to the great problems of human destiny" (xiii).

Such a reinterpretation could be seen as excessively charitable, accommodating, or even fatalistic, but it is more appropriately evaluated as subversively ennobling. Responsibility for slavery was transferred to higher planes and the heroism of the slaves was magnified. Slaves had been agents of cosmic truth, sacrificial lambs who became the means for national redemption. As the chosen instrument of a divine omnipotence, their importance was crucial, while slavery was revealed as a demonic moment and the authority of their masters was deflated. The slave protagonists could be portrayed in more heroic terms, as people whose survival bore witness to the ultimate power of Good, whose special sufferings had earned them special rewards, whose rise would be all the more stellar because of the depths from which they have traveled. The postbellum protagonist could be characterized as the epitome of the American Dream, surpassing Benjamin Franklin's rise from poverty to power by moving from being property to becoming proprietors. In Elizabeth Keckley's case, she had gone from being a slave girl, repeatedly told she would never be worth her salt, to become a modiste and friend to Washington's political elite, the indispensable designer, the stage manager for the roles played by the families of the Confederate and the Union presidents.

In consenting to write her autobiography, Elizabeth Keckley believed she could again be the means by which a major wrong could be righted. She had been behind the scenes and knew the truth that could set free. Her testimony could correct misunderstandings and promote positive actions. But her social position and the story that she had to tell required rhetorical structures and language for which there were not yet existing models. The postbellum slave narrative provided useful elements, but as a woman and a mother Keckley had experienced pressures and problems unreported by male slave writers. The manner and moments of her assertion and triumph were different from those of male slaves. In the cases where her defiance or her victories did resemble theirs, her violation of gender restrictions could work against her. Keckley's text was to the postbellum slave narratives as Harriet Jacobs's had been to slave narratives of the antebellum period. It could be accommodated within the basic structure of the genre but that genre needed modification to fit the form of female experience.

As the preceding discussion has shown, the antebellum elements restricted the usefulness of the model that Harriet Jacobs devised, but parts of that were useful also. The circumstances of the two women were similar enough to allow Keckley to adopt several of Jacob's strategies. Keckley, too, intended to write across the color line and, therefore, could anticipate an audience dominated by women readers willing to concede their ignorance about her subject but not to accept easily the authority of her rendition. And, like Harriet Jacobs, Elizabeth Keckley's determination to tell the truth required her to confess to incidents that could destroy her credibility and negate her claims to sisterhood. For example, she too felt compelled to report that she had been sexually harassed by a white man. In her case, Keckley had been unable, or unwilling, to confound her nemesis by choosing another, but she does not claim to have been raped. Indeed, her self-characterization and the abrupt, brief, and vague manner in which she relates that incident suggest otherwise. While she doesn't dwell on the sexual dilemma as Jacobs did, Keckley too refused to be labeled a victim or judged a criminal for having conceived a child without benefit of marriage. In fact, Keckley politicizes the question and disenfranchises the women as adequate jurors even more sharply than did Jacobs. The subject is one "fraught with pain," she says, and she chooses not to dwell upon it. But the only opinion that truly matters to her is that of her child and the implication here is that were it not for society's ill-advised reactions, he would not have cause for discomfort. "If my poor boy ever suffered any humiliating pangs on account of birth, he could not blame his mother, for God knows that she did not wish to give him life; he must blame the edicts of that society which deemed it no crime to undermine the virtue of girls in my then position" (39).

Both authors wrote of selected incidents in their lives, choosing from their histories those moments they deemed most significant to their authorial enterprises. And both confronted the issues of authority and authenticity in the preface. Keckley begins, as does Jacobs, by conceding that her narrative might seem like fiction to some and asserting the truthfulness of her statements by confessing that she has not told the entire truth. "My life, so full of romance, may sound like a dream to the matter-of-fact reader, nevertheless everything I have written is strictly true; much has been omitted, but nothing has been exaggerated" (xi) was Keckley's version. In these and other ways, Elizabeth Keckley's *Behind the Scenes* resembles Harriet Jacobs's *Incidents in the Life of a Slave Girl*. But its differences are critical.

Some are fairly subtle and were it not for the effect of them in aggregate, could be attributed to differences of personality or publishing prerogative.

For example, Elizabeth Keckley does not call upon another individual to authenticate or to apologize for her narrative. Elizabeth Keckley assigns to herself the role that Lydia Maria Child played in Jacobs's text, absolving Jacobs for any possible "indecorum" in discussing "delicate subjects" and "willingly tak[ing] the responsibility for presenting them with the veil withdrawn" (3–4). But Elizabeth Keckley matter-of-factly declares "In writing as I have done, I am well aware that I have invited criticism; but before the critic judges harshly, let my explanation be carefully read and weighted" (xi). And a few pages later she writes, "It may be charged that I have written too freely on some questions, especially in regard to Mrs. Lincoln. I do not think so; at least I have been prompted by the purest motive" (xiii). Clearly she relies less on the mask of polite deference or strategic withdrawal than did Harriet Jacobs with her "Pity me and pardon me, O virtuous reader, but . . ." approach. Keckley's assumption of equality, indeed her authority to instruct and to correct is made quite clear by the end of her preface when she writes

> I do not forget, . . . that ladies who moved in the Washington circle in which [Mary Lincoln] moved, freely canvassed her character among themselves. . . . If these ladies could say anything bad of the wife of the President, why should I not be permitted to lay her secret history bare, especially when that history plainly shows that her life, like all lives, has its good side as well as its bad side? None of us are perfect, for which reason we should heed the voice of charity when it whispers in our ears, "Do not magnify the imperfections of others." (xv)

Keckley's narrative stance not only demonstrates a difference between two individual women writers, it also suggests that in the postbellum era, women could claim a greater freedom for themselves and their literature. Before the war, they generally found it strategically helpful to present themselves as long-suffering and nonviolent victims of oppression. For example, Harriet Jacobs needed to persuade her readers that slaves were women and sisters and that as women they could and should extend more than their sympathies to them. Therefore, she offered a more radical alternative to the True Womanhood construct, but she also downplayed the slave women's abilities to help themselves, chose incidents common to domestic fiction, and modulated her tone to effect the greatest sympathy and strongest support. They and she were as ladylike as possible. Linda Brent used sass[106] and manipulation in resourceful and generally effective ways, but when slapped or pushed, she screamed, trembled, or fainted. Elizabeth Keckley, on the other hand, was freer to describe physical confrontation and resistance. Both antebellum and postbellum whites might consider it unseemly for a black or a woman to raise a hand against a white man, but the heroism of both during the Civil War made postbellum readers a bit more inclined to tolerate, excuse, perhaps even admire, a black woman's desperate attempts to defend her virtue and to preserve her pride by any means necessary.

Elizabeth Keckley included an incident when she physically defended herself. Here again was the image of the black woman betrayed by her white sister, for it was Mrs. Burwell, a "morbidly sensitive" and "helpless" woman, who urged the local schoolmaster to subdue Keckley's "Stubborn pride." As Keckley describes the situation, it was not the undeserved beating that precipitated her violent reaction. It was this man's refusal to respect her as a woman. Mr. Bingham instructed her to take down her dress and Keckley in a direct address to her readers says: "Recollect, I was eighteen years of age, was a woman fully developed, and yet this man cooly bade me take down my dress." Such an indignity was not only intolerable but justified further defiance, and she continued, "I drew myself up proudly, firmly, and said: 'No, Mr. Bingham, I shall not take down my dress before you. Moreover, you shall not whip me unless you prove the stronger. Nobody has a right to whip me but my own master, and nobody shall do so if I can prevent it'" (33). Here clearly she restricts the grounds of grievance. She continues to address him as "Mr. Bingham" and she does not challenge the male prerogative to discipline females who show too much spirit. She does, however, refuse to submit herself to the view or abuse of a man who has not legal claim to her body. Though she fought vigorously, she was brutally beaten. Moreover, her adherence to social mores was not rewarded, for when she reported her abuse to her master and insisted that he justify his failure to protect her, he picked up a chair and knocked her down. Keckley continued to display self-respect and they continued to try to destroy it. She won. Her resorting to physical defense compelled the men to abandon their rope and rawhide and to snatch chairs, sticks, brooms, and whatever they could to subdue her. In resorting to such weapons, they abdicated the symbols of power and authority. Instead of inflicting punishment and discipline, they were humiliating and defeating themselves.

Keckley carefully showed that her violence was a reaction of extreme desperation and that each of her transgressors came to repent and to pay for their sins. She does not present the confrontations and the victory as purely personal episodes. After Mr. Bingham's third attempt to conquer her spirit, Keckley reports, "As I stood bleeding before him, . . . he burst into tears, and declared that it would be a sin to beat me any more. My suffering at last subdued his hard heart; he asked my forgiveness, and afterwards was an altered man. *He was never known to strike one of his servants from that day forward*" (emphasis mine 37). And just as important as the divine intervention that caused the schoolmaster (and eventually the minister and his wife) to repent was the solidarity of the community. For Keckley's self-respect could not allow her to submit passively to unjustified brutality, but she chose to limit her violence to self-defense. Revenge was not a motive, but justice was her due. It was not enough that the men stop abusing her, and she writes that "These revolting scenes created a great sensation at the time, were the talk of the town and neighborhood, and I flatter myself that the actions of those who had conspired against me were not viewed in a light to reflect much credit upon them" (38). Since it is unlikely that the men took it upon themselves to spread the news of their confrontations, one must conclude that Keckley herself reported it. The victory then was a common one. The good whites joined the aggrieved blacks and forced the transgressors to desist. The analogy to postbellum readers was clear.

Descriptions of physical resistance such as this one were fairly common in postbellum narratives. However, they were carefully contextualized to avoid arousing fears among whites. Whites in the postbellum period may have been slightly more tolerant toward slave rebels, but even with the care taken to assuage their fears of violent reprisals, the enormous number of newly freed slaves caused them considerable concern. Again, Elizabeth Keckley's narrative demonstrates how many writers responded. Unlike the antebellum slave narrators who downplayed their individual initiative and self-discipline to enhance their argument against the insidiousness of slavery as an institution, postbellum narrators needed to convince their readers that the former slaves, especially those who had passively endured their bondage, were capable of assuming the responsibilities of freedom.

This was partly accomplished by increasing the length of time that the narratives covered. Although many antebellum narratives were written years after the authors had escaped from slavery, most climaxed with their arrival in the free North. Postbellum narratives, by contrast, normally went beyond that arrival to describe the actual or anticipated achievements of the former slave. From one perspective, to depict life in slavery as a character-building experience or as one very difficult preparatory school which developed the skills and courage to go on to bigger and better things might seem to be excessive, naive, or far too accommodating. Keckley's story is actually more that of an ambitious and calculating hero who is recounting the cost of her success and impressing the value of her achievements upon others who were inclined to underestimate it. She made it clear that from her childhood she was industrious and ambitious to prove herself worth her salt. At age four, she cherished her appointment as a nursemaid because it was a way to leave the rude cabin and move into the master's house. While such desires could have been as childish as simply wanting better food and warmer quarters, they also show the early stages of the personal attributes that would move her into the White House. Her story testified not simply to her own strength of character but it represented the strength and courage that enabled her fellow slaves to emerge from the crucible, and it typified that of other black achievers whose autobiographical offerings would follow her model. In this way, *Behind the Scenes* is a prototype for later black success stories such as *Elizabeth, A Colored Minister of the Gospel, Born in Slavery* (1889), *From the Virginia Plantation to the National Capitol; or, The First and Only Negro Representative in Congress from the Old Dominion* (1894) by John Mercer Langston, *From Slave Cabin to the Pulpit: The*

Autobiography of Reverend Peter Randolph: The Southern Question Illustrated and Sketches of Southern Life (1893), and Booker T. Washington's *Up from Slavery* (1901).

As is evident from their titles, the emphasis upon black achievement in these works was manifest before the first incident in the life of a former slave was related. Authorship, integrity, transcendence, authority, and authenticity are equally important. In Keckley's case, her declaration of authorship interrupts the title and subtitle and makes a single statement of integrity, authority, and transcendence. Equally spaced on the title page are "Behind the Scenes," "by Elizabeth Keckley, formerly a slave, but more recently modiste, and friend to Mrs. Abraham Lincoln," and "Or, Thirty Years a Slave, and Four Years in the White House." "By Elizabeth Keckley, formerly a slave" is in the tradition of "Phillis Wheatley, servant to . . ." and "Frederick Douglass, an American Slave." But while it immediately and prominently identifies its author with slavery, *Behind the Scenes* also modifies that form by stressing a movement up from slavery. Keckley's identification as "formerly a slave, but more recently modiste, and friend" and her juxtaposition of "Thirty Years a Slave, and Four Years in the White House" rejects a static definition as "slave" or even "former slave." It suggests progressive movement, and it emphasizes the social distance traveled.

In "Reunion in the Postbellum Slave Narrative," William Andrews discusses the preponderance of joyful reunions between former slaves and former slaveholders. Andrews rightly concludes

> reunions with former enslavers were motivated by a complex of desires, some psychological, some sociopolitical, and some literary. Underlying them all, however, was . . . "a strange inexpressible longing . . . to see again the home of my boyhood" where an answer might finally be found to the question of what, if anything, the slave past had to give to a self-respecting, forward-looking black man or woman in the late nineteenth century.[107]

My reading of Keckley's text upholds that conclusion, but I would add that at the time of the writing, the answer had already been found. She knew what the slave past had to give. She was about the business of instructing those readers to whom it had not yet been made clear. The nation had no cause to fear that former slaves held grudges or were a threat to safety or security. It was the institution, not the people, that deserved condemnation.

Elizabeth Keckley describes herself as having come "upon the earth free in God-like thought, but fettered in action" (17). From her earliest memories, she had believed that the rude slave cabin was not her natural place. When she was but four years of age, she welcomed her assignment as a nursemaid for her mistress's baby because through it she could move from the slave cabin to the master's house. That assignment earned her many cruel beatings as the child that she nursed "grew into a self-willed girl, and in after years was the cause of much trouble to me" (21). And though she was repeatedly told she was inferior, that she would "never be worth my salt," Keckley is pleased to note that the time came when she was the sole support of her master's entire family. "With my needle I kept bread in the mouths of seventeen persons for two years and five months. While I was working so hard that others might live in comparative comfort, and move in those circles of society to which their birth gave them entrance, the thought often occurred to me whether I was really worth my salt or not; and then perhaps the lips curled with a bitter sneer" (45–46).

Thus, the reunion scene, which served complex and multiple psychological, sociopolitical, and literary purposes could also be used as an assertion of authority and transcendence. When Elizabeth Keckley visited her former mistress after the war, Keckley admitted that her "one unkind thought" toward their former relationship was that the mistress had denied her a good education. Ann Garland confessed that she regretted that also. But she also believed that Keckley had overcome that obstacle. "You get along in the world better than we who enjoyed every education advantage in childhood" (257), she rejoined.

Unlike the male narrators, however, Keckley depicts two reunions. After Keckley's visit to her mother's house, Maggie Garland was a guest in Keckley's home. Keckley calls her reader's attention to Garland's "expressed surprise at seeing me so comfortably fixed" and to the fact that Maggie Garland identifies herself as "Your child, Mag." These inclusions combined with the insertion of letters from her "child" and from her former mistress, the "child's" biological mother, call attention to Keckley's progress, a progress which had in fact surpassed that of those women who by law and custom had been considered superior to her. Ann Garland's letter expressed the hope that Keckley had been sufficiently pleased with their hospitality to accept an open invitation to be their guest "whenever you have time to come; provided, of course, you have the wish also" (262–63). Not only does this evidence a solicitousness of Keckley's pleasure but it also extends formal recognition of the former slave's right to choose how and with whom to spend her time. In that same letter, Ann, the wife of a former Confederate officer, complains, "I have had to be at times dining room servant, house-maid, and the last and most difficult, dairy-maid." Maggie Garland is now "buried in the wilds of Amherst" (265) where she works as a governess and where her fingers are too cold to write long letters. Maggie concludes her letter to her former mammy by saying, "I am sure that I was made to ride in my carriage, and play on the piano" (266). The lesson is clear. Slavery had illsuited the Garlands to adapt to changes of fortune as mature women should. Their present discomfort contrasts glaringly with Keckley's position. She had performed competently as a slave and now as a free woman she had gone on to become confidante and enabler for major players in the great American drama then unfolding. The pride, dignity, and self-worth that she once had to defend fiercely against local school teachers and ministers was acknowledged by the president of the United States, who routinely addressed her as "Madame Elizabeth" and by the First Lady, who used the more sisterly "'Lizabeth." Moreover, the former slave mammy was an independent, modern woman, a "modiste" for whom some twenty other women worked. Thus, the reunions in *Behind the Scenes* reinforce the interpretation of slavery as a trial that prepared the slaves to triumph. They reassure the readers that these ex-slaves bore no ill will and posed no threat to the nation's recovery, that they, in fact, could be the means by which the American Dream would be realized for them all.

Behind the Scenes is a pivotal work, one that qualifies in Robert Stepto's terms as a "response" to the slave narratives' "call"; that is, an "artistic art of closure performed upon a formal unit that already possesses substantial coherence" (*Veil* 6). It is clearly a major moment in the African American woman's literary tradition. It makes good use of the literary strategies developed by Harriet Jacobs and it joins Maria W. Stewart, Jarena Lee, Nancy Prince, and Harriet Wilson in contributing alternatives to the literary stereotypes of the passive victim and the tragic mulatto. However, the virulent reaction to Keckley's reports of activities behind the scenes made hers a cautionary tale that undoubtedly dissuaded many African American women who might have been considering adding their written testimonies. It is a little explored but obvious incongruity that during what appears to have been a most propitious moment for women and for African Americans to enter the public discourse, very few African American women published their stories. The postbellum and Reconstruction period was a complex time, and in the next chapter I suggest some very practical and probably more significant reasons for this silence, but the sensationalism engendered by Elizabeth Keckley's efforts was certainly a factor in African American women's choosing other modes of social involvement and other forms of public discourse.

Before she wrote *Behind the Scenes,* Elizabeth Keckley had enjoyed a reputation, particularly within the black community, as a lady of impeccable taste and high standards. She had created a thriving business and had earned access to the homes and confidences of the wives of the Washington power elite. Because it was well known that both the president and the First Lady were subject to her influence, prominent people from all races sought her support for their projects. She numbered among her personal friends and acquaintances Frederick Douglass, Henry Highland Garnet, Martin Delany, several congressmen, and other successful African American women including the twelve black school teachers in the District of Columbia system. Elizabeth Keckley was an active member of and a generous financial contributor to the Fifteenth Avenue Presbyterian Church where, it is reported, her manner was so dignified and her attire so grand that many worshipers arrived early in order to witness the arrival of the woman they knew as "Madame Keckley." According to her minister and friend, the Reverend Francis Grimke, hers was a genuine piety. In his eulogy he named her "a true child of God. She loved the Lord Jesus Christ in sincerity and truth."[108] And, Grimke also reports, "She was a woman who thoroughly respected herself. . . . She had a high sense of what was befitting, and held herself up to it, and held others up to it also" (5–6). Madame Keckley knew that she was a witness to and a participant in historic occasions and that she had become an example and an exemplar. She cherished her reputation for its personal vindication of her against a former mistress who predicted that Keckley would never "be worth her salt" (21). She was gratified that her achievements were viewed as inspiration for other blacks and as proof of racial progress to whites. It was her sense of history, her piety, and her pride that made her decide to write *Behind the Scenes* at the time and in the manner that she did.

Her book was first of all intended as an autobiography. She had long collected materials for a history of her life and times. And her wealth of interesting stories had often moved her listeners to urge that she record them. But the catalyst for her writing was Mary Todd Lincoln's involvement in the "Old Clothes Scandal." Believing that she was facing a life of poverty, Lincoln had decided to sell her clothing and had convinced her very skeptical but ever loyal "dear Lizzie" Keckley to help her. The men that Mary Lincoln engaged to sell her goods induced her to become involved in increasingly questionable conduct: writing letters designed to embarrass the Republican party, allowing her clothing to be exhibited as relics of the former presidency, and finally engaging in an acrimonious exchange over the return of the unsold goods and the distribution of the cost of the venture. In all of this Keckley had a part and while the public attention was focused upon the notorious widow of the recently assassinated president, Elizabeth Keckley believed that the slander affected both their reputations. She also believed intentions and results should be weighed on the same scale of justice, that censure should be reserved for deliberate trespasses, and that it be passed by those who were themselves blameless. Mary Lincoln, she believed, had been imprudent, but if the public only knew her motivations and the private acts that had taken place outside of their view, they would judge both Mary Lincoln and herself calmly and fairly. This, she determined, was the time for her to set the record straight about a lot of things, including: slavery and the incidents that molded her character, the family life of Jefferson Davis and of Abraham Lincoln, and in the words of chapter titles in her book, "Washington in 1862–3," "The Origin of the Rivalry between Mr. Douglas and Mr. Lincoln," and "The Secret History of Mrs. Lincoln's Wardrobe in New York."

It didn't work. Elizabeth Keckley, who had been so many times the voice of reason and the pillar of strength for others, found herself duped, abandoned, and reviled. It was a fate to stop the flow of ink from many a less courageous and trusting writer. In some ways, Keckley was responsible for the tragedy. She was not unsophisticated and she had been betrayed before, but her previous successes were her undoing. She allowed her faith in the efficacy of truth, or her belief in her own specialness, to blind her to the clear evidence that Anglo-Americans routinely resented and resisted any African American volunteering any opinion on any matter that did not focus upon slavery or racial discrimination. Yet, being Elizabeth Keckley, she might have pulled it off, had the people she enlisted to help her not betrayed her instead. Much of the responsibility for her failure rests upon her editor and her publisher.

Like Jarena Lee, Harriet Jacobs, and many other African American women writers, Elizabeth Keckley was articulate and literate, but she had no formal education. Her penchant for perfection, those "high standards" to which Grimke referred, no doubt influenced her to rely heavily upon her publisher and other professionals for advice and editing. The identities of all involved and their exact contributions to her manuscript are not known. But according to Mary E. Brooks, who lived in the house and was "constantly in her room and the parlor," Elizabeth Keckley wrote for long hours every night and met in the parlor every morning with several "white men." James Redpath was a frequent visitor and, according to some scholars, the person whose zeal for exposing the truth behind the scenes exceeded Keckley's and indirectly destroyed her business and irreparably harmed her reputation.

Keckley had met James Redpath during her tenure at the White House; he was a political activist, a war correspondent, and an advisor to Lincoln on issues such as the independence of Haiti. Redpath was also an abolitionist and democrat who had edited and published works by Louisa May Alcott, Wendell Phillips, Balzac, Swift, and Hugo in his "Books for the Times" and "Books for the Campfire" series. Perhaps more important to Keckley, Redpath had published William Wells Brown's *Clotelle* and *The Black Man, His Antecedents and His Genius,* a biography of Toussaint L'Ouverture, and his own *Public Life and Autobiography of John Brown.* His *Palm and Pine* had published poems by Frances Harper and the Lyceum Bureau, which he was in the process of establishing during the year that Keckley's book was being published, represented Emerson, Greeley, Beecher, Sumner, and Wendell Phillips.

Small wonder then that Keckley might accept his counsel and trust him with her private papers. According to John Washington,[109] Keckley loaned Redpath her letters from Mary Todd Lincoln because he wanted to help her choose the most appropriate excerpts. But Redpath never returned the letters and, without Keckley's consent, the publishers printed them almost verbatim. Without those letters, Keckley's revelations about behind-the-scenes actions and the unscripted comments of the Abraham Lincolns would have been interesting but not scandalous. With those letters, the intrinsic interest of her book was eclipsed by the scandal of their inclusion.

Identifying her book as the latest in a series of scandalous exposés, the editor of the *New York Citizen* pronounced it "grossly and shamelessly indecent . . . an offence of the same grade as the opening of other people's letters, the listening at keyholes, or the mean system of espionage which unearths family secrets with a view to blackmailing the unfortunate victims."[110] Mary Todd Lincoln never spoke with Keckley again. Robert Lincoln demanded the book be suppressed, and whether it was from Lincoln's influence or not, the book was withdrawn from the shelves. Elizabeth Keckley received no royalties and she lost most of her wealth. In the past, she sometimes supplemented a healthy income from her clothing design and manufacturing with occasional stints as a nurse and companion for thirty-five dollars a week plus expenses. Now, her wealthy clientele disappeared. Whites denounced her as an example of the traitorousness of blacks. Within the black community, some believed she had been victimized but most were angered by their fear that the backlash from her actions would jeopardize their own positions. After the book, she could depend only upon the twelve dollars a month pension she received as a widow whose only son was killed in combat.

In retrospect, perhaps Elizabeth Keckley should not have been so surprised or personally pained. Her publisher, G. W. Carlton, well known as a publisher of sensationally successful books, had earned this reputation by publishing fast and advertising widely. While he was respected as an honest and caring businessman, one who paid his writers fairly and promptly, he was not above editing drastically and accepting less than well-considered work. So intrusive had his alterations become on the manuscripts of the best-selling humorist, Artemus Ward, that Ward advised Carlton that "The next book I write I'm going to get *you* to write."[111] And, in another telling example, Carlton had Michelet's *La Femme* translated in seventy-two hours and the "450 page volume was set, cast, printed, bound, and 20,000 copies were sold in less than thirty days" (Hern, 201).

Carlton began advertising the book before it was completed. At first, it was promoted as an autobiography. The advertisement in the April 1, 1868, edition of the *American Literary Gazette and Publisher's Circular* announced "G.W. Carlton and Co. Will publish in early April A Remarkable Book entitled *Behind the Scenes*. . . . the book is crowded with incidents of a most romantic as well as tragic interest, covering a period of forty years. It is powerfully and truthfully written and cannot fail to create a wide world interest not alone in the book, but in its gifted and conscientious author" (Washington 231–32). Three days later, the work was promoted in *The New York Commercial Advertiser* as "A Literary Thunderbolt . . . by Mrs. Elizabeth Keckley." Yet the emphasis was still upon the overall autobiographical flavor. Keckley, the advertisement tells us, was "for 30 YEARS household slave in the best Southern families. . . . She has much to say of an interesting, not to say startling nature, in regard to men and things in the White House, Washington, and New York" (Washington 232–3). But less than a month after the book was published, it was being advertised by the dual title "White House Revelations or Behind the Scenes" (Washington 233). And by the end of May, *The New York Library* found it sufficient to simply declare "Behind the Scenes The Great Sensational Disclosure by Mrs. Keckley $2.00" (Washington 234).

The reading public took its lead from the advertisements. Rather than developing an interest in this "gifted and conscientious author," readers focused upon the book's description of the private lives of Abraham and Mary Todd Lincoln. In words remarkably similar to those with which Lydia Maria Child introduced *Incidents in the Life of a Slave Girl,* Elizabeth Keckley had acknowledged in her preface that some might consider her subject indelicate, but "The veil of mystery must be drawn aside; the origin of a fact must be brought to light with the naked fact itself" (xiv). She had trusted that her readers would sympathize with her motives or at least recognize that what she revealed was less damaging than the malicious rumors being spread in the press. She repeated this in the letter she wrote to the *New York Citizen* after its editors had published their indictment under the heading "Indecent Publications." "I maintain," Keckley wrote, "that all I have written of Mrs. Lincoln has had a tendency to place her in a better light before the world. To see how bitterly and shamelessly Mrs. Lincoln has been assailed, it is only necessary to turn to the files of the various journals in the United States, THE CITIZEN not excepted. . . . Let any one read my book, with a few choice extracts before him or her, clipped from the respectable and leading newspapers of the country, and then if it is decided that I have scandalized Mrs. Lincoln, I will calmly submit to the decision. . . . The impartial reader of the book, if I mistake not, will also agree that it is not written in the spirit of 'an angry negro servant.'"[112] But Elizabeth Keckley was mistaken.

Keckley had tested the ability of language and literature to communicate the truth as experienced by an African American woman. Her design was workable and her testimony eloquent. But with the help of many whose assumptions and intentions were not the same as hers, she discovered that in this competition for authority and authenticity her pen was not mightier than the money and media of Anglo-America. She wrote to "stifle the voice of calumny," but her contribution increased the volume to irrational shrieks—a noise that certainly frightened off many less intrepid African American women writers.

EIGHT

Doers of the Word

The Reconstruction Poetry of
Frances Ellen Watkins Harper

Although Elizabeth Keckley initiated relief efforts designed to aid the newly freed slaves and although she was friend and colleague to many prominent black activists, her writing is relatively silent on racial issues. She knew that insofar as her dramatic rise from chattel to entrepreneur could be used to refute notions of black inferiority or to inspire people to emulate her courage and determination, her book would help improve the image, and perhaps the status, of African Americans. However, the immediate impetuses for Elizabeth Keckley's book were the scandal concerning Mary Lincoln and Keckley's concern about its effect upon her own reputation. Keckley undoubtedly realized that the account of a black woman who had struggled up from slavery to a position of owning her own business and of participating in matters of national import was in the mode of the most popular postbellum slave narratives. But *Behind the Scenes* is, first of all, Elizabeth Keckley's *apologia pro sua vita,* her personal account of some of the "events that moulded [her] character."

The emphasis in *Behind the Scenes* upon advancement via individual determination was one literary model for Reconstruction writers. Postbellum Americans needed to believe that the worst of times were over and that the best of times had begun. African American writers, like other American writers, responded to the need to repair the psychic damage of a war between the states and to adjust to a land without slavery but with an awesome number of former slaves. They believed that their stories of strength through adversity, of struggle and achievement, of hard work and discipline replacing the slave's rags with the decorous attire of proper citizens, could serve to inspire other blacks, assuage the fears of some whites, and help revive the American Dream. As did most survivors of the Civil War, African American writers saw themselves as architects for the rebuilding of the nation, who would salvage the best of its past, make the most of its present, and integrate its future. They sought to accomplish this through a revised literature that spoke more broadly to and of American society, a literature that celebrated national diversity even as it affirmed national unity.

If, as Fred Lewis Pattee argues, "It was not until after the war that our writers ceased to imitate and looked to their own land for material and inspiration. . . . [I]t was not until after the Civil War that America achieved in any degree her literary independence. One can say of the period what one may not say of earlier periods, that the great mass of its writings could have been produced nowhere else but in the United States,"[113] then, despite Pattee's curious silence about their writings, African Americans were among the original designers of American literature. If, as Arna Bontemps and others have argued, a true American genre had developed before Pattee's "Second Discovery of America," that the antebellum slave narratives were the first genre indigenous to North America, then one must simply note that African American writers intended themselves to be part and parcel of the American Renaissance. In either case, their contributions as much as any writer's confirmed Pattee's assessment of the postbellum era as a time of "a new spirit—social, dramatic, intense" (15), when the "intellectual life of the nation no longer was to be in the hands of the aristocratic, scholarly few" (15) but new ideas, new literary forms, and new attention to the "voice[s] of all the people" (21) were the rule.

Historians, economists, and political scientists have long acknowledged what literary scholars have not, that the years between 1865 and 1877, commonly known as the Reconstruction era, were largely shaped by concerns about the role of black people in American social systems. On the whole, scholars of American literature have not placed race so squarely in the center of that era. While the editors of *The Norton Anthology of American Literature,* for example, note that racial inequality was the problem "perhaps the most persistent and resistant to solution" of the period, that comment is almost an afterthought, coming as it does with no elaboration in the penultimate paragraph of the introduction to the literature from 1865–1914. Scholars of American literature have preferred to emphasize this period as a time of "transformation," a time when "the central material fact of the period was industrialization."[114] Their key words for postbellum American literature are "realism, naturalism, and local color" (6). Their descriptions bury race within more ambiguous terms such as "collective discontinuities" and "civic life" as they intone, "The more enduring fictional and nonfictional prose forms of the era . . . come to terms imaginatively with the individual and collective dislocations and discontinuities associated with the closing out of the frontier, urbanization, intensified secularism, unprecedented immigration, the surge of national wealth unequally distributed, revised conceptions of human nature and destiny, the reordering of family and civil life, and the pervasive spread of mechanical and organizational technologies" (10). While they acknowledge that a prevailing occupation during this time was "the quest for a usable past," they tend to ignore the implications of many of the subjects and forms used by authors they consider "major," writers such as Mark Twain and Joel Chandler Harris.

Without a doubt, Fred Lewis Pattee and most literary scholars did not have African American writers in mind when they spoke of the new American literature. But the changes that they identify, the nationalism and populism, the regionalism and the realism—these changes influenced and were influenced by African American writers. Writers on both sides of the Mason-Dixon line and on both sides of the color line were inspired by the folk tales, the black literary types and stereotypes, and the music and language of the black South.

For African American writers the "quest for a usable past" had a special urgency. They knew that by confronting that past and its literary stereotypes, they could affect their present condition and help shape the American future. African American writers took it as their social responsibility as well as their literary right to revise history, report the present, and envision a future in which their people and their people's contributions and potentials would be fully appreciated. In terms of literary techniques, for example, this meant expanding their subjects, creating new characters, and experimenting with genre and style. Some chose to concentrate upon nonfiction and journalism. Others contributed to the American literary transformation by writing fiction and poetry that conveyed the attitudes and experiences of their people in ways more true to the ways in which those attitudes and experiences were expressed among themselves. Frances Ellen Watkins Harper chose to do both.

Harper was not a new literary voice. During the antebellum era, writing as Frances Ellen Watkins, she had produced numerous letters, essays, and poems as well as what is generally considered the first published short story by an African American. Harper's literary reputation had been greatly influenced by the popularity of particular poems such as "The Slave Mother," "Eliza Harris," and "Bury Me in a Free Land"; by her own indefatigable efforts as an abolitionist; and by the general tendency to associate blacks and their literature with slavery. Her poems, though never exclusively devoted to topics of race or slavery, had been recognized as providing, along with the spirituals and the slave narratives, the most authentic rendition of the slave's point of view available to nineteenth-century readers.

Like Whittier, Stowe, Douglass, and many others of her time, Frances Harper based most of her writings upon incidents and themes which her readers could acknowledge as "real." She wrote of heroic historical figures, of pressing contemporary issues, and of timeless moral and philosophical ideals. For Harper, literature was one of the many tools necessary to create a better world. As an anti-slavery lecturer and a member of the Underground Railroad, she had covered thousands of miles carrying her messages of abolition, Free Produce, women's rights, and other reform issues to audiences throughout the free states. During her travels, Harper strategized with local and national leaders, interviewed fugitive and ex-slaves, and witnessed the conditions under which free women and men lived. With the money that her books and appearances generated, she further supported the causes to which she devoted her voice and pen. It was entirely in keeping with Harper's activist poetics that immediately after the War between the States had ended, she went to the South to determine what could be done to aid the freedpeople and to bind the nation's wounds.

From 1864 to 1871 Frances Harper crossed and recrossed the South, visiting every state but Arkansas and Texas, teaching and lecturing to Southern audiences and recording her impressions for Northern readers. The time that she spent in the deep South was a period of physical danger, intellectual challenge, and intense self-discovery. The poverty was beyond any she had previously experienced, but the hospitality, optimism, and hard work of most blacks and many whites surpassed her expectations. There Harper found "ignorance to be instructed; a race who needs to be helped up to higher planes of thought and action; and whether we are hindered or helped, we should try to be true to the commission God has written upon our souls" (*Brighter* 125–26). There Harper rededicated herself to her literature and her causes. On February 20, 1871, Harper wrote, "I am standing with my race on the threshold of a new era, and though some be far past me in the learning of the schools, yet to-day, with my limited and fragmentary knowledge, I may help the race forward a little" (*Brighter* 127).

The texts of most of Frances Harper's Reconstruction lectures are not available. Apparently she was too busy traveling and speaking to write them out. Some of her words were recorded by news reporters and a few lectures such as "The Colored Woman of America" were reprinted almost verbatim in periodicals. Other lecture titles, such as "The Mission of War," "The Work before Us," and "The Colored Man as Social and Political Force," suggest that her general themes were the same as those in her letters to William Still. It is these letters—some of which were published in Northern papers and others which Still included in his book, *The Underground Rail Road* (1871)—that most directly inform us of Harper's Reconstruction concerns.

Frances Harper generally developed two themes in her Reconstruction lectures. One was that the future of the nation depended upon the ability of its citizens to unite behind a common goal. She argued, "Between the white people and the colored there is a community of interests, and the sooner they find it out, the better it will be for both parties"; yet, Harper continued, "that community of interests does not consist in increasing the privileges of one class and curtailing the rights of the other, but in getting every citizen interested in the welfare, progress and durability of the state."[115] Her other theme, and the one that increasingly dominated her published writings, was that the Emancipation had opened a new era—a time for blacks, particularly black women, to "lift up their heads and plant the roots of progress under the hearthstone" (*Brighter* 127).

The poems and letters that appeared in the press and the fact that the earliest existing text of *Moses: A Story of the Nile,* published in 1869, is marked as the second edition suggest that the indefatigable Mrs. Harper did continue to write during her Southern tour. However, we have no new collection of poems until fifteen years after *Poems on Miscellaneous Subjects* first appeared. Then in rapid succession, Frances Harper published three collections: *Moses: A Story of the Nile* (1869), *Poems* (1871), and *Sketches of Southern Life* (1872).

Frances Harper's activities and interests are more important to the subject of her Reconstruction poetry than simple biographical context alone. To Harper, literature was not separate from life. Her writing was but one of the ways in which she sought to live her convictions and to work for the betterment of the world within which she lived and the people with whom she identified. In her earliest extant prose piece, "Christianity" (ca. 1853), she enunciated her aesthetic convictions by saying that literature is an "elegance" achieved by toil of pen and labor of pencil. Its purpose is "to cultivate the intellect, enlighten the understanding, give scope to the imagination, and refine the sensibilities" (*Brighter* 98). But, she also admonished, it is important only to the extent that it inspires individuals to high and noble deeds. Over the years she reaffirmed this idea in several texts. For example, Jenny, Harper's fictive self in her "Fancy Etchings" series (1873), tells her Aunt Jane:

> Aunty I want to be a poet, to earn and take my place among the poets of the nineteenth century; but with all the glowing enthusiasms that light up my life I cannot help thinking, that more valuable than the soarings of genius are the tender nestlings of love. Genius may charm the intellect, but love will refresh the spirit. (*Brighter* 225)

Wanting to "earn and take [her] place among the poets of the nineteenth century" indicates a recognition of a tradition to be entered, a standard to be surpassed, a "genius" to be expressed. But personal satisfaction and public acclaim are secondary objectives. Jenny continues, "It is just because our lives are apt to be so hard and dry, that I would scatter the flowers of poetry around our paths; . . . I would teach men and women to love noble deeds by setting them to the music, of fitly spoken words" (*Brighter* 225).

Frances Harper's commitment to a pragmatic poetics did not exclude concern with literary techniques or experimentation with genre and style. It was during her travels throughout the war-torn South and as a part of her Reconstruction efforts that she created one of her most experimental texts. *Moses: A Story of the Nile* is transitional between the structure that Harper had used in poems such as "Ruth and Naomi" (1856) and "The Two Offers" (1859), and that she would use again in the novel *Iola Leroy* (1892). Each of these works begins, as does *Moses,* with a dialogue between two major characters that is interrupted by an omniscient narrator who describes or interprets for the reader. The first eight stanzas of *Moses* alternate between the words of Moses and his adopted mother, Charmian. But here she prefaces these first stanzas with the name of the speaker and thereby frames the dialogue as dramatic scenes. She restages the life and times of the Jewish leader who led his people from slavery in seven hundred lines of blank verse. Her characters and the scenes she creates reenact the Bible story in ways that are obviously useful for the religious inspiration and instruction of women and children and, as such, entirely in keeping with notions of "women's literature" and "women's concerns." At the same time, in *Moses,* as in many other biblically and classically inspired poems by African American women, the central participants are women and the themes are applicable to the contemporary issues of race and sex.

Frances Harper revises the Old Testament story to make manifest its relevance in two major ways. First, she subordinates the unique circumstances of Moses's life and focuses instead upon the decision that he makes to sacrifice his immediate pleasures and privileges in order to help his race. Second, she gives the women larger, more active parts in the liberation story. The Old Testament mentions the women only in terms of their roles in preserving the infant's life and summarizes Moses' childhood by noting that "the child grew," was taken "unto the Pharoah's daughter, and he became her son" (Exod. 2:10). Frances Harper invents a childhood characterized by deep love and devotion between Moses and his two mothers. She presents these women as strong, intelligent, and morally courageous and suggests that Moses' heroism was nurtured by their examples.

The first part of *Moses* echoes Harper's earlier depictions of idealized motherhood and the grief of separation in poems such as "Eliza Harris" and "A Mother's Heroism," "The Slave Mother" and "The Slave Auction." She emphasizes the separation theme by entitling the first section "The Parting." Her opening scene depicts the conversation between adoptive mother and son. Moses's salutation emphasizes Charmian's high rank, goodness, and generosity as well as his personal esteem for her:

> Kind and gracious princess, more than friend,
> I've come to thank thee for thy goodness,
> And to breathe into thy generous ears
> My last and sad farewell. . . . (*Brighter* 138–39)

Despite his personal attachment to her, he can no longer live "in pleasure" in her household while his people "faint in pain." Charmian, on the other hand, calls him "my son" and tries to dissuade him from a decision that she believes will make his life less comfortable and his future less secure. Charmian, as we learn from her argument, is a noble and loving woman who defied the law and braved her father's wrath to save the infant Moses' life. She succeeded because of her steadfast determination to protect with her own the life of that child. As her narrative indicates, Charmian has inherited this strength and courage from her own mother and it is this resemblance to his beloved wife that vanquishes her father's anger and resolve. The Pharaoh's words are quoted by Charmian to Moses:

> Charmian, arise,
> Thy prayer is granted; just then thy dead mother

> Came to thine eyes, and the light of Asenath
> Broke over thy face. Asenath was the light
> Of my home; the star that faded out too
> Suddenly from my dwelling, and left my life
> To darkness, grief and pain, and for her sake,
> Not thine, I'll spare the child. (*Brighter* 142)

Harper shows that although Charmian is not Moses' biological mother and is, in fact, of another "race," she sincerely and unequivocally loves Moses as her son. She has rescued him from drowning in the Nile and from the death decree of her father, the Pharaoh, and this, she declares, makes him

> Doubly mine; as such I claimed thee then, as such
> I claim thee now. I've nursed no other child
> Upon my knee, and pressed upon no other
> Lips the sweetest kisses of my love. . . . (*Brighter* 142)

Moses is fond of Charmian, but he would not forswear his race in order to live with her. During their conversation, Charmian recognizes in Moses a nobility, courage, and self-sacrifice that surpasses her own, and before "the grandeur of the young man's choice, / . . . she bowed / Her queenly head and let him pass" (*Brighter* 145). In Frances Harper's version of the Old Testament story, Charmian, the foster mother of Moses, claims as much, if not more, of the reader's sympathies as does her son, the ostensible protagonist. Charmian's was a claim and a devotion that Moses recognized and to which he responded. However, Moses could not accept an individual freedom while others of his race were excluded from similar experiences. He chose the greater needs of his race over the smaller pleasures of his personal affinities. This dilemma is one that Harper pursues from a slightly different perspective later in her novel, *Iola Leroy*. Then Iola, Henry, and Dr. Latimer all repeat, in almost the same words, Moses' decision to reject the offers of "adoption" into the dominant society and to "share the futures of my race."

Harper again enhances the role of women and, in this instance, privileges women's writing with the insertion of a poem she calls "Miriam's Song." In the Old Testament after the crossing of the Red Sea, "Moses and the children of Israel" sang a song of victory and thanksgiving that detailed the destruction of the enemy and celebrated a God who evoked "fear and dread." Moses' song gets nineteen verses, then in one quick mention, we learn that Miriam, "the prophetess, the sister of Aaron" led the women in dancing and singing Moses' song (Exod. 15:1–21). Miriam was sister to both Aaron and Moses, and Harper chooses to identify her not with Aaron but with Moses, the heroic leader. Harper increases the halo effect created by Miriam's close kinship with the heroic leader by describing Miriam's great joy and having Miriam "live the past again" as she reviews her role in protecting and nurturing Moses. As in the biblical version, Miriam leads the women in music, dance, and songs of celebration, but in Harper's account, "Miriam's Song" is not the repetition of a refrain from Moses' song. It is "another song of triumph" (*Brighter* 160) that is heard to rise over the first song and to change both the tune and the tenor of the occasion. Instead of celebrating the details of destruction, "Miriam's Song" contrasts the past with the present and emphasizes the Passover when "Egypt wakes up with a shriek and a sob / To mourn for her first-born and dead" (*Brighter* 161). In *Moses: A Story of the Nile,* women have been crucial actors in bringing this moment to pass and a woman now becomes its poet and historian. Harper emphasizes Miriam's perspective by setting the song apart from the rest of the text and presenting it as a separate poem with its own distinctive rhythm and rhyme patterns. "Miriam's Song" interrupts the narrative, it identifies individual ambition and pride as increasing the suffering of an entire nation, and it illustrates two of Harper's themes, the pain and grief of divided families and the opportunity for each individual to assist in the eventual triumph of good over evil. In focusing upon Miriam and her song, Harper implicitly makes a case for women's active participation in politics and she gives a biblical precedent for women as poets and social analysts.

In her characterization of Moses' mother, Frances Harper merges feminist and racial themes. It was the mother's ancestral stories that gave Moses his strong identification with his race. In vivid imagery Harper depicts the scene of the young children, gathered, fascinated and inspired, around the woman as she related what Moses calls "the grand traditions of our race that float, / With all their weird and solemn beauty, around / Our wrecked and blighted fortunes" (*Brighter* 143). It was his mother, Moses asserts, who instilled in her children their hope of freedom and their understanding of the necessity of their faith and obedience to God's will as conditions of that moment when ". . . the God our fathers loved and worshiped, / Would break our chains, and bring to us a great / Deliverance" (*Brighter* 144).

In *Moses: A Story of the Nile* Frances Harper creates an allegorical piece from Judeo-Christian mythology that reinterprets the roles of women and women's stories but does so in a distinctively African American manner. The subtitle, "A Story of the Nile," suggests, for example, the whole of Africa and not simply the small area indicated by "Egypt." It also shifts the focus from the hero to the situation, thus implying that the story is larger than that of one individual, one family, or even one nation. Just as Phillis Wheatley did with "Goliath of Gath" nearly a hundred years earlier, with *Moses* Frances Harper chose a subject and emphasized details that invite comparisons with the conditions of African American people. Were there more texts by African American women writers available, I might be able to chronicle a continuous progression from Wheatley to Harper. As it stands, I can assert that the literary model did exist and that in *Moses,* as with her other biblically and classically inspired poems, Frances Harper claimed her legacy by asserting the contemporaneousness of history and its applicability to issues of race and sex.

The roots of *Moses* grew not only from the African American women's literary tradition, but also from the more general folk culture. As Kenny Williams points out, Harper's *Moses* is her "most ambitious and her most symbolic work. . . . it never mentions the Negro's position in America nor the problems which immediately occurred as a result of the Emancipation Proclamation; yet it is quite obvious that the poem is an attempt to use the story of Moses very much as the poets of the spirituals had done in order to emphasize the need for a racial leader."[116] Williams's suggestion that *Moses* is a symbolic work in the tradition of "the poets of the spirituals" is insightful and is easily corroborated by many elements of Harper's poetry. Perhaps the most obvious is the Moses motif, itself, a staple in African American cultural, as it was in Harper's personal mythology. Spirituals such as "Go Down, Moses," "On the Rock Where Moses Stood," "Deep River," and "Steal Away" emphasize the liberation, escape, and vindication themes that her own *Moses* echoes. And Harper's emphasis upon the attitudes and roles of women find precursors in such ancestral songs as "Mary, Don't You Weep" as it conflates the Old and New Testament mythologies and invites the woman to take courage from her knowledge of similar moments in history.

However, we find other possible sources for themes and images in Harper's poem in the African American secular folk tradition. For example, Harper's characterization of Moses' mother as not only the culture bearer but also the nurturer of resistance resembles similar imagery in songs such as "De Ole Nigger Driver." In this piece, the narrator recalls his mother's teachings about the oppression of his people and the sources of that oppression when he says,

> Fust ting my mammy tell me,
>   O, gwine away!
> Tell me 'bout de nigger driver,
>   O, gwine away!
> Nigger driver second devil,
>   O, gwine away!

And, as Moses did with the Egyptian overseer, the narrator decides

> Best ting for do he driver,
>   O, gwine away!
> Knock he down and spoil he labor,
>   O, gwine away![117]

In African American folklore, the Moses figure was well established as a literal and symbolic device. Harper's Moses is the liberator of both the Old Testament and of the spirituals. Moreover, Moses in African American folk culture is androgynous. Moses is also Harriet Tubman, the African American woman of the antebellum Underground Railroad. Tubman, like

Moses, had escaped the fate of her enslaved people. And, like Moses, Tubman refused to bask in the luxury of her individual freedom while her people remained enslaved. Moses symbolized the sacrificing of personal gain, the risking of personal safety for the good of one's people. In a speech at the Eleventh Woman's Rights Convention on May 10, 1866, Harper explicitly identified Harriet Tubman with the Old Testament Moses when she said: "We have a woman in our country who has received the name of 'Moses,' . . .—a woman who has gone down into the Egypt of slavery and brought out hundreds of our people into liberty."[118]

In referring the overwhelmingly white Protestant delegates to the Eleventh Woman's Rights Convention to the Jewish Moses and the black Harriet Tubman, Frances Harper was mediating between cultures. She was reminding them that the Old Testament stories directly condemned racial oppression and she was requiring them to absorb African American symbology into their frames of reference. Harper's poem, then, resonates with multiple allusions and would have sparked interest and identification with a variety of readers ranging from the newly literate to the more experienced and well educated. Several news accounts indicate that Harper recited *Moses: A Story of the Nile* to "large and delighted" audiences. While these reporters do not indicate their personal awareness that the poem had any particular relevance to current issues, on at least one occasion Frances Harper explicitly identified its contemporary application. During the Woman's Rights Convention, after identifying Harriet Tubman as a Moses, Harper expanded the definition of those needing to be saved to include not just black slaves but also white women of leisure. Harper said:

> While there exists this brutal element in society which tramples upon the feeble and treads down the weak, I tell you that if there is any class of people who need to be lifted out of their airy nothings and selfishness, it is the white women of America. (*Proceedings* 48)

Her words echo those that Harriet Jacobs used as an epigraph to *Incidents in the Life of a Slave Girl* when she quoted Isaiah's warning to the "careless daughters."

Moses: A Story of the Nile is a Reconstruction poem in other ways. To the antebellum symbolism of a black Moses, Harriet Tubman, Frances Harper added a second, modern day Moses. Harper, like many other nineteenth-century blacks, called Abraham Lincoln "Moses." In a letter to William Still dated April 19, 1869, Harper writes:

> Moses, the meekest man on earth, led the children of Israel over the Red Sea, but was not permitted to see them settled in Canaan. Mr. Lincoln had led up through another Red Sea to the table land of a triumphant victory, and God has seen fit to summon for a new era another man. It is ours then to bow to the Chastener and let our honored and loved Chieftain go.[119]

Postbellum readers would recognize *Moses: A Story of the Nile* as a call to all citizens of the United States to choose the larger social good over their own personal gain. The African American oral tradition had long since established Egyptian bondage as a metaphor for American slavery and the abolitionist movement had taught many whites to recognize this. Therefore, *Moses* as a symbolic retelling of African American history would be clear to many. At the same time, this poem would not unduly disturb those readers who wished to concentrate upon the building of a united nation and ignore its past mistakes. Moral decisions that faced the reunited states also included the proper relationship between individual aspirations and community responsibilities. If the term, "the Gilded Age," had not yet been applied, the manifestations of such an era were fast becoming evident. As the story of an individual who renounced material success, identified with the downtrodden, and accepted the tasks assigned him by his God, Moses could also serve as a model for American society at large.

As a writer who saw her art as means of educating and uplifting, Harper was careful to choose figures who were familiar to and instructive for the greatest number of readers. As a teacher, she recognized the inclusiveness of the Moses symbol that made it effective as a text in day and Sabbath schools. In focusing her first major postbellum work upon a figure as well established in African American folk culture as Moses, Frances Harper increased the significance of her poem for African American readers. However, her message was one of renewal and rededication for all people of good will. It made it easier to see, for example, the work of the Freedmen's Bureau and the American Missionary Society as enacting contemporary versions of the biblical story. The teachers, nurses, and social workers who left their homes and loved ones to join the survivors in the devastated South could identify with Moses, as individuals who answered God's call to prepare a way out of the wilderness into the Promised Land.

In 1871, Frances Harper published *Poems,* her second Reconstruction volume. It does not obviously continue the Reconstruction themes and the bold experimentation with form of *Moses: A Story of the Nile,* but presents a number of poems that in style, theme, and subject echo those of her antebellum best-seller, *Poems on Miscellaneous Subjects.* Since many of the selections in *Poems* had been published separately before and during the war, it might seem more fitting to consider this work as a miscellaneous collection rather than a sustained new work. However, in his essay "The South in African American Literature: 1877–1915," Dickson D. Bruce, Jr., makes a point worth heeding here. Bruce notes that post-Reconstruction black poets organized their books with "easily recognizable structural principles" designed to appeal to a diverse readership.[120] To understand the poet's intention, one must consider the effect of the entire volume, the order of its poems and its dominant tone, as well as the themes and subjects of individual poems. While Bruce's concern is with a slightly later group of writers, his idea holds true for Harper as well. In fact, since Harper was a precursor to and model for those writers and since she exercised great authority over the composition of her books, indeed published and distributed most of them herself, it is altogether reasonable to suggest that Harper's *Poems* may have set the pattern that Bruce finds common during the period of his study.

The individual works in *Poems* generally focus on three subjects: motherhood, death, and public celebration. Though these are not new subjects for Harper, her Reconstruction social and artistic ideals inspired modifications and additions, especially in tone and theme. For example, in *Poems* she writes about infants and children not as objects of pathos but as sources of love and faith. As in her earlier volumes, Harper still idealizes motherhood, but to the fugitive mother running with infant in arms and to the sorrowful slave mother being auctioned away from her child she adds a new figure, a mother who says, "Hope and joy, peace and blessing, / Met me in my first-born child" (*Brighter* 181).

Many of the death poems in this volume also focus upon divided families, especially those created by dying mothers or children. Again, however, Harper modifies her antebellum images. Rather than the kinds of poems that appeared in her antebellum collection, "The Slave Mother" grieving over her imminent parting with her child or even the central figure in "The Slave Mother, a Tale of Ohio" choosing to kill her infant rather than see it return to slavery, this volume offers other, less tragic separations. "The Dying Mother" with her last words blesses her children, comforted by the knowledge that her husband and family remain together, that God will watch over them, and that they will be united in "the brighter world above" (*Brighter* 184). From the horrific and unnatural experiences that slavery created, Harper's poems now turn to the redemptive suffering of divinely ordained separations.

The new poems about children, the death poems, and the celebratory poems of public experiences such as "The Fifteenth Amendment," "Lines to Miles O'Reilly," and "President Lincoln's Proclamation of Freedom" establish a Reconstructive ideal, that of heroic effort, sacrifice, and courage rewarded or continued through new life.

Poems has about twice as many death poems as did Harper's earlier collection. In her introduction to *The Complete Poems of Frances Ellen Watkins Harper,* Maryemma Graham suggests that this may be a response to Frances Harper's own fragile health and to her husband's death in 1864, less than a decade before.[121] It is quite likely that personal grief was a factor. Furthermore, such an autobiographical perspective also suggests reasons for the unusually high number of pieces that celebrate infants and children. When *Poems on Miscellaneous Subjects* appeared in 1854, its author was a single woman. During her brief marriage to Fenton Harper, Frances Harper had become mother to Mary and stepmother to her widowed spouse's three children. This could account for works such as "To a Babe Smiling in Her Sleep," "The Mother's Blessing," and "Thank God for Little Children."

Reading the poems from an autobiographical perspective enhances their meaning in the context of the total volume.

In general, *Poems* strikes a more mature, contemplative, but hopeful tone than the earlier collection. This shift undoubtedly reflects Harper's personal experiences, but it also mirrors the Reconstructive social spirit with which Harper aligned herself. And this perspective, I believe, is more in keeping with the relationship Harper maintains between her life and her art. Since the early days when she dedicated her life to public service, Frances Harper did not usually allow her private life to diverge from her public stance. Her literature is remarkably formal in that it does not divulge her own feelings or allude to her own life except, as in the example of her being ousted from the Philadelphia streetcars or in her letters from the South to abolitonist friends and the reading public, when her experiences illustrated larger social themes. From this perspective, the more general sorrow over the deaths of countless soldiers and of Abraham Lincoln which Harper shared with her readers was as important as Harper's own mother-hood and widowhood in shaping the new emphases upon life and death in this volume.

Poems concludes with "Light in Darkness," a work that can be read as representative of the collection and of the hopeful period within which it was published. In the heavily iambic rhythm and ABCB-rhymed stanzas that typify other poems in this collection, the narrator of "Light in Darkness" declares that even though "We've" lost much due to mistakes and bad choices, and we have been punished for our sins, there is, nonetheless, "room to build holy altars / Where our crumbling idols lay" (*Brighter* 195). The poem suggests that the loss of material goods and the assault upon their spirits are actually gifts for which "the chastening angel" might be thanked because from the "shadows" of their suffering they could more clearly see "the light and beautiful visions" (*Brighter* 195). The poem becomes a meta-phor for the experiences of the Civil War period. In the concluding stanza, the narrator credits poetry for making survival easier and foreshadows the words of Jenny in "Fancy Etchings" some five years later:

> Our first view of the Holy City
> Came through our darken'd years,
> The songs that lightened our sorrows,
> We heard 'mid our night of tears. (*Brighter* 195)

Frances Harper's third Reconstruction volume, *Sketches of Southern Life,* was published in 1872. It is a small volume of poetry—only nine poems—but its small size belies its great significance. *Sketches* summarizes Frances Harper's earlier themes and anticipates her later writings. It is a true benchmark in her own poetic career and a touchstone for African American literature. *Sketches* combines the themes of *Moses* and of *Poems* while returning to the stylistic experimentation of the earlier work. *Sketches*

continues Harper's earlier emphasis on female characters and their perspectives, explores further possibilities concerning civil rights, social responsibilities, and spiritual progress, and it initiates a bold new direction in African
American poetics. As Maryemma Graham concludes, "*Sketches of Southern Life*, . . . shows a mature poet at her best. It is both a culmination of
the formal structure Harper had used in her earliest poetry and an incorporation of a vernacular mode" (xli).

Sketches echoes the dramatic narrative technique with which Harper
was experimenting in *Moses* and earlier works. In fact, as Graham indicates,
Moses and *Sketches* "may be seen as complementary texts. For Harper,
they represent an intellectual exploration into the meaning and nature of
freedom. Taken together they form an important link in the evolution of the
quest or journey motif in African American autobiographical, poetic and
fictional discourse" (xlii). While the biblical sources, the theme, the characterizations, and even the structure of *Moses* bear some resemblance to
earlier writing, equally important are the ways in which that text reflects
Harper's Reconstruction ideas and anticipates *Sketches of Southern Life*, a
work that consciously and clearly incorporates elements of African American folk culture and was intended to contribute to the Reconstruction of
American literature.

Sketches of Southern Life articulates Frances Harper's basic Reconstruction theme that the future of the nation depended upon the ability of
its citizens to unite behind a common goal. Poems such as "Learning to
Read" and "Church Building" promote community effort in establishing the
institutions whereby individuals may reach their highest development. Finally, *Sketches* anticipates Harper's later work. Many of its ideas, situations,
characters, and techniques reappear and are reworked in later poems such
as "Dialogue on Women's Rights" and in her novel, *Iola Leroy*.

The remainder of my discussion of the Reconstruction poetry of Frances
E. W. Harper will center on *Sketches* as I seek to demonstrate three ideas
which basically apply to all three books: (1) Frances Harper wrote as a
popular poet with a clear sense of the aesthetics and concerns of popular
literature. (2) She did not limit herself to simply imitating the popular poetry
of the day but instead experimented with form, character, and language. (3)
Sketches, like Harper's other collections, not only shares characteristics
with nineteenth-century American popular literature in general, but represents the literature of other African American women writers of that era.

Sketches of Southern Life begins with a poem of appreciation to "Our
English Friends" for their support of the American anti-slavery struggle. It
includes several poems told by one persona, Aunt Chloe, and it concludes
with two poems titled respectively, "I Thirst" and "The Dying Queen."

The first poem, dedicated to "Our English Friends," acknowledges the
international readership that Harper anticipated for this volume. From the
earliest extant published book by an African in the American colonies
through the slave narratives, the earliest novels by African Americans, and

up to Harper's own time, England had provided an enthusiastic reception for African American literature. Moreover, during the antebellum period, British abolitionists had worked to block an effort to enlist England in support of the Confederacy and Harper, of course, was well aware of this. There was an important difference, however, between this poem and antebellum works, such as William and Ellen Craft's narrative, that heralded the British as the antithesis of Americans, as those who proclaimed a monarchy but offered freedom while those who spoke of democracy deliberately maintained slavery. "Our English Friends" does not play up the irony of an Old World monarchy that nurtured democratic movements more fervently than the New World republic which had declared its independence in pursuit of equal rights for all. The slave era is portrayed, instead, as a time of mortal affliction, when "Slavery full of wrath and strife, / Was clutching at the Nation's life" (*Brighter* 196). The brave Britons had reached out to this nation in its "hour of need," and the poet, on behalf of the country itself, thanks them for their nobility and courage, for putting their love of freedom ahead of "paltry gain," for encouraging and supporting the winning cause. In speaking not as a member of a freed race but as a citizen of a revived country, the narrator aligns herself and the freedpeople with the best elements of United States society, those individuals who had recognized the peril and righteously fought to overcome it.

The title of the penultimate poem, "'I Thirst,'" evokes the Crucifixion as related in John 19:28–30 when Jesus said "I thirst," drank the vinegar, and died. In this way, biblical scholars tell us, Jesus fulfilled the final prophecy and his mission was completed. He was allowed to die. As she had done in *Moses,* Harper writes this as a drama which she embellishes with the details that suit her immediate goals. "'I Thirst'" is a dialogue between two voices, one longs for death to end earthly suffering and the second rebukes that longing. The second voice reminds the first that death is God's decision as to when human work has ended and that until God had determined that they had fulfilled their obligations, each individual must rely upon the "living fount" within for renewal of strength and restoration of faith.

The final poem, "The Dying Queen" recounts the last moments of a woman who chooses to die as she had lived, with her eyes wide open. The epigraph of this poem is "I would meet death awake." Although the resolution is different, the words echo those of Cleopatra, the African Queen, who also had "met the battle's shock, / And born the cares of state" (*Brighter* 209). Both Harper's and Shakespeare's dying queens reject the death scene urged upon them by friends and dictate their own terms upon which they would meet death.

"Our English Friends," "'I Thirst,'" and "The Dying Queen" frame the series of poems that obviously inspired the volume's title. This structure, which defines the context within which the Aunt Chloe narratives will be read, anticipates similar strategies by writers such as Joel Chandler Harris, Charles Chesnutt, Thomas Nelson Page, and Octavia Albert. The first and the last two poems in the volume not only separate the "Aunt Chloe" section but their tone and narrative personae establish a relational distance wherein the writer and the personae in the framing poems stand closer to the reader as they all become the audience for the world being depicted in the middle section. Such a relationship allows greater freedom in the Aunt Chloe series to sketch with all its peculiarities and without omitting the abuse and pain of her slave experiences, a history that is both individual and social but a history not intended to implicate all readers. The framing poems "balance" the volume and mediate between the Aunt Chloe voice and that of the book as a whole. At the same time that it balances, the volume also privileges Aunt Chloe's voice. Since two-thirds of the poems and the title itself relate to Aunt Chloe and her friends, the variety within the remaining three poems emphasizes the priority of that single subject.

The "Aunt Chloe" poems form at once an autobiography of an ex-slave woman and a history of slavery and Reconstruction as narrated by that woman. Whereas Harper's antebellum poetry often told stories about slaves, in these poems a slave speaks for herself. Aunt Chloe is the voice of the slave mother, heretofore only seen from a distance, now being heard and understood from her own perspective.

The opening poem, which serves as the exposition to the overall saga, is a revised slave narrative. The Civil War and the constitutional amendments that followed it had made the proclamation of humanity less an issue than the quality of character that these new citizens possessed. Thus Harper's narrator did not need to begin with "I was born" and other attestations of being. Like Elizabeth Keckley, Harper assumed the task of demonstrating the potential of newly freed slaves to become responsible and contributing citizens. Chloe, like Elizabeth, concentrates on the incidents that molded her character. Chloe begins with her separation from her children. As in many slave narratives, their sale was not a deliberately punitive action in response to any inadequacy or guilt of the enslaved, but the result of the insolvency that the master's death exposed.

As Keckley had implied in her work, white women were also victimized by slave economics. When Aunt Chloe heard that her children had been sold, her first impulse was to ask her mistress to intercede. She undoubtedly knew that the widowed woman had no legal power, but she quickly learned that the news of her insolvency had reduced her mistress to tears and that she was emotionally incapable of helping Chloe with her crisis. Here, Harper reverses the situation in much abolitionist literature. Instead of an Angelina Grimke or a Lydia Maria Child or any other white woman describing the sufferings of black women, the ex-slave woman is the one who reports the sufferings of white females in the antebellum South.

The poem is not about the plight of women, however. It is about a particular group of women, American slave women as represented by Aunt Chloe. Chloe is a part of a community. Her fellow slaves warn her of the impending sale, they sympathize with her in her grief, and they rejoice with her in their freedom. Their stories are used to supplement Chloe's personal experiences and to provide a context within which the protagonist can be better understood.

Aunt Chloe identifies her feelings when her children were sold away, suggests that the slaves had a mutual support system, and describes the development of the faith that allowed her to survive that separation. When her fellow slaves whispered to her that her children had been sold, Chloe says:

> It seemed as if a bullet
>   Had shot me through and through,
> And I felt as if my heart-strings
>   Was breaking right in two. (*Brighter* 196)

The importance of the slave community to Chloe's survival stands in stark contrast to accounts in the slave narratives by men, whose protagonists were usually alienated from mothers, friends, or support systems; they were, in Phillis Klotman's words, "running men." However, Frances Harper's depiction is quite in keeping with the accounts by slave women discussed earlier. As was the case with Harriet Jacobs, the women sympathized with and supported one another; and as with Jacobs, the protagonist prefers to remain within the community. She leaves only to insure the safety and survival of herself and her family.

The second poem, "Deliverance," is a sixty-stanza history of Chloe's life from the sale of her children until the present telling. Chloe's frequent use of the first-person plural encourages the reader to see her experiences as representative of those of other slaves as well. The poem's three subplots exemplify the themes of retribution, release, and responsibility. Retribution, or the "justice in the kingdom," ultimately comes after liberation, but it is also manifested in the reversals that the slaves witness during slavery. For example, Aunt Chloe, whose sons have been sold from her, sees her mistress lose her son to war. In a scene ironically reminiscent of the parting between Moses and Charmian, Mister Tom chose his higher calling (i.e., joining the Confederate forces) over the tearful entreaties of his loving mother who would keep him safe at home. Chloe's acknowledgment of the woman's suffering may well have been the attitude of Moses' mother toward Charmian's grief. Chloe says, "'Now, old Mistus feels the sting, / For this parting with your children / Is a mighty dreadful thing'" (*Brighter* 200). But as certainly as Moses' mother was not overly troubled by the Egyptian princess's loss, Chloe recognizes her mistress's suffering without misunderstanding the differences in their circumstances. Though the grief of separation is a "mighty dreadful thing," the "now" and the "old" that describe "Mistus" suggest the satisfaction of retribution realized.

In telling the story of the slaves' release from bondage, Harper focuses on the liberator more than on any active participation of the liberated. Like the children of Israel during the plagues and the Passover, the slaves "were praying in the cabins, wanting freedom to begin" (*Brighter* 200) while a noble and courageous individual carried out the liberation. In "Deliverance," not only does Harper identify Abraham Lincoln as the Moses figure but she implies that he is a second Christ. When the news comes that the South has been defeated, the former slaves "just poured our prayers and blessings / Upon his [Lincoln's] precious head" (*Brighter* 201). Their jubilation brings to mind the scene in *Moses* after the Red Sea has destroyed the pursuing army. Like the Israelites, the slaves just "laughed, and danced, and shouted, / And prayed, and sang, and cried" (*Brighter* 201). Lincoln's assassination was "one awful sorrow," one that aroused an immediate desire for someone else to "be the Moses of all the colored race" (*Brighter* 202). However, the emancipated people must learn that with freedom comes great responsibilities, and the subsequent poems demonstrate that the freed slaves, like the children of Israel, could not rely upon Moses to bring them to the promised land.

This third theme, responsibility, supplements the acclamation of a divinely inspired liberator with attention to the subsequently important roles of the liberated. Leaders can open the way, but the journey is ultimately made by the followers. The poem rejects the subordination of one to the other and suggests that those who follow might at some point need to lead. It does assert the necessity of each doing what one can. The final section of "Deliverance" concentrates upon the importance of intelligent suffrage and the roles that women can play to insure clean politics even when disenfranchised. By listing several cases wherein men misused their votes and by contrasting their stupidity with the strong and corrective actions of their wives, Harper demonstrates that lack of political rights is not necessarily lack of power and that enfranchisement based solely upon gender is incorrect and dangerous to the country's reconstruction.

The final stanza makes the lesson of "Deliverance" clear. Though there are still too many who don't know the facts and obligations of their liberation and though liberation, especially that of women, has not been complete, it is vital to "rally round the cause"—for each individual must recognize that

> . . . their freedom cost too much
> Of blood and pain and treasure,
> For them to fool away their votes
> For profit or for pleasure. (*Brighter* 204)

"Aunt Chloe's Politics," "Learning to Read," and "Church Building" are shorter poems that elaborate on the three issues that Harper believed would make a reconstructed nation strong: equal rights, education, and spirituality. The final poem of the sequence, "The Reunion," serves as the narrative denouement. It completes the circle by moving from Chloe's communal experiences back to her more personal story. The social achievements of learning to read, participating in community development, and acquiring her own property are most satisfying when shared with loved ones. The promise of reunification contained in the first poem fulfilled, this postbellum slave narrative closes with the vision of a unified family in a home "that will hold us all." Reunited with her children and now a proud grandmother, the slave, Aunt Chloe, has become "Mrs. Chloe Fleet," woman and citizen.

To Frances Harper, as to many nineteenth-century writers, "songs for the people" should be "sweet anthems of love and duty" (*Brighter* 371), and her desire was to inspire that "deeper sense of justice and humanity" in as many people as she could. Like nineteenth-century women, particularly, Frances Harper resisted the trend toward secular materialism and wrote with a firm grounding in militant Christianity. Such literary goals were shared by nineteenth-century American readers. They expected their literature to record, argue, or exhort, to point out the lessons in their everyday experiences, to be a weapon with which to defend good, to expose hypocrisy, and to abolish evil. However, readers in the mid-nineteenth century were by and large, as Roy Harvey Pearce states, "literate but not literary, thinking but not thoughtful, caught up in the exhilarating busyness of day-to-day life."[122] Therefore, as Pearce concludes, "the rule was this: that the poet who would reach the great audience had, willy-nilly, to cut himself down to its size. Such a cutting down . . . implies also the production of an art in some respects different in kind from high art, and to be judged and valued accordingly" (246). The privileging of utility over pleasure and of inclusiveness over exclusivity not only required a particular kind of writing but it encouraged the merging of oral and written forms.

One way in which Harper achieved this—incorporating folk symbology into her writing—has already been discussed. Another method is that described by Pearce. Harper adapted her writing to the "great audience" and created popular art. Not only did she intend her work to be printed, but like Dickens, Twain, and others, Frances Harper gave public readings that were exceptionally well received. It could be said of her poetry as Theodore Parker said of Emerson's works, that they were "published before they were printed; delivered by word of mouth to various audiences."[123] From her presentations, if from nothing else, Frances Harper knew that nineteenth-century readers preferred poems with rhythms and rhymes that were easy to memorize and to recite. Other requirements for popular poetry included familiar verse forms such as the sonnet and the ballad, simple and didactic metaphors, and readily comprehensible and prosaic word order. When one recognizes this, then the fact that Harper's poetry often sounds better in recitation than it scans may be attributed to factors other than what later critics decided were errors in her construction of meter.

Frances Harper was also adhering to aesthetics of postbellum popular literature in writing literature that was designed to appeal to a broad spectrum of American society. Frances Harper was herself a radical civil rights activist, who had a clear-eyed and realistic perspective of difficulties: par-

ticularly of the poverty, the abuse, and the devastation that permeated the
postbellum South. However, Harper chose to mitigate with humor the mis-
ery of slavery and the atrocities of Reconstruction and to emphasize themes
of progress, unity, and determination. For example, in "Deliverance," the
key poem of *Sketches,* Harper devotes four stanzas to the disappointment
of the Johnson era, but she treats it ultimately as merely an aggravating
interruption of the nation's progress:

> But everything will pass away—
>   He went like time and tide—
> And when the next election came
>   They let poor Andy slide
>
> But now we have a President,
>   And if I was a man
> I'd vote for him for breaking up
>   The wicked Ku-Klux Klan. (202)

    The rhythm is lively and light, but within these lines, Harper acknowl-
edges the unwillingness of Andrew Johnson to support Reconstruction efforts, the failure of the country to allow women to vote, and the existence
of the Ku Klux Klan. Her audience may well have noticed her gentle deri-
sion in referring to the former president as "poor Andy," especially when
contrasted to her consistent references to Abraham Lincoln as "Mister Lincoln" and to the next line which says "But now we have a President." In
other writings of the same period Harper does not treat the vicious Ku Klux
Klan so gently, but in this poem her use of the term "wicked" deflects the
controversy that more forceful adjectives would have engendered.

    Certainly her colleagues in the suffrage movement would appreciate the
irony of Aunt Chloe, the narrator who is competent to recite history but not
to vote; the contrast in "Deliverance" between the men who sold their votes
for three sticks of candy or for white sand topped with sugar and their wives
who brought them back in line; and the declaration that despite their inability to vote, "we women radicals" had nonetheless defeated Curnel Johnson's
election efforts. These are all obviously critical statements. Yet they are
made with wit and humor and with the clear implication that things are
getting better, thereby encouraging the assent of less radical but politically
important readers.

    As she did in *Moses,* Harper chooses characters that a wide and diverse
group would recognize but with which the freed slaves would be particularly
familiar. For example, there is a biblical precursor to Aunt Chloe that
strengthens the poem's applicability to the Reconstruction era. In the New
Testament, Paul's first letter to the Church at Corinth came during a time
when various groups were trying to establish their own places within the
emerging Christian society. The Corinthian congregation included a woman
named Chloe. Paul's letter came in response to information from Chloe's

people about certain factions; he was writing to revive their unity and to assure that each individual was accorded proper respect. Readers who associated the New Testament Chloe with Harper's would recognize similarities in the current American situation and that of Corinth. They would remember that Paul began his letter by asserting Christian equality. The Corinthians were "called to take their place among all the saints everywhere who pray to our Lord Jesus Christ; for he is their Lord no less than ours" (I Cor. 1:2). Readers could even have compared Paul's literary aesthetic and Harper's, for Paul, too, wrote "not with any show of oratory or philosophy, but simply to tell you what God has guaranteed" (I Cor. 2:1).

A second connection that would have been made by nineteenth-century readers is that between Frances Harper's Aunt Chloe and Harriet Beecher Stowe's. Both Harper and Stowe based their characters on cultural types. In the *Key to Uncle Tom's Cabin,* Stowe argued that she drew upon personal accounts and contemporary literature for her people and incidents. But while the mammy figure may have been a part of contemporary literature or even of African American culture, Stowe's Aunt Chloe was a caricature. As Trudier Harris explains in *Mammies and Militants,* the Southern mammy figure had begun as a complex literary rendition of a type, but quickly began to degenerate. Harris says:

> Mammy's self-respect was lost in groveling before and fawning upon her mistress, master, and young white charges. Her loyalty became self-effacement and her affection anticipated the exaggeration of the minstrel tradition. Her piety and patience worked more often than not in favor of the whites, and her tyranny was most ruthless when it was exercised over other Blacks.[124]

Harriet Beecher Stowe's *Uncle Tom's Cabin* was one of the early examples of this, and Frances Harper's Aunt Chloe was an early African American response. Harper's own familiarity with Harriet Stowe's work is well established. In the 1850s, she had written a poem "To Mrs. Harriet Beecher Stowe" that praised Stowe's abolitionist efforts, and she had based at least two earlier poems, "Eliza Harris" and "Eva's Farewell," upon characters from *Uncle Tom's Cabin.* Perhaps Harper did not take on Stowe's depiction of the mammy earlier because she did not wish to lessen the abolitionist value of the novel, or perhaps at that time Frances Harper herself, a freeborn, middle-class black woman, was not sufficiently knowledgeable about slave women of the rural South. But as her letters document, Harper's postwar experiences in the South gave her a new appreciation of and respect for these women. And her postbellum resolve, which was shared by most African Americans, to become even more aggressive in articulating African American realities from the perspective of African Americans gave a new urgency and new direction to her feminist concerns. Thus, it is not entirely coincidental that the experiences and attitudes of Harper's Aunt Chloe revise several of those of Stowe's character.

Several critics have recognized Harper's experimentation with language in *Sketches*. J. Saunders Redding, for example, notes that "In all her verse [Harper] attempted to suit her language to her theme. In *Moses* she gives her language a certain solemnity and elevation of tone. In her pieces on slavery she employs short, teethy, angry monosyllables. Her use of dialectal patterns [in *Sketches*] was no accident" (Redding 43). While a few critics have misjudged Harper's language as "dialect," it is more appropriately recognized, as Redding notes, as "dialectal patterns." Harper's folk characters speak with "a fine racy, colloquial tang" (Redding 42). Eschewing misspellings and linguistic signals that befuddle the reader and constrain the speaker within preconstructed dialectical boundaries of pathos and humor, Frances Harper avoided the problems that ensnared Paul Laurence Dunbar and worried James Weldon Johnson.

Paul Lauter has pointed out that Harper's language was "clearly a conscious and . . . political choice." Lauter describes Harper's technique and distinguishes it from that of Harriet Stowe in the following analysis of "Aunt Chloe's Politics":

> Here, however, [Harper] wishes to draw a shrewd and upright woman of the people who is not, like Stowe's Aunt Chloe, distanced from her audience, white or middle-class black, by the "color," so to speak, of her language. Like most Americans, this Aunt Chloe uses some slang—like "honey-fugle round," to cajole or wheedle, and "a heap"—some non-standard grammar—"have took it"—and the mock ignorance of the savvy: "I don't know very much About these politics." Harper carefully establishes in the third line—"Though I think that some who run 'em"—Aunt Chloe's control of standard, informal English before, in the next to last line—"Though I thinks a heap of voting"—she presents her using a specifically Southern black locution. Aunt Chloe's language is, I believe, designed to legitimate her keen political commentary.[125]

Frances Watkins Harper was an innovator among African American writers. According to Joan Sherman in *Invisible Poets: African Americans of the Nineteenth Century*:

> in every decade since 1850, Harper's work remains the prototype of black poetry. As early as 1871 she forgave the oppressor and combined her appeals for civil rights with a confident vision of racial brotherhood. During the last two decades of the century she leads the poets in uplifting verse, directed not only at raising black moral, educational, and economic status, but also at reforming the national evil of alcoholism and the double standard of sex.[126]

Frances Harper was an innovator among American writers generally. At least a dozen years before Walt Whitman's essay "The Poetry of the Future," Frances Harper was writing along the lines that Whitman visualized. In his 1881 manifesto, Whitman called for a poetry that would "arouse and initiate more than to define or finish."[127] He called for epic poetry about the "real history of the United States" (208), works that would sum up "the tremendous moral and military perturbations of 1861–5, and their results" (209).

According to Whitman, the new poetry would recognize that "the real, though latent and silent bulk of America, city or country, presents a magnificent mass of material, never before equalled on earth," and that "Poetry of the Future" would unite "closer and closer not only the American States, but all nations, and all humanity." Exhorted Whitman, "That, O poets! is not that a theme worth chanting, striving for? . . . Perhaps the most illustrious culmination of the modern may thus prove to be a signal growth of joyous, more exalted bards of adhesiveness, identically one in soul, but contributed by every nation, each after its distinctive kind" (205).

Frances Harper anticipated Whitman in her use of the Civil War and its aftermath as her subject. Her choice of black American farmers was more radical than Whitman probably intended but it did give voice and visibility to a "real, though latent and silent bulk of America." As she sang songs of her "distinctive kind" she also emphasized the unification of the peoples of the United States.

Frances Harper's Reconstruction poetry is among the relatively few extant volumes published by African American women of that time. That which we have confirms that Harper's poetry was innovative in many ways but that her themes were generally those of her African American sisters. They, too, wrote about morality, social reform, and freedom. They wrote odes to leaders such as Abraham Lincoln and Charles Sumner, and they wrote tenderly of children, musingly of death, and passionately about outstanding women in history. For example, Adah Isaacs Menken's *Infelicia* is filled, as Joan Sherman tells us, with "'shrieks and groans' like the 'ghosts of [her] dead hopes'"[128] and is seemingly far removed from the rural Christian South that dominates *Sketches*. But Menken, like Harper, depicts independent, aggressive women, and views literature as a social corrective without assuming that *utile* negates *dulce*. In "My Heritage," Menken shows that she, too, would make songs for her people. Menken writes that her legacy is

> To think, and speak, and act, not for my pleasure,
> But others'. . . .
> To hear of fraud, injustice, and oppression,
> And feel who is the unshielded victim.

Her heritage, she says, is the "high/Free spirit: strength, sorrow-born, that bends/But breaks not in [Poverty's] clasp. . . ."[129]

Sketches of Southern Life was well received by Reconstruction audiences, but it was the last original volume of poetry that Frances Harper published for twenty-three years. She did write at least three serialized novels for the *Christian Recorder* and contributed a series of dramatized commentaries on contemporary issues of political and social concern. But with the exception of a few reprints and short pieces, it was not until the enlarged version of *Sketches of Southern Life* appeared in 1888 that Harper published another volume of her work.

NINE

Confrontation and Community in Octavia Victoria Rogers Albert's *The House of Bondage*

As the poetry of Frances Ellen Watkins Harper shows, African American women's literature continued to develop during Reconstruction. But that period was probably the first time in the history of the United States that African American women could count on something besides their pens and the pulpits to initiate their concepts of social change, and as autobiographical accounts and collective biographies such as Gertrude Mossell's *The Work of the African American Woman* (1894) and Hallie Q. Brown's *Homespun Heroines* (1921) documented later, African American women took advantage of this postbellum opportunity to work individually and collectively in a variety of newly accessible occupations. Rather than write imaginatively about changes, many of them acted to realize their ideas in more physical fashion. They became professional nurses and teachers and they volunteered to work with refugees and newly freed people. They participated in the temperance movement and they worked for suffrage and equal rights. They established schools and orphanages, and asylums for the aged, the poor, and single women. They did not abandon the Word, but now African American women could meet their audiences face to face in public auditoriums, in schoolrooms, churches, and even, on special occasions, the halls of government. A steady trickle of poems, essays, and short stories flowed during those years and, for many, journalism made a vital confluence of word and deed. But judging from the texts now extant, African American women were too busy to do much writing in the genres that required sustained concentration and time. Few novels, dramas, or other long texts are known to have been published. Frances Harper did accompany her three early Reconstruction volumes of poetry with a serialized novel, *Minnie's Sacrifice* (1869), that proselytized for more women activists and Maria W. Stewart contributed a revised *Productions* in 1879, but it appears that it was not until the end of the eighties that African American women writers took up the longer literary forms in any significant numbers.

The turn to larger literary tasks was in part a concession to failure. Despite their dedication and earnest efforts or perhaps because of their amazing successes, their dreams of a new, more inclusive democracy had been opposed by powerful white males who, with stunning rapidity, had been able to halt Reconstruction and to dismantle its accomplishments. While some leaders continued to speak of diversity and democracy, in cruel consistency with the previous War of Independence the pragmatics of political financiers overcame the idealism of certain social architects. The colonization of Hawaii and Cuba, of the West and Southwest and other territories inhabited by people of color, accompanied by an unprecedented influx of displaced white Europeans caused defections among the advocates of equal rights for all and swelled the ranks of those whose American Dream was unblushingly white. As the fracture created by the Fifteenth Amendment clearly demonstrates, white women very consciously separated themselves from the other Others. The Trail(s) of Tears, the Asian Immigration Act, the Jim Crow Laws, all expose the pervasive assumption that a comely portrait of a country of pointed firs and homes on the range could allow people with different contours but should color itself locally and internationally in monochromic white.

As African American women once again found themselves being shoved into roles of service and subordination, they were forced to return to their pens for power. Though it was a time when race relations were at an all-time low, a time that Rayford Logan called "The Nadir of Black Experience in the United States," African American women echoed Maria W. Stewart's refrain when she withdrew from the podium in 1833: "nor will I, although a female of a darker hue, and far more obscure than they, bend my head or hang my harp upon willows; . . . I will virtuous prove" (71). Frances Harper was among the first to submit substantial proofs of virtue and perseverance. She began by reprinting and revising *Sketches of Southern Life* (1886) and *Moses: A Story of the Nile* (1889) and by publishing three new novels. The titles of two, *Sowing and Reaping* (1876–77) and *Trials and Triumphs* (1888), are emblematic of the attitudes and persistence that African American women writers again displayed. Harper's third and most successful novel, *Iola Leroy* (1892), a fictionalized history of slavery and Reconstruction, directly addresses their goals when, near its conclusion, the following dialogue occurs:

> "Doctor," said Iola, . . . "I wish I could do something more for our people than I am doing."
> "Why not," asked Dr. Latimer, "write a good, strong book which will be helpful to them?" (262)

This exchange illustrates the seriousness with which many African American women, and men, viewed literature. It articulates their continued belief that literature could elevate and enlighten. Dr. Latimer's faith in the power of "a good, strong book" was shared by most Americans of the late nineteenth century; however, for African Americans that faith was grounded in a particular historical experience which had once known literacy as the basis of

literal freedom and identity. Latimer's advice to Iola manifested itself in
works such as Clarissa Minnie Thompson's *Treading the Winepress* (1885),
A. E. Johnson's *Clarence and Corrine* (1890), Emma Kelley's *Megda* (1891),
Lucy A. Delaney's *From Darkness Cometh Light; or, Struggles for Freedom*
(1892), Katherin Davis Chapman Tillman's *Beryl Watson's Ambition* (1893),
and Pauline Hopkins's *Contending Forces* (1900), works that signaled the
determination of African American writers to use their pens as both process
and product. Insofar as they described their culture, chronicled achievements, and exhorted readers to contribute to racial progress, their writings
were part of a process of "lifting as they climbed."[130] To the extent that they
demonstrated by felicity of form and artistry of language the results of the
writers' own formal education and cultural sophistication, these productions
also proved the kind of progress already made.

The dedication of African American writers to literature of conviction
and conversion was matched by an equally serious commitment by other
Americans, many of whom had diametrically opposed agendas. The post-
Reconstruction period saw a renewed literary pragmatism. An increasing
number of readers turned to nonfiction to clearly interpret the meanings of
their recent past and very contradictory present. Interest in local history
and culture, in folk tales and folkways expanded. And many fiction writers
responded with a new emphasis upon history, regionalism, and "local color."
At the same time, they entertained a definite nostalgia for a simpler, more
romantic past. Given the desire to unite the nation in its march toward
progress and the increased tendency to define that nation as white, this was
a perfect opportunity for Southern whites to polish their tarnished images.
According to J. V. Ridgely, almost every white Southern writer contributed
to the effort to explain and defend slavery. It was, Ridgely reports, "a deadly
serious business" for white Southern writers "to fictionalize their pasts and
to mythify their present institutions, and to cast these imaginative constructs
with themselves in self-satisfying roles."[131]

Some of these writers fed the paranoia of those in the United States
who feared the cultural changes which the accommodation of the masses of
immigrants and free blacks necessitated. These writers contrasted a fanciful
bygone era of culture and refinement with warnings of devastating confusion
and corruption if the natural social hierachy were disturbed. Blacks by nature, they claimed, were primitive, lacking aptitude or aesthetic appreciation,
immoral, and potentially dangerous. Full citizenship, it seems, would trans-
form Uncle Tom into Mr. Hyde. Others wrote in the less violent but equally
dangerous milieu known as the Plantation School, a movement that climaxed
with Margaret Mitchell's *Gone with the Wind*. Writers such as Thomas Nelson Page misrepresented slavery as a benign institution, conjuring images
of stately mansions, hoop-skirted belles, and gallant gentlemen. Slaves were
depicted as "simple, contented, comic, credulous, picturesque, and sometimes philosophical character[s], gifted in singing, dancing, tale-telling, and
reuniting estranged white loves."[132]

No one was more aware of the seriousness or deadliness of these Southern apologists than the slaves and descendants of slaves who were compelled to engage them in linguistic combat. As the Plantation School's myth of the antebellum South gained increasing public acceptance and as attacks against black intelligence and integrity increased, black literature became more aggressive. Some traditional literary strategies were still useful. By and large, African American writers continued to present themselves as exemplars and racial spokespersons. They depicted African Americans as embracing essentially the same ethics and values as those attributed to the early Puritans, the founding fathers, and the best of the New England middle class. They described slavery as an institution that was temporarily dehumanizing to both slaves and slaveholders, as a sorry moment in the nation's past and the pit of degradation from which African Americans, at least, had ascended. And many African American writers helped gild the age by writing glowingly of the contributions of African Americans to the advancement of the United States and to western civilization.

Some of the avant-garde literary conventions were well suited to their ends. Adhering to the tenets of literary realism, African American writers also wrote about "real" people in the "real" world and they experimented with dialect and other local color devices. In this, however, African American writers relied more heavily upon irony than upon humor and their literature did not so much celebrate black folk culture as it presented it for inclusion among the various entities to be stirred into the melting pot. The popularity of the Horatio Alger stories provided a model that was easily adapted to accommodate the requests of nineteenth-century African American leaders to create stories of progress, stories of "men and women who have struggled up from slavery," stories that "witness[ed] in behalf of the capability of the American Negro."

African American writers consciously and clearly wrote in rebuttal to particular trends and stereotypes but generally those rebuttals were couched in the terms of those against which it argued. Their racial loyalty is indisputable, but many of these writers were also determined that their white middle-class readers recognize the viability of a black middle class which had as much, if not more, in common with them than with the illiterate and impoverished elements of the black community. Phillis Wheatley had a more celestial concept of refinement but her proclamation of a hundred years before summarizes the attitudes of many nineteenth-century African Americans who repeated her admonishment that readers remember that "Negroes, black as Cain, / May be refin'd, and join th' angelic train" (53).

Despite the applicability of contemporary modes and the continued usefulness of earlier strategies, African American writers still needed to fashion strategies more appropriate to the current racial situation. Many of the strongest advocates for the improvement of the conditions of African Americans were dead, impotent, or no longer interested. The postbellum dismissal of the slavery issue had extended to a general indifference to or suspicion of stories about the plight of African Americans. As early as 1874, John Hope Franklin says, "The North had grown weary of the crusade for the Negro. . . . younger people, with less zeal for the Negro, . . . were loyal party men, practical politicians who cared more about industrial interests in the North and South than Radical governments in the South" (266). By the early 1880s, most of the political and economic gains established during Reconstruction had—by legal and extralegal means—been eliminated. Many African Americans who had been employed as skilled craftspeople and professionals were losing their positions to European immigrants and poverty and illiteracy were major problems, yet a large percentage of whites believed that America's obligations to those of African descent had been fulfilled with the abolition of slavery and the new amendments to the Constitution.

A quotation from Sutton Griggs's *The Hindered Hand* both delineates some of the problems and demonstrates the beginnings of a strategy to confront them:

> Ensal thought of the odds against the Negro in this literary battle: how that Southern white people, being more extensive purchasers of books than Negroes, would have the natural bias of the great publishing agencies on their side; how that Northern white people, resident in the South, for social and business reasons, might hesitate to father books not in keeping with the prevailing sentiment of Southern white people; how that residents of the North, who essayed to write in defense of the Negro, were laughed out of school as mere theorists ignorant of actual conditions; and finally, how that a lack of leisure and the absence of general culture handicapped the Negro in fighting his own battle in this species of warfare.[133]

The odds as Griggs enumerates them are formidable enough, but Griggs has, in fact, carefully couched his language in terms calculated to be as inoffensive as possible. For example, he limits the hesitancy to "father books" to those Northern whites who are residing in the South and he attributes the reluctance of large publishing houses to concerns about jeopardizing a sizeable Southern market. Harriet Jacobs's admission that what she writes is "strictly true" but that it "fall[s] far short of the facts" (1) could have been Griggs's as well. For Griggs knew, as did most African American writers, that racism in the United States was not a regional phenomenon, and yet he was aware that racism was not a subject to be approached head on if he hoped to reach a white audience.

What Sutton Griggs was doing was modifying a technique that had been successful in the antebellum period. Though they did not write exclusively for members of the Northern white middle class, antebellum black writers had wanted to win their approval and support and had made them a primary target. They had, for example, hedged their bets by consistently equating the South with the sin of slavery and the North with the virtue of courageous Christianity. The Southern miasma choked the aspirations of true women and mèn but the free air of the North revived their industry, honesty, and integrity. In the wake of slavery's abolition and the reconciliation movement of the present moment, geographic qualifiers, which had always been more useful than truthful, were less effective but did retain some residual value.

Not only was the Mason-Dixon line less helpful in uniting the African American writer and Anglo-American readers, but Northern whites had almost as much at stake in a mythification of the antebellum South as did the Southerners. They too desired to lessen the burdens of guilt for a sinful past and to diminish their responsibility to atone for slavery's atrocities. Given the devastation of the war-ravaged South, the resources to rehabilitate the masses of illiterate, unskilled, and impoverished former slaves had to come from Northern pockets. The children were tired of paying the bills of their forebears. And the difficulty in recognizing the learnedness of a Phillis Wheatley, the devotion of a Jarena Lee, or even the womanhood of a Harriet Jacobs faded in comparison with the problem of accepting their commonality with the masses of ex-slaves who had neither the opportunity nor the inclination to change from cultural values and practices that were startlingly, and often frighteningly, different.

To the exacerbated problems of race and class that the post-Reconstruction period presented to writers was added for African American women the problem of sexism. The barriers against women's public presence and particularly against their leadership in political and social issues were more easily scaled when supported by others. But before the wall of sexism, African American women found themselves separated from African American men and from Anglo-American women. Black men on the whole were becoming as sexist as white ones. Being head of household was about the only privilege they could still claim as free men and even that right was severely circumscribed. They were decidedly disinclined to abdicate the slight patriarchal power that they had. On the other side, Northern women who had earlier identified their status as a form of slavery now preferred to join with their Southern white sisters. The implicit answer to the question, "Am I not a woman and a sister?" posed during the anti-slavery movement was now explicitly answered "Well—maybe . . ." or "Yes, but . . ." and "No, not really." White women now gave priority to the feelings of former slave mistresses and opted for a segregated woman's movement. A few worked to insure the existence of colored women's auxiliaries but on the whole they preferred separate meetings, separate conventions, and separate projects.

Such was the milieu then for the African American women writers at the end of the nineteenth century. Their response is clearly articulated by Rosetta Douglass Sprague, the author of a biographical sketch about her father and mother, Frederick and Anna Douglass. Speaking at the first Annual Convention of the National Federation of Afro American Women, Sprague summarized the attitude of post-Reconstruction black women:

While the white race have chronicled deeds of heroism and acts of mercy of the women of pioneer and other days, so we are pleased to note in the personality of such women as Phyllis Wheatley, Margaret Garner, Sojourner Truth and our venerable friend, Harriet Tubman, sterling qualities of head [and] heart and that hold no insignificant place in the annals of heroic womanhood. . . Our progress depends on the united strength of both men and women—the women alone nor the men alone cannot do the work. We have so fully realized that fact by witnessing the work of our men with the women in the rear. This is indeed the *women's era,* and we are coming.[134]

In unprecedented numbers African American women edited ladies' columns and ladies' pages in the black press. They supported magazines, such as *Our Women and Childen* (1888), *Ringwood's Journal* (1891), and *Woman's Era* (1894), created expressly for black women. They wrote to educate women in the domestic sciences and to support the establishment of Young Women's Christian Associations, Women's Christian Temperance Unions, Sunday schools, and women's clubs that they named after African American women such as Phillis Wheatley and Frances Harper. They set about to create a body of texts that was distinctly an African American woman's literature, but they did not limit their interests to the home or to polite subjects. For example, determining that Ida B. Wells's data on the relationship between lynching and rape should be widely distributed, two black women's clubs in New York held benefits to raise funds for its publication.

They confronted the contradictions of their present and created new literary forms to explore new directions and to counter the newest assaults upon their progress. Experienced writers were joined by the new ones. To Maria W. Stewart's revised *Productions,* Julia Foote added *A Brand Plucked from the Fire* (1886). To Frances Harper's serialized novels was added Clarissa Thompson's *Treading the Winepress; or, A Mountain of Misfortunes* (1885–86) and Garrison's *A Ray of Light* (1889–90). In 1890 Amelia Johnson published a novel, *Clarence and Corinne; or, God's Way;* Josephine D. Henderson published a volume of poems called *Morning Glories,* and Octavia Victoria Rogers Albert contributed *The House of Bondage; or, Charlotte Brooks and Her Friends.* It is the latter text that this chapter explores as representative of this period.

Albert's debt to her sister writers may be illustrated by the ways in which her work resembles Frances Harper's Reconstruction poetry. Published not long after the reprinting of *Sketches of Southern Life, The House of Bondage* is similar in both structure and characterization. Just as Harper adapted the slave narrative form to accommodate Aunt Chloe's account of slavery and freedom, Octavia Albert extends that tradition by presenting her book as a collection of slave narratives, with the central story being that told by Aunt Charlotte, who resembles Aunt Chloe in spirit and experiences. *House of Bondage* includes several characters and incidents similar to those in *Sketches* and in *Iola Leroy.* The poem with which Albert concludes her text is one that celebrates the freedom of the Israelites from captivity and makes explicit the subtext that words and allusions have created throughout. And two lines of that poem may signal Albert's intention, if not to revise *Moses: A Story of the Nile,* then at least to answer Harper's consistent calls for more Moses-like individuals. One answer to the question, "Who shall return to tell Egypt the story / Of those she sent forth in the hour of her pride?" is the narrator of *The House of Bondage,* who has done just that.[135]

Albert expands the postbellum slave narrative tradition by introducing Charlotte Brooks and her friends as ordinary black people. Unlike Aunt Chloe, Charlotte Brooks doesn't take an active role by building churches or schools or by monitoring the voting practices of black men. She is barely able to sustain herself from day to day, but she takes delight in the progress of others, representing another of the good people who, in Frances Harper's words, "pinched, and scraped, and spared, / A little here and there" (206) to build the churches and to send their children to the Freedmen's Bureau schools. Moreover, Charlotte Brooks and her friends are from Louisiana, an area rarely represented in African American literature at that time. Albert highlights Louisiana's unique characteristics and distinct differences from other regions, not to argue for special consideration but in a conscious effort to complement the literary depictions of black life. Hers too are strong, solid, Christian survivors of slavery, but their survival has taken place in a predominantly Catholic area which has increased the difficulty of practicing their religious faith.

The intertextuality of *The House of Bondage* is not limited to the African American literary tradition. It also fits within the regionalist or local color movement then in vogue. Her characters speak a form of black English distinguished by occasional vernacular expressions particular to their region. Albert provides details of their honest and simple lives and explains many folkways as derived from their rural culture. The narrator, a sympathetic individual whose careful questions and thoughtful interpretations reveal her sophistication, education, and fine moral character, represents gentility and social progress. In short, *The House of Bondage* was intended to document, through the examples of Charlotte Brooks and others, the horrors of slavery, to prove that slavery was a crime against God and mankind, and to demonstrate that the current problems of blacks in American society were the legacy of slavery. At the same time, *The House of Bondage* was to be an inspirational work, a chronicle of the African American people's rise from the "depths of disgrace and infamy" and proof once more of "the exceeding mercy of God" (xiii).

The House of Bondage, as its title indicates, is obviously intended as a historical record of the life and legacy of slavery and it concentrates upon the experiences of ordinary slaves. But it does not neglect those who have made extraordinary achievements. With the examples of Colonel Douglass Wilson, Rev. Dr. Daniel Minor, and as we will develop later, the narrator herself, it serves as a creative reconstruction of the lives and times of exemplary African Americans. In this manner it resembles earlier works such as Josephine Brown's *Biography of an American Bondman* (1856) and Frances

Rollin's *Life and Public Service of Martin R. Delany* (1868). However, *The House of Bondage* is less personal and sentimental, more anthropological and evangelical than these.

The House of Bondage is a complicated piece. Like Wheatley and Terry before her, Albert appropriated techniques and forms from a multitude of literary sources, thereby demonstrating her familiarity with various conventions and techniques while asserting her privilege as a writer to modify them to fit her own needs. Just as Harriet Jacobs asserted the priority of her account over works such as Harriet Stowe's *Uncle Tom's Cabin* by presenting her life story in the form of the domestic novel while assuring her readers that "this narrative is no fiction" (1), so did Octavia Albert intend *The House of Bondage* as an act of appropriation and redesign. It is another example of African American women writers using literature to testify and to test.

And it is as a post-Reconstruction text of confrontation and community that it is most important here. *The House of Bondage* challenges the remythologizing of the Plantation School by confronting the authority and authenticity of writers such as Thomas Nelson Page. It seems intended by structure and content to be consciously reversing the images and attitudes presented in texts such as Page's *In Ole Virginia*. And *The House of Bondage* demonstrates an African American narrative strategy revised in response to the demands of the post-Reconstruction era, a strategy that emphasizes community via the mediation of a "new" African American. It establishes a viable alternative to the Mason-Dixon line method of aligning Northern Anglo-American readers against their Southern kin in order to identify with African American writers.

The House of Bondage; or, Charlotte Brooks and Other Slaves was published first in serial form in the *South-western Christian Advocate*. Before the series could be gathered into a single volume, Octavia Victoria Rogers Albert had died. The publication that appeared in 1890 contains three documents that introduce the author, the circumstances of the writings, and the authority which they display. These prefatory documents were all written after Octavia Albert's death, but they are part of the text as received by the readers at that time. They are important for this study because in the points that they present, the details that they introduce, and the order in which they appear, they underline the areas deemed most problematic for the appropriate reception of the book. The concerns that occupied the sponsors of Albert's text are the same ones to which she gives special consideration within the text. Thus, the authenticating devices substantiate what a close analysis of Albert's writing suggests, that narrative stance and correction of falsifying literature were major concerns of Octavia Albert and others. The prefatory documents help verify Albert's narrative strategies as conscious and representative.

The problematic areas were those that persistently haunted the words of an African American woman writer: her expertise on the subject about which she writes, the appropriateness of her writing about such a subject, and her authority as a woman to speak publicly on issues that are political and social rather than domestic and private. But as familiar as they were to African American women writers, for reasons discussed earlier, the ambiance of the post-Reconstruction period demanded new responses. Albert's solution was to use an I-witness narrative voice but to reject the status generally signified by the gender, race, and class which it encompassed and to relocate the stance and redefine the points of contact generally assumed by the writer and the reader in discourse on the subject of slavery and race relations.

In part, Albert's problem was similar to that faced by any writer in the United States who was not born free, white, and male. In "The Poetics of Point of View: Status, Contact, Stance," Susan Lanser discusses this situation in detail. For our purposes the following synopsis should suffice. Unless there is information to the contrary, readers, then as now, automatically assume that the "unmarked" narrator is a literate white male. When the title page or the book jacket or any other sources mark a different identity, certain sets of cultural assumptions come into play. Those assumptions are "determined by the ideological system and the norms of social dominance in a given society."[136] This social identity is never totally irrelevant, but when the subject content of the text coincides thematically with the readers' assumptions about the writer's or narrator's social identity, status becomes particularly significant to the discursive context. "Social identity and textual behavior," Lanser concludes, "combine to provide the reader with a basis for determining the narrator's *mimetic authority*" (169).

The level of authority and reader cooperation that Octavia Albert needed to accomplish her purposes required that she identify her personal and professional status, but in so doing she would encounter problems of social identity that could undermine that very authority. To confront her readers with the issue of slavery, to resurrect a past that many wanted to forget and to posit a future that many feared, was an audacious act. But for a black freedwoman to write of historical and political subjects was to grievously transgress the bounds of womanly propriety, racial discretion, and class privilege. Although African American writers had managed to establish some authority in matters of slave life and their personal responses to it, readers were not accustomed to entertaining any other ideas, experiences, and concerns of those who by race, sex, and class were legally and customarily inferior. To initiate a discourse upon issues as vital as slavery and racial discrimination, issues which she depicts in fundamentally different ways from the "master" groups, was to enter a narrative minefield.

Considerations such as these account for the careful presentation of the text and the weaving progression of subject, tone, and point of view. The movement begins with an abrupt assertion of ability, of knowledge and skills superior to the readers. It continues with an objective series of anthropological or scientific disclosures, case histories that sometimes seem almost randomly revealed but which move the text from the relatively safe historical past into the more treacherous present. It ends by linking the entire endeavor to Old Testament tradition and, in the poem that concludes the text, posits the journey as one assumed in response to the question "Who shall return to tell Egypt the story / Of those she sent forth in the hour of her pride?" (161).

The House of Bondage begins by reporting a series of "conversations" between an interviewer, who is new to the area, and several elderly freedpeople, who tell her about their lives in slavery and afterwards. Charlotte Brooks is the primary informant. The testimonies of the others supplement or verify hers. The last part of the book includes a lengthy dissertation by "Colonel Douglass Wilson, a colored man of considerable prominence, not only in Louisiana, but in the nation" (129). It concludes with the narrator herself as subject describing her personal experiences and observations of the accomplishments that former slaves and their children had managed despite their history of bondage and the shackles of contemporary racism. The text presents a vision of community possible if everyone obeyed the laws of God and the best instincts of humankind. Preceding all this are the three authenticating texts that empower Albert to deal with the subject by evoking her status as a former slave, her training as a college student, and her endorsement by clergy. A compiler, a bishop, and her surviving family all assure the reader that her academic training and evangelistic reformism have prepared her for this writing but have not "unsexed" her. These narratives "are not imaginary, but actual, and given as they actually occurred." "An only daughter unites" with her learned father in pronouncing them "an unpretentious contribution" by "a devoted mother and wife" (vi).

The emphasis upon Albert's text as retold stories is a conscious manipulation of the "discourse of distrust." Again, Albert had to assume that many of her readers would be unable or unwilling to concede that former slaves could or would act, think, or write in ways contrary to those that the readers were accustomed to seeing in literary depictions by white writers. She knew that in her situation when she intended to present original, individual, and revisionary ideas, she had to disrupt her readers' normal reading act. Without establishing her narrative authority and the authenticity of her text immediately, she could not trust her readers to grant either.

Some thirty years after Harriet Jacobs had grappled with this problem, Octavia Albert found herself in a remarkably similar situation. But Albert took almost the opposite tactic from Jacobs. She presented true situations, the data that she had gathered from numerous anthropological interviews, and presented them as if they were folktales. She created a storytelling frame and, without actually saying so, suggests that the reader apprehend her book as if it were fiction. As Stepto has pointed out, the discourse of distrust works quite well with the storytelling mode. It subverts the model that he describes as "creative reading and/or authoring" that invites the ingenious reader to grapple with and possibly subdue a devious or elusive text. "In Afro-American storytelling texts especially," he explains, "rhetoric and narrative strategy combine time and again to declare that the principal unreliable factor in the story telling paradigm is the reader (white American readers, obviously, but blacks as well), and that acts of creative communication are fully initiated not when the text is assaulted but when the reader gets 'told'—or 'told off'—in such a way that he or she finally begins to *hear*" (309).

The effectiveness of this getting told is often heightened by apologies that disarm the reader and only in retrospect are recognized as exaggerated and inauthentic. Examples of these include the assurance found in Phillis Wheatley's preface that these poems were written "for the amusement of the author" with "no Intention ever to have them published" (iv) or in Frederick Douglass's confession that "the idea of speaking to white people weighed [him] down," that it was a "severe cross" that he took up only because of the enormous importance of "pleading the cause of [his] brethren,"[137] and in the prefatory materials of *House of Bondage.*

In disclaiming pretensions to authorship or authority, the writers posit the lack of artifice, the authenticity, if you will, of their texts. The preface to *The House of Bondage,* for example, claims "no special literary merit"; each informant, it says, "speaks for himself" (v). Such declarations are not accurate, nor were they meant to be. Wheatley regularly wrote poems on assignment and had been publishing for years by the time she wrote her preface. Douglass's own text, his report of how a slave becomes a man, betrays the racial humility implied in his concluding statements. And far from being a transcriber of each slave speaking for herself or himself, the narrator in Octavia Albert's text is the protagonist, who initiates, controls, and interprets the testimonies of her informants.

These disclaimers are masks adopted for the race rituals. Professing the ambition to humbly, sincerely recite known and common facts for clearly defined and positive purposes is not to be mistaken for playing the fool or being, in the popular (and literarily inaccurate) sense, an "Uncle Tom." This creative communication is more appropriately understood as a literary counterpart to the innovative music of African Americans. Like blues or jazz, the lines may appear repetitious or the melody sound familiar, but they do not repeat exactly or they riff the readers away to new, different, and compelling interpretations. By using elements such as character, language, and tone in seemingly familiar ways, but deliberately disrupting such elements with ambiguous or subtly confounding variations, the writer becomes something like Ray Charles singing "Georgia on my Mind."

Albert's first sentences in chapter 1 get the reader told and no doubt in the serialized publication were sufficient unto themselves. The narratives were first published in the *South-western Christian Advocate,* a paper described by I. Garland Penn as "a great and powerful church organ, having the largest circulation of any paper in New Orleans," with a readership that included "thousands of white Methodists, as well as thousands of Afro-American Methodists."[138] Readers would recognize "Mrs. A" as the wife of the man who was both their bishop and the editor of their official church paper. As a Methodist "first lady" writing to Methodist laity, Octavia Albert could expect her integrated audience to give her a polite hearing and to be in general agreement on theology and the basic responsibilities of Christian living. And even if they did not know that she had a college education, Albert had the advantage of having studied the same curriculum as the most educated of her readers and therefore could manipulate those shared literary experiences and assumptions.

But as the simultaneous publication in New York and Cincinnati of the complete volume suggests, its sponsors had targeted a larger and more diverse readership. The prefatory matter seems calculated to supplement Albert's "telling" narrative stance. By emphasizing her credentials, credentials which in themselves violate stereotypes of blacks, women, and former slaves, they begin the process of reader disorientation that sets the readers up to be told off. The prefatory documents that precede Albert's own words are a preface presented as a joint testimony from Albert's husband and daughter, an introduction signed by Willard F. Mallalieu, a Methodist bishop with an international reputation as a writer and scholar, and a biographical statement about the author by an unnamed "compiler."

The first sentence of the preface asserts textual authenticity and authority. It begins: "The following pages, giving the result of conversations and other information gathered, digested, and written by Mrs. Octavia V. Rogers, deceased wife of the Rev. A. E. P. Albert, A.M., D.D., first appeared in the columns of the *South-western Christian Advocate*" (v). A halo effect of authority is extended to the female author by virtue of her marriage to a minister with both a master of arts and a doctor of divinity degree. Naming her as "Mrs. Octavia V. Rogers" identifies her as a wife but in using "Rogers" and not "Albert" as her surname, it emphasizes her individual claim to authority. That the information was gathered, digested, and written by her verifies its authenticity, and this research having been printed in *The South-western Christian Advocate* further suggests the sanction of the Methodist Episcopal Church. The preface not only implies theological and academic authority for the writer but it also evokes the sanctity of heaven, for it describes Mrs. Octavia V. Rogers as having been a "precious and devoted mother and wife" of "angelic spirit" and "subtle and holy influence" (vi). And she is now "deceased," a status that implies she has completed her duty and been rewarded with heavenly rest. The signateurs are her husband and her daughter, who affirm the text's authority with their personal testimony. The place of their signing being designated as the "editorial rooms" of the *South-western Christian Advocate* reminds us of the professional and theological environment within which she wrote.

The introduction is the second authenticating device. It is signed from Boston, by Willard F. Mallalieu, who as a prominent white theologian lends the blessings and endorsement of white male church leaders to the text. Mallalieu extends this endorsement to include the founder of the Methodist

Church, John Wesley, by quoting him on the abomination of slavery and the need for every Christian to oppose it. Mallalieu argues that the story must continue to be told so that Christians will "know from what depths of disgrace and infamy they rose when guided by the hand of God, they broke every yoke and let the oppressed go free." And he supports the claim that Octavia Albert herself makes in the beginning of her text that those who had experienced slavery were the most reliable informants about it. Mallalieu grants Octavia Albert specific authority to interpret slavery by identifying her as a former slave, one who "had known the accursed system" and who had known "the joy of deliverance" (xiii).

The "compiler" begins with the assertion that "The author of this volume, Octavia Victoria Rogers, wife of the Rev. A. E. P. Albert, D.D., was born in Oglethorpe, Macon County, Ga., of slave parentage, December 24, 1853, and was educated at Atlanta University, in that State." The first sentence repeats several signifiers of authority made in the preface. The author is the wife of a minister who possesses the doctor of divinity degree and she herself is college educated. Her credentials, therefore, are impeccable and rare. But it goes beyond the testimony of her family to note, as did Bishop Mallalieu, that the author was born "of slave parentage" (xv)—that is, she was a slave and her heritage was that of a slave. Her authority begins with her personal experience with, and her descendance from, slave culture, but that authenticity is buttressed by the discipline and guidance of the academy and the teachings of the church.

The House of Bondage is constructed as a story of stories. The narrator is both listener and teller. She has heard the testimonies of those who lived the experience and she now tells them to others. Although the subtitle of the book and chapter 1 are entitled "Charlotte Brooks," the first voice is that of the narrator who declares: "None but those who resided in the South during the time of slavery can realize the terrible punishments that were visited upon the slaves. Virtue and self-respect were denied them" (1). In asserting that only those who lived the experience can tell the true story, she "tells her readers off" by privileging the lived experience over any and all contrary notions that the readers may have accumulated by observation or report. With the second sentence, she positions herself as the interpreter of that lived experience by summarizing the "terrible punishments" and naming the results as loss of virtue and self-respect. The narrator positions herself somewhere between the subjective realities represented by the testimonies of the ex-slaves and the more abstract understanding available to her readers. Like her slave informants, the narrator knows that "the half was never told concerning this race that was in bondage nearly two hundred and fifty years" (2), but she is also a part of the literate society who knows that "much has been written concerning the negro" and that from that evidence "we must confess that the moral standing of the race is far from what it should be" (1).

That the narrator uses terms such as "the negro" and "this race" is important here. For while the prefatory materials identify the author as a former slave and though the narrator is addressed in the text as "Mrs. A," the narrator, as characterized in the text, is racially ambiguous and personally unfamiliar with the lived realities of slavery. The narrator effects a scholarly distance, referring to her subjects as "the slaves," "this race," and "them." In offering to introduce her audience to "some characters that will amply illustrate what I mean" (2), she offers to share her knowledge and to support her interpretation with evidence assumed to have been heretofore unavailable to her readers. The narrator does not refute allegations of black immorality, but restricts that weakness to Southern illiterates, places the blame for this condition upon slavery, and promises to document this thesis through the subsequent biographies. Her strategy lies in acknowledging the differences between the black masses and her readers while attributing these differences to historical conditions and emphasizing their common identity as Christians and Americans.

The narrator further asserts her primacy by introducing Charlotte Brooks's narrative with these words: "It was in the fall of 1879 that I met Charlotte Brooks . . . I have spent hours with her listening to her telling of her sad life of bondage" (2). In this manner the narrator establishes herself as the medium through which Brooks's life will be revealed. Through her ears, the reader will hear the story. Through her consciousness, the characters will be introduced, the conversations will be reconstructed, and the interpretations will be provided. Says the narrator, "I remember one morning as she entered my home I said to her, "Good morning, Aunt Charlotte; how are you feeling to-day?" (3). "I remember one morning" implies the resulting dialogue is representative of many such but it also makes clear that the narrator is the one selecting the experiences and determining the picture of slavery that the reader will receive. In addressing her as "Aunt Charlotte," the narrator establishes the level of respect to be accorded her informants. Charlotte Brooks emerges as a character through her folksy response that "La, my child, I didn't sleep hardly last night; my poor old bones ached me so bad I could not move my hand for a while" (3). Aunt Charlotte attributes her present infirmity to injuries received during slavery, thereby revealing the continuing effects of that institution. But she does so in language which also positions her below the narrator, whose vocabulary and syntax mark her as part of the educated elite, the group with which her white readers, particularly, would choose to identify.

Most of Brooks's story is presented through her own words as reported by the narrator. Indeed, the narrator allows Brooks to sketch without comment the more familiar tales of physical hardship and family separation. However, the narrator interrupts Brooks's recitation to emphasize, to request elaboration, or otherwise shape the image the reader is to retain. For example, her interruption highlights Brooks's regret that separation from her family also meant an end to regular church attendance. She says, "Aunt Charlotte, did you say you *never* attended church any more after leaving

Virginia? . . . What did you do on the Sabbath?" (5). The questions link the sale of human beings with the forced separation of families and with the breakdown of religious observances. In this manner, Charlotte Brooks's experiences become evidence that "the sadly immoral condition of this illiterate race" (1) is the masters' fault, not the slaves'. Moreover, her interruption sustains the narrator's characterization as the voice of the concerned Christian who is scandalized at this new evidence of slavery as a sin against God and mankind. Charlotte Brooks has been thrice victimized. Not only was she physically enslaved, but she was torn from her mother's embrace and she was forced to violate the commandments of her heavenly father.

In chapter 2 the reader learns that Aunt Charlotte and some of her fellow slaves struggled to retain their spiritual integrity. Despite their masters' persecutions, they retained a form of religious community and worshiped as often as their circumstances would allow. Others were not so fortunate or so strong. Thus, the narrator emphasizes the heroic efforts of many slaves to maintain any religious practices at all over the failure of the entire race to be perfect models of piety. It is notable here that Albert does not choose to cite the numerous instances of white reprobation. Her relationship to her audience is too tenuous to allow that argument. Instead she aligns herself and the ex-slaves with the American religious majority, Protestant Christians. Much of the reason for Charlotte's suffering came because her owners were Catholics. Good Protestants, such as the narrator and her readers, can avoid condemnation by understanding the origins of immorality and undoing the work of the sinful Papists.

The narrator provides a transition from the possibly excusable sin of failing to observe the Sabbath to allegations concerning other kinds of immorality by beginning chapter 3 with a question about Charlotte's children. The reader learns that Charlotte Brooks had been forced to bear the children of her master's son, then was denied the security and comfort of those children in her old age. Since Aunt Charlotte's master required her to leave her babies and go off to work the canefields, all her children died, she says, "for want of attention" (14).

This basic pattern continues throughout the book. The details of slavery that are similar to those found in slave narratives serve to introduce younger readers to the recent history upon which their present is based and to remind those who had been inclined to forget or to romanticize the horrors of that institution. And through the narrator's interrogation and commentary, the readers gradually realize the more profound implications of their shared legacy of slavery. Charlotte Brooks, as slave mother, is the primary example of the many tenants in the house of bondage. Uncle John's response to the narrator's suggestion that Charlotte Brooks must be an extraordinary person to have withstood such trials emphasizes this. "Why ma'am," Uncle John replied, "Sister Charlotte just suffered like the most of us did" (62). The narratives of Charlotte Brooks's friends serve to introduce other types who peopled the house of bondage. Sallie Smith, a Louisiana native, gives the experiences of the runaway slave. John Goodwin provides a comparison of Georgia slavery with that in Louisiana. Lorendo, his wife, is a Creole convert from Catholicism. Stephen Jordan gives an insider's view of the slave coffles.

The actual protagonist in *The House of Bondage* is the narrator, who mediates between the former slaves and her readers, some of whom were certainly former slave holders. The antagonist is the readers themselves. In refusing to romanticize slave-owner relations, to palliate the slaves' sufferings, or to verify claims that former slaves are unfit, if not by nature then by nurture, for full citizenship, *The House of Bondage* challenges its readers to a radical revisioning of slavery and Reconstruction. It emphasizes their common identification as Protestant Christians, a religious commitment that allows the slaves to bear no ill will and pose no threat, and that obligates them all to join hands in Christian fellowship. Since Octavia Victoria Rogers Albert, as an African American woman, cannot trust her readers to set aside cultural assumptions of superiority, she uses the storytelling mode of the discourse of distrust to abort the contest for authorship and authority that writerly texts tend to produce. She constructs instead a cooperative context of stories shared with sympathy, thus establishing a basis for affirmation and community and expanding a narrative strategy that was inherited from earlier African American writers and that would be further developed by those who came after her.

The narrator connects the black former slaves with white readers, some of whom were certainly former slave holders, through their common status as committed Christians. In keeping with the evangelical context and to reassure those readers whose fear of retribution might prove stronger than their guilt, Albert emphasizes the strong religious faith of her subjects, a faith that not only sustained them during slavery but restrains them from any vengeful thoughts. Despite their hardships, the ex-slaves profess to have forgiven their oppressors. They are content to know that their suffering will be avenged on Judgment Day. They encourage their young to work and to study, to save their money, and to take their legitimate places as members of a free society. Uncle Cephas sums up their feelings thus: "Education, property, and character, to my mind, have ever been the trinity of power to which I have looked and do look for our complete redemption in this country" (127).

Having reviewed the historical past with subtle revision and delicate shadings but in familiar terms, having told, as it were, stories of hardship and survival, of the triumph of good over evil, stories similar in ways that the narrator mentions to *Pilgrim's Progress,* she has encouraged the readers to adopt a cooperative role. To support the positive direction of her book, from the chronicle of the African American people's release from the house of bondage to the advertisement for their acceptance into the promised land of a free United States, the narrator moves from Charlotte Brooks and her friends to their children and the members of the black middle class. This is more dangerous terrain and Albert introduces Colonel Douglass Wilson to provide an analysis of the present and a plan for the future. With Colonel Wilson as the spokesperson for these controversial ideas, Albert is using the conventions of female rhetoric discussed with reference to Harriet Jacobs in chapter 6. Colonel Wilson is the only informant who is not addressed by the familiar "Uncle" or "Aunt" and who is not described as an acquaintance but as a family friend. He does not come to her house to be interviewed but they converse while the two families are vacationing at a resort. Colonel Wilson articulates the position of the narrator and of the black middle class. Colonel Wilson relates the bravery and gallantry of black soldiers and the trials of the newly freed people. He tells of riots against blacks and of school children being attacked. "When we sent our children to school in the morning," he says, "we had no idea that we should see them return home alive in the evening" (139). Wilson was wounded during the war and his son was wounded during his struggle to attend school. "We both call our scars marks of honor" (140), Wilson said. They are marks of honor because in spite of legal and illegal opposition, Wilson is proud that "no people similarly situated have ever made the progress in every department of life that our people have made, since the world began" (144). The present is difficult, but Wilson believes American racial problems are solvable. "The negro problem," he believes, is "all a matter of condition and national and constitutional authority. Get the conditions right [and] . . . 'life, liberty, and happiness,' will follow" (145). These conditions are not emigration or colonization. Colonel Wilson's plan is for blacks to "stay right in this country with the white people, and to be so scattered in and among them that they can't hurt one of us without hurting some of their own number. That's my plan, and that is one of my reasons why I am in the Methodist Episcopal Church" (146–47). Thanks to the prefatory notes, Albert's readers know that she converted from the African Methodist Episcopal Church to the Methodist Episcopal Church and the identification of Colonel Wilson's ideas with those of Octavia Albert could be an easy transference. Since his first name is Douglass (with the double *s*), Colonel Wilson's (and Octavia Albert's) ideas evoke the authority of Frederick Douglass also. Wilson's plan for racial progress echoes the sentiments of most of the nineteenth-century black intelligentsia and many whites as well. Editors and writers of *The Colored American* and *The Anglo-African,* like those of *McClure's* and *Harper's,* believed in the efficacy of Protestantism, industrialism, and nationalism. They preached democracy even as they perpetuated what Alan Trachtenberg has called "a particular idea of culture as a privileged domain of refinement, aesthetic sensibility, and higher learning."[139] In such a way, Albert gradually assumes an authority that exceeds the limits of gender, class, and even race.

In the last two chapters, Albert becomes a character relating her own experiences during the last few years. In chapter 19, Albert reports on the General Conference of the Methodist Episcopal Church. It was "the most representative body" she had ever witnessed. She is especially proud of the cordial reception of the "fifty-three colored delegates, sandwiched promiscuously everywhere like so much black pepper in a vessel of salt" (148). During this conference the black delegation called upon Mrs. General U. S. Grant and was represented by the eloquence of Dr. Minor, "the son of Uncle Jacob Turner, one of Uncle Cephas's fellow-servants" (150). Albert is the reader's on-the-spot reporter, naming the senators and other prominent people present to receive the African American delegates, describing the order of events, and including the text of Dr. Minor's speech because, she writes, "I tell you, his speech was a real masterpiece of polished eloquence, and was delivered with such marked effect as to charm, subdue, and bring forth tears from many that stood and heard it. I know you would have been glad to have been there and to have heard it; so I shall try to repeat it for you" (150). Knowing her readers would have "been glad" to have been in her place and respecting masterpieces that markedly "charm, subdue, and bring forth tears" indicate her privileged status as narrator even as it implies her own appreciation of and ambition to create words that "charm, subdue, and bring forth tears."

The final chapter, "A Touching Incident," is a deliberate denouement that reunites separated family members, recalls the first part of the book, and firmly situates the narrator as a spokesperson for and instigator of political and social integration. She begins: "I cannot close *my* story until *I* tell *you* of a very touching incident which I can never forget. . . . *I know you will enjoy it,* and therefore I don't feel that it is necessary for me to make any further apology for going back to recall it" (emphasis mine 156). The incident involves the highly successful speech of the Rev. Dr. Coleman Lee at the 1884 Cotton Centennial Exposition to sixty thousand enraptured listeners. Here she does not report the speech; her own actions are the focus of this chapter. She does mention that the leading papers of the nation were also impressed with his eloquence and quotes a review in *Harper's Magazine* to substantiate her opinion that the black speaker was the most gifted and eloquent of the many fine orators that participated in the program. The young man's performance so pleased her that afterwards she pressed her way to the front of the crowd of well-wishers "to thank him, in the name of the race, for the honor he had reflected upon himself and his race" (158). In their ensuing conversation, he mentioned enough details of his life history that she recognized him as someone whose story Aunt Charlotte had related to her. "Just as I was about to tell him about Aunt Charlotte and what she told me of Aunt Jane Lee," the narrator says that his mother "rushed wildly" (159) to him. Here again, the narrator's prestige is enhanced. The mother apparently could not recognize her son until she heard his story as told to "Mrs. A." The next two paragraphs are replete with "I's," as the narrator tells how she felt ("almost like one of the family" [160]), how she cried tears of joy and how she took them to her house where they spent nearly half the night with her, her family, and her friends. The narrator concludes by asking

"When will all this scattered race be reunited . . . ?" (161) and with a poem celebrating the release of the Hebrew children from Egyptian bondage, a poem that implicitly answers her question. The conclusion allows three things to happen. The middle-class and the lower-class blacks are presented as distinct but part of the same fabric, the lower status being, in fact, more a situation of chance than of choice. The story of Charlotte Brooks is brought again to the forefront of the reader's attention. And *The House of Bondage* ends as it began with the narrator's voice.

In linking the African American enslavement with that of the Old Testament implicitly in several places throughout the text and explicitly at the conclusion, Albert makes the antebellum past one to repent for, not one to glorify. She presents the slave experience as a trial endured by God's chosen people and not the manifestation of a natural hierarchy. In this way she resists the Plantation School, which was recreating the antebellum past as the golden days of Camelot when natural aristocracy ruled with a fine sense of noblesse oblige. *The House of Bondage* also challenges the Plantation School by refusing to romanticize slave-owner relations, to palliate the slaves' sufferings, or to substantiate the notion that freedom meant license for immorality.

In fact, the close formal resemblance to *In Ole Virginia*, a collection published three years earlier by the leading practitioner of the Plantation School, Thomas Nelson Page, suggests that it may well have been directed against that work. My point in advancing this thesis is not to prove that Octavia Albert had a vendetta against Thomas Nelson Page. I would not argue that there exists clear and irrefutable evidence that she had even read *In Ole Virginia*. But, like Harriet Beecher Stowe's *Uncle Tom's Cabin,* the images and the attitudes of *In Ole Virginia* were known beyond the covers of their volume and had spawned a plethora of imitations. Albert need not have read the book or consciously designed hers after Page's in order to have written such an obvious reversal of it.

According to John Herbert Nelson, Page "felt it a duty to interpret a glorious past to an uncomprehending world. . . . [he] was not so much the literary artist as the faithful clansman, the historian, as he would have it, of Virginia's "first families.""[140] For Page it was crucial that the historian of the South be a Southerner. He believed that the South had been "misjudged" and "misinterpreted" because it allowed others to tell its story. It is "a sad fallacy," he says, to think that authorship is not important, for "In [authorship] lies the difference between fame and infamy, between corruption and immortality" (360–61).

Both Albert and Page wrote to correct misrepresentations and to preserve the truth about the antebellum South but they totally disagreed about what that truth was. According to Page the antebellum South represented a Golden Age "when men treated women chivalrously and women relied on men implicitly, when success bore no relation to wealth, and when the seventh commandment was not deemed a proper subject for conversation in mixed company."[141] According to Albert, however, the antebellum South was characterized by a system more brutal than even the Spanish Inquisition, a system of slavery so corrupt that "the half has never been told" (2). Albert does not mention whether the seventh commandment was an appropriate subject for discussion but in identifying miscegenation as a common practice among slaveholders, she shows that whether discussed or not, that commandment was regularly violated. Page maintained that slavery had "Christianized the negro race in a little over two centuries, impressed upon it regard for order, and gave it the only civilization it has ever possessed since the dawn of history" (Gross 45). But Albert declared that Americans should "all thank God and rejoice that the unearthly institution has been swept away forever in a sea of blood never to rise again" (161).

The two books' titles, *The House of Bondage; or, Charlotte Brooks and Her Friends* and *In Ole Virginia; or, Marse Chan and Other Stories,* are structurally similar. Both "the house of bondage" and "ole Virginia" are common metaphors for the slave South, but their connotations are antithetical. *In Ole Virginia,* like *The House of Bondage,* is a collection of narratives about the antebellum South told by participant-informers to outside inquirers. But the narratives told by Charlotte Brooks and her friends are autobiographical: the slave experience is the subject of their discourse. The stories told in *In Ole Virginia* are narrated by the slaves, but they are about the slaveholders.

Page's volume begins with the story of "Marse Chan" told to an unidentified traveler who, "One afternoon, in the autumn of 1872" in a place where the "outer world strode by . . . while [its inhabitants] dreamed," comes upon an elderly black man talking to a dog. Curious about the "once splendid mansions, now fast falling to decay," the traveler questions the man about the history of this area. His informant, it turns out, is a former slave of Marse Chan, who spends his remaining days looking after his master's old dog and the grave yard. Page's choice of an outsider, one unfamiliar with the experience but curious about "the handsome old place" that gave evidence of having "once been the seat of wealth" is designed to establish a rapport with the reader which both offers a sense of direct experience while at the same time guiding the perceptions.[142]

Albert also chooses a narrator who is a curious but objective outsider, who relays to the reader the stories she's heard from former slaves. But Albert's narrator may claim more credibility for her stories because she is not passing through and chancing upon an individual informant who claims to know the answers to his questions. Mrs. A. has come to live in the community, she has established a rapport with the people before selecting those whose stories would be most helpful. At one point in the narratives she says, "After my conversation with Uncle Cephas in the last chapter I did not get to see anyone particularly for a month or more who could add materially to my story any thing that might interest you" (129). This statement suggests that from an abundance of data, the narrator is selecting that which provides the most complete and representative accounts. This and other statements seem designed to point out an inherent weakness in Page's work. When her narrator says, "people who never knew any thing about slave-life in the south can hardly credit the reports that have been circulated by those who have resided here" (42), she could be commenting upon the gullibility of those passing through who chance upon their informants.

At the same time that she establishes the credibility of the informants and the situations within which the narrator interacts with them, Albert is careful not to identify her narrator with the ex-slaves. Just as Page is careful to create a narrator who "may be Southern or Northern. . . . who may be Page himself or the reader" (Gross 23), so too does Albert create a narrator with whom the reader is more likely to identify. In Page's text, however, the informant becomes the focus of attention and the stranger to whom he speaks merely serves as a vocalized pause, filling in the moments of silence and serving as a transition to the next part. The dominant voices in Page's text are those of slaves who tell stories in an almost unreadable dialect. The reader, having to continuously translate while reading, feels distant from the scene and identifies with neither the stranger nor the slave informant. On the other hand, while Albert's subjects may speak with idiomatic expressions and occasionally ungrammatical speech, the narrator does not. Her refusal to use dialect as a mode of communication removes the distance between reader and subject, encourages their greater identification with the narrator, and eventually merges the perspective of the insider narrator and the reader observer. Thus, while using the framing that Page uses, she exchanges the distance of a folk tale of a bygone era for the collected data of a present-day historian. She challenges the authority of the storyteller on the very basis upon which he has established that authority: the authenticity of the witness-observer.

Page's slave informants regale the stranger with tales of duels and deaths, lost loves and cruel jokes aplenty for their masters and mistresses, but when answering queries about their own experiences, they inevitably reply as did Marse Chan's Sam:

> Dem wuz good ole times, marster—de bes' Sam ever see! Dey wuz, in fac'! Niggers didn' hed nothin' 't all to do—jes hed to 'ten' to de feedin' an' cleanin' de hosses, an' doin' what de marster tell 'em to do; an' when dey wuz sick, dey had things sont 'em out de house, an' de same doctor come to see 'em whar 'ten' to de white folks when dey wuz po'ly. Dyar warn' no trouble nor nothin'. (10)

In contrast, Albert's narratives do not focus on the experiences of the masters of large plantations as witnessed by their self-identified faithful retainers, but on the experiences of the field slaves and those who lived on small farms. Like Page's Sam, Charlotte Brooks is originally from Virginia and tells her story in the decade after emancipation. However, unlike Sam, who reports "no trouble nor nothin'," Aunt Charlotte says "nobody knows the trouble we poor colored folks had to go through" (4). Charlotte's master did not provide doctors or send things to sick slaves. To the contrary, her present infirmities directly result from her mistreatment as a slave. To further combat the idea of the "good ole times," chapter 4 in *The House of Bondage*, "Cruel Masters," is devoted to examples of slave oppression and suffering.

While Thomas Nelson Page did not claim that *In Ole Virginia* was nonfiction, he refers, in his dedication, to the work as "this fragmentary record" of the life of his people and implies scholarly objectivity in his prefatory notes on the techniques of replicating the actual language of that area. Says Page, "The dialect of the negroes of Eastern Virginia differs totally from that of the Southern negroes. . . . The elision is so constant that it is impossible to produce the exact sound, and in some cases it has been found necessary to subordinate the phonetic arrangement to intelligibility." He then offers a set of rules to "aid the reader."[143]

Similarly, the preface to *The House of Bondage* identifies it "as a panoramic exhibition of slavelife, emancipation, and the subsequent results" (v). Its characters, we are assured, are "most interesting and life-like" (vi). Its conversations "are not imaginary, but actual" (vi). Without referring to any specific writer, it proclaims the superiority of Albert's work by asserting that "No one can read these pages without realizing the fact that 'truth is often stranger than fiction'" (vi). Moreover, Albert suggests that these stories are not only true, but they are almost sacred. In a conversation with one informant the narrator says that "we should not only treasure these things, but should transmit them to our children's children. That's what the Lord commanded Israel to do . . . and I verily believe that the same is his will concerning us and our bondage and deliverance in this country" (130).

The *House of Bondage* is significant not only for its factual evidence but also for the fact of its existence, which belies myths of black illiteracy, intellectual inferiority, and lack of historical perspective. Its dual function as artifact and as tool made the form as important as the content. Like other nineteenth-century African-American women writers, Octavia Albert was working toward the realization of a community that recognized the freedom of all its members to contribute to its stories of its past and its dreams for its future. To do so required that she confront her opponents, expose their misrepresentations of history and the fallacies of their propositions for the future. Her task did not end with confrontation. She had to exhibit evidence to support her own alternative suggestions, to define her vision of the community that the United States could become.

As an African American woman and a former slave, this task required strategies that were different from those of others who by race, gender, or class did not share her social identification. To that end Octavia Victoria Rogers Albert incorporated versions of the discourse of distrust that her literary tradition had developed and she appropriated techniques and models from the literary traditions of other Americans as well. With her *House of Bondage: or, Charlotte Brooks and Other Slaves* she opposed the Plantation tradition and anticipated the directions of African American women's writings in the women's era.

TEN

"A Woman Question and a Race Problem"

The Black Woman's Era

In 1890, the same year that Octavia Victoria Rogers Albert's *House of Bondage* appeared in the *South-western Christian Advocate,* Josephine Heard published a volume of poetry, *Morning Glories,* and Amelia E. Johnson published a short novel, *Clarence and Corrine. Morning Glories* was possibly the first volume of poetry to be published by an African American woman since Frances Harper's *Sketches of Southern Life* almost two decades earlier. In her preface, Heard wrote that she intended her poetry to inspire and to encourage African American youth. Amelia Johnson's novel is a sentimental tale of two orphans whose survival and triumph were the direct results of their faith and perseverance and the lived Christianity of their benefactors. Clarence and Corrine, like the majority of the characters in the story, are racially ambiguous. The book's illustrations show that they are not dark skinned but the textual references to their thin faces, their high cheekbones, and their dark eyes may be as readily applied to African Americans as to Anglo-Americans. This is a direct reflection of Johnson's attempt to write across the color line on a subject that was important to everyone; however, the reviewers' regular identification of Amelia E. Johnson as the first black novelist to be published by the American Baptist Publication Society reveal that this book was considered an act of racial progress. The tendency to emphasize personal moral and religious themes over those more specific to race is reflected also in Emma Dunham Kelly's *Megda* published in 1891. Since African American women writers had consistently refused to limit their discourse to slavery and race, writings such as these reflect one strand of the tradition that began with Lucy Terry's "Bar's Fight" and Phillis Wheatley's *Poems on Various Subjects, Religious and Moral.* However, the greater tendency at the end of the nineteenth century was toward the deliberate discussion of race and racism.

Lucy A. Delaney's *From the Darkness Cometh the Light; or, Struggles for Freedom* (1892) is one example of the decision to synthesize the secular and the spiritual accounts into a deliberately racial account. Combining the religious imperatives of writers such as Julia Foote with the themes of postbellum narrators such as Elizabeth Keckley, Delaney confesses that she "cannot recur with any happiness" to slavery days but she posits, nonetheless, the benefits that came from that time of trial and proclaims that she and other former slaves find comfort and pleasure in looking backward and reviewing their early days. Delaney wrote to provide those "who have never suffered as we have" with the vicarious experience that would enable them to look upon former slaves with "interest and sympathy" and to know what slavery meant to them all.[144] She assumed a dispassionate narrative persona similar to that of Octavia Victoria Rogers Albert, but instead of using a Charlotte Brooks as the nucleus around which the other narratives clustered, Lucy Delaney claimed that position as her own. And she is right in line with her contemporaries who were writing to remind men and white women that African American women knew themselves to be and were hereby proclaiming themselves as entitled to full participation in the life of the nation and of the world:

> As this is a world of varied interests and many events, although we are each but atoms, it must be remembered, that we assist in making the grand total of all history, and therefore are excusable in making our affairs of importance to ourselves, and endeavoring to impress them on others. (viii)

It is this attitude that characterizes not only Lucy A. Delaney's book but the other three significant publications by African American women that appeared in 1892. Each bears obvious resemblances to earlier texts and each became a means and a model for later works of twentieth-century writers. From this perspective, 1892 may be regarded as the midwife to modern American literature. Since most discussions of African American women's literary tradition begin with 1892, the relationship of Harper, Wells, and Cooper especially to twentieth-century African American literature has been treated, richly and lucidly.[145] It is therefore sufficient that I conclude my discussion of early African American women writers by suggesting a few of the ways in which the literature published in 1892 represents the trends and the diversity of this transitional period.

Besides Lucy A. Delaney's *From Darkness Cometh the Light,* there appeared in 1892 Ida B. Wells's *Southern Horrors: Lynch Law in All Its Phases,* Frances E. W. Harper's *Iola Leroy; or, Shadows Uplifted,* and Anna Julia Cooper's *A Voice from the South by a Black Woman of the South.* It is important to our understanding of their times and their testimonies to note that for each of these women, literature was but one of the tools they employed to bring into being the new world order they envisioned. Lucy A. Delaney proudly concludes her narrative by summarizing her lifetime of activism and her intentions for her book:

> I became a member of the Methodist Episcopal Church in 1855; was elected President of the first colored society, called the "Female Union," which was the first ever organized exclusively for women; was elected President of a society

known as the "Daughters of Zion"; was matron of "Siloam Court," No. 2, three years in succession; was Most Ancient Matron of the "Grand Court of Missouri," of which only the wives of Masons are allowed to become members. I am at present, Past Grand Chief Preceptress of the "Daughters of the Tabernacle and Knights of Tabor," and also was Secretary, and am still a member of Col. Shaw Woman's Relief Corps, No. 34, auxiliary to the Col. Shaw Post, 343, Grand Army of the Republic. . . . if this sketch is taken up for just a moment of your life, it may settle the problem in your mind, if not in others, "Can the negro race succeed, proportionately, as well as the whites, if given the same chance and an equal start?" (62–64)

At the same time as they were writing their books, the other three women were campaigning to participate in the planning and execution of the 1893 World's Fair, or to extend the metaphor by which the Columbian Exposition came to be known, they were claiming their right to reside in the "White City." Their writing was for them, as writing had been for Lucy Terry and Phillis Wheatley, prompted by an intrinsic artistic ardor informed by a continual struggle for freedom and a resolve to be included in the written record of this country as it was, is, or should be. Two of these women, Frances Ellen Watkins Harper and Anna Julia Cooper, had extensive and successful experiences with other civil rights battles. Ultimately, they would be selected as two of the six African American women grudgingly allowed to address the World Congress of Representative Women which was a part of that World's Fair. Their young fiery friend, Ida B. Wells, would not be invited to participate. However, with the backing of other African American women and men, she would stand within the White City's gates and distribute her essay, *The Reason Why the Colored American Is Not in the World's Columbian Exposition.* Hers would be a bold and decidedly unladylike action and a sequel to the pamphlet that she had published in 1892, a pamphlet that was certainly one reason that Ida B. Wells had not been invited to participate in the World Congress of Representative Women.

In *Southern Horrors: Lynch Law in All Its Phases,* Ida B. Wells had chosen a topic not easily assigned to the ladies' pages of most newspapers. She had written about an impolite topic with a candor unprecedented among female journalists. It was not so much that no respectable woman writer had written critically about law, justice, and the American way. Nor was it that they had not mentioned murder or other acts of violence or alluded to the relationship between lynching and racial prejudice. But Ida B. Wells eschewed euphemisms and wrote about rape using its own four letters. And she identified and discussed the logical conclusions and the alternative interpretations of the attitudes that portrayed all black males as inherently dangerous to white womanhood.

Ida B. Wells was quite aware that her boldness invited criticism and she used many of the literary strategies employed by African American women before her to establish her authority and her veracity; however, Wells impatiently stripped these rhetorical techniques of their more feminine trappings.

For example, she prefaces her texts with the same sort of apology as did Jacobs, Keckley, and Albert. She, as did they, acknowledges that her subject matter might offend many of her readers and asks that they accept as justification the critical urgency of her ends. "It is," she wrote, "with no pleasure I have dipped my hands in the corruption here exposed. Somebody must show that the Afro-American race is more sinned against than sinning, and it seems to have fallen upon me to do so."[146]

Here, she sings the song of subordinating personal preference and decorum in order to do her duty to the afflicted and suffering. Her apology echoes the traditional justifications employed by Harriet Jacobs, Jarena Lee, and Maria W. Stewart, the latter of whom wrote in 1832: "Methinks I heard a spiritual interrogation—'Who shall go forward, and take off the reproach that is cast upon the people of color? Shall it be a woman?' And my heart made this reply—'If it is thy will, be it even so, Lord Jesus!'" (45). And indeed, in candor and explicitness on subjects of political, economic, and legal significance, Ida B. Wells is most clearly a literary child of Maria W. Stewart.

Ida B. Wells continued another tradition of African American women by specifying women as a significant part of her intended audience and of her supporters. A little over a century earlier, Phillis Wheatley had accepted the affidavit signed by Boston's most prominent Anglo-American males, but she had named the Countess of Huntingdon as her book's patron. Ida B. Wells echoes Wheatley's dedication "To the Right Honourable the Countess of Huntingdon, the following poems are most respectfully Inscribed, by her much obliged, very humble, and devoted Servant" with an apostrophe to "the Afro-American women of New York and Brooklyn, whose race love, earnest zeal and unselfish effort . . . made possible its publication" (15). With *Incidents in the Life of a Slave Girl,* Harriet Jacobs had modified the tradition of including authenticating affidavits by white men by substituting letters from two white women and George W. Lowther, "a highly respectable colored citizen of Boston" (205). Ida B. Wells dispenses with white endorsements altogether. She publishes a letter from Frederick Douglass which supplements the endorsement implied by the patronage of the New York African American women and which in this context privileges their place in the public discourse. For Douglass hails her as a "Brave Woman" and allows that her writing on this subject is more powerful than his own: "I have spoken, but my word is feeble in comparison. You give us what you know and testify from actual knowledge. You have dealt with the facts with cool, painstaking fidelity and left those naked and uncontradicted facts to speak for themselves" (15).

Wells's structure was factual and her testimony was certainly naked. Ignoring the sentimental diction with which others had cloaked their critical analysis, she presented instead a strong and compelling series of quotations and examples taken from the public media. So important was her stance of well-documented argument that she often quoted her own published words rather than summarize or rephrase them. The literary and social significance of *Southern Horrors* is made clearer by another comparison with Jacobs's *Incidents*. Jacobs took on the delicate subject of miscegenation by relating her personal experiences in the language and manner of the novel of seduction. Her title, *Linda; or, Incidents in the Life of a Slave Girl,* is but one example of her embodiment of political and social commentary in the form of a woman's whisperings into the ears of other women. Wells presents her discussion as a dissertation informed by her personal experiences but based upon diligent research and presented to a general readership.

Briefly, *Southern Horrors* documents the following sequence. On May 21, 1892, Wells had published in her newspaper, *Free Speech,* an editorial that identified lynching as ritual murder based upon racism and justified by a hypocritical argument which besmirched the very reputations of those white women they pretended to protect. What Wells wrote was this:

> Eight negroes lynched since last issue of the "Free Speech" one at Little Rock, Ark., last Saturday morning where the citizens broke (?) into the penitentiary and got their man; three near Anniston, Ala., one near New Orleans; and three at Clarksville, Ga., the last three for killing a white man, and five on the same old racket—the new alarm about raping white women. The same programme of hanging, then shooting bullets into the lifeless bodies was carried out to the letter.
>
> Nobody in this section of the country believes the old thread bare lie that Negro men rape white women. If Southern white men are not careful, they will over-reach themselves and public sentiment will have a reaction; a conclusion will then be reached which will be very damaging to the moral reputation of their women. (16–17)

Strident in tone, armed with copious examples, Wells had determined to test the limits of "Free Speech" with her testimony on behalf of African American men and their mothers, sisters, wives, friends, and children. It is not clear whether Ida B. Wells realized the intensity of the rage her words would evoke, but when the fury burst forth, she was out of town. A mob destroyed her newspaper offices and she was informed that her return to Memphis would be a return to her death. The alacrity with which other black people rallied behind her shows that she had dared to write what they might have but had not. T. Thomas Fortune hired her to work for the New York *Age* and on June 25, 1892, that paper published a sequel that documented in more detail Wells's earlier editorial. Wells argued that racial prejudice and the betrayal of white women were primary causes of the increasing epidemic of lynchings. She pointed out that in only one-third of the 728 lynchings reported between 1884 and 1891 was rape even alleged. And by citing case after case wherein it was discovered that rape charges had been concocted by desperate white women whose newborn infants betrayed their indiscretions or who had been surprised in compromising positions with their black lovers, Wells makes it clear that the vast majority of those accused were not guilty of rape.

The demand for Ida B. Wells's writings was so extensive that the resources of the New York *Age* could not satisfy it. But in a historical convergence of African American women's lives and literature on October 5, 1892, two black women's clubs staged a benefit in New York to raise funds to publish their sister's writings. And, on October 26, 1892, when Ida B. Wells signed the preface to *Southern Horrors,* her words might be understood as prefacing the emerging Black Women's Era:

> The Afro-American is not a bestial race. If this work can contribute in any way toward proving this, and at the same time arouse the conscience of the American people to a demand for justice to every citizen, and punishment by law for the lawless, I shall feel I have done my race a service. Other considerations are of minor importance. (15)

Determining other considerations as of minor importance to the opportunity of serving one's race is exactly the stance of Frances Ellen Watkins Harper as she approached what would become another major publication in 1892. Harper, who had distinguished herself as a fearless freedom fighter several decades earlier and who had years before Ida B. Wells braved physical dangers and social approbation in order to speak the truth on subjects of national importance, did not use such naked language as the younger Wells. But it may not be insignificant that Wells had been Harper's guest during much of the commotion over the *Free Speech* editorial and that "Iola" is both the name of the title character in Frances Harper's book and the nom de plume for many of Ida B. Wells's editorials.

Iola Leroy is another tale constructed to replace certain "threadbare" lies. I have written about *Iola Leroy* in greater detail elsewhere.[147] Here it is sufficient to repeat only that Frances Harper intended to write a book "of lasting service to the race." She, like Octavia Albert, wanted to refute stereotypes, whether malicious or well intended, that defamed or diminished African Americans and to record a more accurate history of slavery, the Civil War, and Reconstruction. The subtitle, *Shadows Uplifted,* implies both the theme of *Iola Leroy* and Harper's intentions for the novel. The imagery obviously refers to Harper's determination to supply the spiritual and intellectual light to eradicate the doubts and disrepute currently being cast over African Americans.[148] Within the text itself, the enlightenment and change are effected by those that social and literary experts were proclaiming as passive, weak, inadequate, or uninterested. In *Iola Leroy* Harper introduces an African American community of various colors, ages, genders, and condition of bondage and shows virtually every member of that community in a joint effort to lift themselves and their race. In the very first chapter, she describes the "phraseology" invented by slaves to communicate war news, their skill in reading both printed material and body language, the multiple functions of "prayer meetings." Her novel chronicles heroic feats and acts of supreme integrity among those who enlisted in the war, those who could but accompany the soldiers as servants and guides, and those who waited and prayed for freedom where they were.

The dominant character in the text is Iola Leroy, a beautiful, educated, refined, and committed mulatto woman. And while many have written about the political implications of Harper's choice to make the most compelling character a mulatto, few have recognized that Iola is a revision of the tragic mulatto stereotype that her mother, Marie, more closely represents. Marie was a beautiful, pious, domestic, pure, and well-educated young slave who had won her master's heart and his hand in marriage. Marie despised slavery and "Like Esther pleading for the lives of her people" (75), she had spoken against it during her commencement speech and she had tried without success to convince her husband to free their slaves and remove their family to free soil. But Eugene Leroy, Harper tells us, was a person "of habit, combined with the feebleness of his moral resistance . . . he had learned to drift where he should have steered" (86). And Marie, though "ever ready to devise plans to ameliorate their condition," (86) was the embodiment of True Womanhood and thus too passive and accommodating. The result was, as typical in tragic mulatto tales, a disaster for them and for their children.

Iola, on the other hand, was as beautiful, as educated, as compassionate, and as refined as her mother. But she possessed something more. She had the insight to perceive the moral weakness of the white man who loved her and the courage to resist the comfortable life that he could offer. Iola speaks essays on feminist, educational, abolitionist, and temperance issues. She was what Harper had described some thirty years earlier in "Our Greatest Want," one of those "men and women whose hearts are the homes of a high and lofty enthusiasm, . . . ready to make every gift, whether gold or talent, fortune or genius, subserve the cause of crushed humanity" (*Brighter* 104). As a mulatto character who truly has reason and means to pass, she is another embodiment of the Moses theme, the theme of genuine self-sacrifice and commitment to the freedom of one's own people.

Consideration of the subtitle, "Shadows Uplifted," and the fact that Iola Leroy's story comes relatively late in the text helps one recognize that while the book is titled with her name, Iola Leroy is best understood as serving a function similar to that of Charlotte Brooks. Hers is a representative story and provides the narrative continuity for the tale, but Iola is merely one member of the African American community. Other significant characters are Iola's uncle, Robert Johnson, her brother, Harry Leroy, the man she marries, Dr. Latimer, and Iola's own model of real womanhood, Lucille Delaney. Iola's brother, her uncle, and her eventual husband are other examples of the Moses motif; each deliberately rejects his very real and specific opportunity to pass for white and enjoy the fruits that his superior talents and energies would bring. Each also refuses to accept the color caste system within African American society as well. Robert remains a staunch friend of the very dark and illiterate Tom and he chooses to live with and support his aged and dark-skinned mother even though it requires him to confront housing discrimination and restricts his own mobility. Harry enlists in an African American regiment because he wants to be reunited with his family and he marries Lucille Delaney, who is attractive to him, in part, because her hair and complexion do not "show the least hint of blood admixture" (199).

Lucille Delaney (whose character and achievements resemble in essence but not in particulars those of the author of *From the Darkness Cometh the Light*) is as important a character as Iola for it is by combining the two characters that Harper's ideal African American women and her intentions for the novel can be realized. Lucille Delaney is older than Iola and has surpassed her young friend in every capacity but is too selfless to realize it. Iola had been able to obtain a teaching position but when her school was destroyed by arson she abandoned that effort. Later when Lucille Delaney hired Iola to teach, Iola had to quit because of ill health. But Lucille had both the physical and mental strength to initiate and to persevere. She recognized a need in the community, designed a curriculum to meet it, created a successful school, and continued in that profession all her life. When Lucille married Harry, they both continued the careers they had established before marriage. Iola, on the other hand, had been unable to keep any of the positions she had obtained and she found her place as the helpmeet to her husband. To Harper, both Iola and Lucille chose legitimate roles and both were to be respected. However, Lucille had the one critical attribute that Iola could never acquire. Lucille Delaney was a woman of sensitivity, intelligence, and generosity who was very dark in complexion and Negroid in features. That she appeared to be an African American without a single Anglo ancestor made her, in Iola's words, "a living argument for the capability which is in the race" (199). This is vital to Harper's mission. In order to embody the unselfish choice to align oneself with the oppressed and to correct the tragic mulatto literary type, Harper needed a character who was white enough to pass, a character who by class and condition could reasonably claim the prerogatives of white True Womanhood. But such a character could not then refute the arguments of racial superiority that attributed the talents and successes of these individuals to their Caucasian ancestry. Separately, neither character could represent the African American experience. Together, the two women represented what Harper deemed the best potential of African American women. And with the other characters, Harry, Robert, Maria, Aunt Nancy, Tom, Uncle Daniel, they could lift the veil of ignorance about slavery, the Civil War, and Reconstruction. They could inspire others of the race to credit themselves agents of progress and the subjects of their own life dramas.

Iola Leroy was intended as a historical novel that rescued the genre from the romanticization of the Plantation School writers. Harper presented a past as a means of critiquing the United States at the present moment and moving it along the road toward a society that in theory and in practice would be an embodiment of Christian democracy. Her characters were not intended to be unique, independent, nor particularly charismatic. They were each to represent a type, they were to articulate positions, they were to demonstrate a lesson or an ideal. *Iola Leroy* was a dramatic essay, standing somewhere between Octavia Albert's *House of Bondage* and Anna Julia Cooper's *A Voice from the South*. From this perspective, Hazel Carby's description of the novels by Frances Harper and Pauline Hopkins as "loci of political and social interests, forming intellectual constituencies, not merely reflecting the interests of a preexisting intellectual elite" (96) is appropriate to the writing of African American women in the 1890s generally.

Anna Julia Cooper, who like Frances Harper would accept the responsibility of speaking on behalf of African American women at the World's Congress of Representative Women, was both convinced of the impossibility of any one individual representing the race and of the necessity of every individual attempting to do so. Anna Julia Cooper, like Lucy Delaney, had been born into slavery but had never defined herself as a slave. Like Ida B. Wells, Cooper essayed to defend her race by intervening into the political process through deeds of defiance and with sharply worded arguments that marshaled facts and examples from history and from current events. In common with these and her other sister writers, she wrote to record, to defend, and to inspire the brave deeds, high thoughts, and lofty aspirations of herself and of her people.

The forthrightness and purpose of Anna Julia Cooper's book were not mere rhetorical strategies. Cooper lived and taught as she wrote. In 1905 she would face a lengthy series of hearings on charges that she had (1) refused to use a textbook authorized by the Board of Education, (2) been too sympathetic to weak and unqualified students, (3) maintained lax discipline and (4) displayed an improper "spirit of unity and loyalty."[149] Despite (or perhaps because of) the fact that through her tutelage several African American students had been admitted to Ivy League universities and as principal of the M Street High School she had guided that institution to its first accreditation by Harvard University, Anna Julia Cooper would lose her job. Eventually she would be reinstated, not as principal but as a Latin teacher. She would rear five children, earn a Ph.D. from the Sorbonne, and found a university dedicated to the liberal education of working-class adults.

Anna Julia Cooper knew that she was not typical but she also knew that she was representative. She knew she was a black woman of the South and she was a progressive woman of the United States. She presented herself as an example of progress being made by a race only a few years removed from bondage and she claimed her identity as a member and example of the human family in historical and international perspective.

Anna Julia Cooper's work does not discard the discourse of distrust, but true to the example of her literary foremothers, she stretched and revised literary strategies to fit her particular needs. Cooper's presentation of her essays as those of a black Southern woman and her choice to speak about issues that she knew to concern her in that specific persona as well as on a more general level is clearly in the tradition of Alice, Maria W. Stewart, and others before her who had refused to be silent or to confine their comments to subjects deemed appropriate to their race, gender, or class.

Some scholars have tended to define *A Voice from the South* simply as an early feminist manifesto, but here we do well to consider what Mary Helen Washington has stated: that Cooper's "position was never narrowly confined to the women's issue because she saw this dominance of the strong over the weak as the critical issue, and she saw that tendency to abuse power in the labor and women's movements, both of which were deeply entrenched in 'caste prejudice' and hostile to the needs and interests of black women" (Washington xliv). Anna Julia Cooper was certainly being very pro-woman when she stated:

> The question is not now with the woman "How shall I so cramp, stunt, simplify and nullify myself as to make me eligible to the honor of being swallowed up into some little man?" but the problem, . . . rests with the man as to how he can so develop his God-given powers as to reach the ideal of a generation of women who demand the noblest, grandest and best achievements of which he is capable. (70–71)

But she contextualized that and other comments with statements such as "All I claim is that there is a feminine as well as a masculine side to truth; that these are related not as inferior and superior, not as better and worse, not as weaker and stronger, but as complements—complements in one necessary and symmetric whole" (60).

Cooper's 1892 volume makes explicit the ideas implicit in the writings of Harper, Delaney, and even Wells. Hers is a theory of inclusion based not upon plaintive pleas or passive endurance but one to be articulated and demonstrated via her own testimony as an African American woman. It is crucial to understanding Anna Julia Cooper's book and the African American women writers of the 1890s that we recognize their arguments and their books, as based upon a firm belief in the propriety and the possibility of diversity and social equality. Neither she, nor they, sought to defend or to promote herself and black women by demeaning or excoriating black men, white women, or any other group.

Cooper's book *A Voice from the South by a Black Woman of the South* manifests in title and structure this concept. Its title has the all-important "A" and "South" repeated twice. "A Voice" is not the only one and "a Black Woman" is likewise singular even as it identifies itself in terms of two categories, race and gender. "The South" is equally important for it does not intend to distinguish between regions within that area in order to align one group against another. As it works in her book, "the South" reminds readers of the reality of *e pluribus unum*. The book consists of eight essays, divided into two sections. The first is called "Soprano Obligato" and offers four essays focusing upon women and their relationship to other groups or their place within the overall human community. The second section, "Tutti ad Libitum," devotes its four essays to explorations of the economic, literary, political, and philosophical constructs that race can and does create.

The breadth, complexity, and diversity of her interests and of the essays in *A Voice from the South* cannot be summarized in a few paragraphs or a few pages. But, as an example of Cooper's rhetoric of inclusion by which she uses a specific subject as the occasion for larger considerations, I will briefly examine one essay, "Woman vs. the Indian." Its basic thesis is that every individual has the occasion and the responsibility to work against inappropriate discrimination. Cooper takes as her title that of a speech recently delivered by Rev. Anna Shaw to the National Woman's Council; however, instead of commenting upon Shaw's paper, Cooper begins by reporting Shaw's involvement in a recent controversy among members of a white women's group over which she presided. Anna Cooper praises Anna Shaw because her personal behavior in this instance matched that of her public rhetoric. Upon discovering that a black woman had been denied admission to a class sponsored by her organization, Anna Shaw threatened to resign. She was joined in this effort by Susan B. Anthony and other members and the group decided to open its community service activities to all women. This particular club had named itself "Wimodaughsis," a word that vaguely evoked a Native American connection and one that offered Cooper fine opportunity to pun upon the arrogance and fallacy of its use. "Wimodaughsis" came from the initial letters of "wives," "mothers," "daughters," and "sisters." Cooper reminds her readers that the group had not only failed to realize that some wives, mothers, daughters, and sisters are not Caucasian but had also allowed its name to imply that all women were wives. Her caustic suggestion that their name might be changed to "whimodaughsis" which would then "mean just *white mothers, daughters and sisters*" (emphasis hers 81) enlarges the conversation beyond the subject of racial exclusivism to question the appropriateness of traditional gender descriptions.

In beginning her essay by praising a woman who said "No" to racial discrimination within a relatively private sphere, Cooper makes her essay speak both to the issue of racial divisions within the women's movement and to ways that individuals who might be uncomfortable addressing issues of public policy can work toward a more democratic society. Cooper uses this incident to demonstrate that "The American woman . . . is responsible for American manners. Not merely . . . of her own drawing room; but the rising and setting of the pestilential or life-giving orbs which seem to wander afar in space, all are governed almost wholly through her magnetic polarity" (86). From this topic, Cooper turns her attention to writings by white women journalists who purport to prove that technological progress and national civility have substantially liberated women in the United States. She agrees that travel is essential to a "true test of national courtesy" (93), but she asserts again that "women" must not be racially exclusive and that given their peculiar social position, black women are better qualified to test this assertion:

> Any rough can assume civility toward those of "his set," and does not hesitate to carry it even to servility toward those in whom he recognizes a possible patron or his master in power, wealth, rank, or influence. But, as the chemist prefers distilled H_2O in testing solutions to avoid complications and unwarranted reactions, so the Black Woman holds that her femininity linked with the impossibility of popular affinity or unexpected attraction through position and influence in her case makes her a touchstone of American courtesy exceptionally pure and singularly free from extraneous modifiers. (93)

Citing her own experience traveling through the South moves her discussion to that of the unnatural influence that the South has had upon the United States: "from the very beginning even up to the present day, [the South has] dictated to and domineered over the brain and sinew of this nation. Without wealth, without education, without inventions, arts, sciences, or industries, . . . the Southerner has nevertheless . . . manipulated Northern sentiment as to succeed sooner or later in carrying his point and shaping the policy of this government to suit his purposes" (101). Personifying the South as a "sullen younger sister" who "pouted, and sulked, and cried" (104) to get her way allows Cooper to weave efficiently and effectively her various discursive threads. In her depiction of the South as a female who failed to outgrow childish selfishness and to assume her role as nurturer of American manners, Cooper connects this "Southern *lady*" (emphasis hers 108) to the essay's beginning example of the Wimodaughsis. For the person who personally barred the black woman's participation in the group had been a white woman from Kentucky. Cooper also blames men, including the "big brother" North and "Father Lincoln," (105) who accept such infantile behavior, implying that they too are deficient in maturity and sophistication. The essay's movement between specific and general continues by reference again to the title of the essay. Now Cooper discloses that even the heroic Anna Shaw had a problem, her "unfortunately worded" title "Woman vs. the Indian." "Woman should not, even by inference, or for the sake of argument, seem to disparage what is weak," (117) she admonishes. Anna Julia Cooper concludes her essay on a grand scale with a summary of its thesis that can serve just as appropriately for the entire book:

> The cause of freedom is not the cause of a race or a sect, a party or a class,—it is the cause of human kind, the very birthright of humanity. Now unless we are greatly mistaken the Reform of our day, known as the Woman's Movement, is essentially such as embodiment, if its pioneers could only realize it, of the universal good. . . .
> It is not the intelligent woman vs. the ignorant woman; nor the white woman vs. the black, the brown, and the red,—it is not even the cause of woman vs. man. Nay, 'tis woman's strongest vindication for speaking that *the world needs*

to hear her voice. It would be subversive of every human interest that the cry of one-half the human family be stifled. (120-21)

The 1890s was a contradictory and complex time. Sandra Gilbert and Susan Gubar conclude, "many literary figures in this period felt that they were living between two worlds, one dead and the other struggling to be born. Nor is it surprising that both sexes frequently associated accelerating historical changes with the rapidly shifting situation of women."[150] Many African American women knew themselves to be an integral part of these accelerating changes. But they did not see themselves as living simply between "two worlds, one dead and the other struggling to be born." The place where they resided was a concourse or a concrescence of many worlds including some which they had been trying to kill for many decades. Their lives and their letters demonstrate that many of them believed that the place where they lived was in fact the place where the true mettle of the nation would be tested. They generally agreed with Anna Julia Cooper, who wrote: "The colored woman of to-day occupies, one may say, a unique position in this country. In a period of itself transitional and unsettled, her status seems one of the least ascertainable and definitive of all the forces which make for our civilization. She is confronted by both a woman question and a race problem, and is as yet an unknown or an unacknowledged factor in both" (134).

In the 1890s many African American women writers knew themselves to be continuing a grand and noble experiment begun by their foremothers. In *A Voice from the South by a Black Woman of the South* Anna Julia Cooper proclaimed "Not unfelt, then, if unproclaimed has been the work and influence of the colored women of America. Our list of chieftains in the service, though not long, is not inferior in strength and excellence, I dare believe, to any similar list which this country can produce" (140). She then listed several examples of African American women who testified to the experiences, hopes, and dreams of themselves and of their communities and who tested the ability of the English language to accommodate and to be appropriated for those testimonies. Anna Julia Cooper's conclusion is an apt conclusion for this study:

These women represent all shades of belief and as many departments of activity; but they have one thing in common—their sympathy with the oppressed race in America and the consecration of their several talents in whatever line to the work of its deliverance and development. (142)

Notes

1. Isaiah Thomas, *Eccentric Biography; or, Memoirs of Remarkable Female Characters, Ancient and Modern* (London, 1803) 1. All references to Alice, unless otherwise noted, are from this source and cited in the text.

2. "Mrs. Stewart's Farewell Address to Her Friends in the City of Boston, Delivered September 21, 1833," *Maria W. Stewart, America's First Black Woman Political Writer: Essays and Speeches,* ed. Marilyn Richardson (Bloomington: Indiana UP, 1987), 71. Subsequent references to Maria Stewart's writings are from this edition and cited in the text.

3. Anna Julia Cooper, *A Voice from the South by a Black Woman of the South* (1892; New York: Oxford UP, 1988) ii. Subsequent references are from this edition and appear in the text.

4. The dynamism of literary scholarship in general and of African American women's literature in particular makes me exceedingly cautious about designating any one or any text as "the first" or "the earliest extant." My basic approach is to avoid such designations but in discussions such as this where priority is important, I am always aware (and indeed hoping) that at any given moment an earlier writer or text will be rediscovered.

5. Richardson, ed., preface, *Maria W. Stewart, America's First Black Woman Political Writer: Essays and Speeches* xiii. Subsequent references are cited in the text.

6. John Hope Franklin, *From Slavery to Freedom: A History of Negro Americans,* 4th ed. (New York: Knopf, 1974), 322. Subsequent references are to this edition and found in the text.

7. *The Work of the Afro-American Woman* (1894; New York: Oxford UP, 1988).

8. *Black Women Novelists: The Development of a Tradition* (Westport, Conn.: Greenwood, 1980), x.

9. Wintrop Jordan, *White over Black: American Attitudes toward the Negro, 1550–1812* (Chapel Hill: U of North Carolina P, 1968) vii. Subsequent references are to this edition and cited in the text.

10. Ed. Gloria T. Hull, Patricia Bell Scott, and Barbara Smith (Old Westbury, N.Y.: Feminist Press, 1982).

11. Eleanor Flexner, *Century of Struggle: The Woman's Rights Movement in the United States,* rev. ed. (Cambridge: Harvard UP, 1975) 5–6. Subsequent references are from this edition and found in the text.

12. Gilbert and Gubar, *Madwoman in the Attic* (New Haven: Yale UP, 1979) xi–xii. Subsequent references are cited in the text as *Madwoman.*

13. *The Poetics of Women's Autobiography: Marginality and the Fiction of Self-Representation* (Bloomington: Indiana UP, 1987) 31.

14. (New York: Oxford UP, 1986) 8.

15. Amy Ling, "I'm Here: An Asian American Woman's Reponse," *New Literary History* 19 (Autumn 1987) 154. Subsequent references are to this source and found in the text.

16. For an extended discussion of how this problem worked during the struggle for abolition and suffrage, see Jean Fagan Yellin's *Women and Sisters: The Antislavery Feminists in American Culture* (New Haven: Yale UP, 1989).

17. Hazel Carby, *Reconstructing Womanhood: The Emergence of the Afro-American Woman Novelist* (New York: Oxford UP, 1987) 18. Subsequent references are from this edition and cited in the text.

18. (Garden City: Doubleday, 1970) xxii.

19. Melville J. Herskovits. *The Myth of the Negro Past* (Boston: Beacon Press, 1958) 115.

20. Janheinz Jahn. *Muntu: African Culture and the Western World.* Trans. Marjorie Grene (1961; New York: Grove Weidenfeld, 1989) 125. Subsequent references are from this edition and found in the text.

21. The *nyatiti*, is a part-time poet who "is called upon to praise friends or relatives, to recount . . . personal experiences, to exalt kindness, hospitality, or courage, and to comment on current affairs" (Ruth Finnegan. *Oral Literature in Africa* [Nairobi: Oxford University Press, 1970] 100). Similarly, the *rara* is a form of lay poetry that a new bride might sing to praise her mother or in anticipation of her new home (Ulli Beier. *Yoruba Poetry* [Cambridge, England: University Press, 1970] 24).

22. "'We Hold These Truths': Strategies of Control in the Literature of the Founders," in *Reconstructing American Literary History,* ed. Sacvan Bercovitch (Cambridge: Harvard UP, 1986) 2–3.

23. Introduction to Phillis Wheatley, *Poems on Various Subjects, Religious and Moral* (1773; New York: Oxford UP, 1988) 7. All subsequent references to Wheatley's poems and letters are from this edition and noted in the text.

24. *The Poetry of American Women from 1632 to 1945* (Austin: U of Texas P, 1977) 37.

25. William Andrews, *To Tell a Free Story: The First Century of Afro-American Autobiography* (Urbana: U of Illinois P, 1986) xi. Subsequent references are cited in the text.

26. LeRoi Jones, "The Myth of a 'Negro Literature'" in *Home: Social Essays* (New York: Morrow, 1966) 112.

27. Fannie Barrier Williams, "The Intellectual Progress of the Colored Women of the United States Since the Emancipation Proclamation" in *World's Congress of Representative Women,* ed. May Wright Sewall. vol. 2 (Chicago: n.p. 1894) 700.

28. Henrietta Cordelia Ray, *Poems* (1910; *Collected Black Women's Poetry,* vol. 3, ed. Joan Sherman [New York: Oxford UP, 1988]) 78. Subsequent references are from this edition and found in the text.

29. Ann Plato, *Essays; Including Biographies and Miscellaneous Pieces, in Prose and Poetry* (1841; New York: Oxford UP, 1988) 111. Subsequent references are to this edition and found in the text.

30. *The Journals of Charlotte Forten Grimke,* ed. Brenda Stevenson (New York: Oxford UP, 1988) 63. Subsequent references are from this edition and found in the text.

31. Frances Ellen Watkins Harper, *Iola Leroy* (1892; New York: Oxford UP, 1988) 262. Subsequent references are from this edition and cited in the text.

32. 1895; *Massachusetts Review* 27 (Summer 1986) 173–74.

33. Quoted in Josiah Holland, *History of Western Massachusetts,* vol. 2 (Springfield, Mass.: Willey and Company, 1855) 360.

34. George Sheldon, *A History of Deerfield, Massachusetts* (1895–96; Somersworth: New Hampshire Publishing Company in collaboration with the Pocumtuck Valley Memorial Association, Deerfield, 1972) 899. Subsequent references are from this edition and found in the text.

35. *Black Poets of the United States from Paul Laurence Dunbar to Langston Hughes,* trans. Kenneth Douglas (Urbana: U of Illinois P, 1973) 17.

36. In using Dunbar's "masked," DuBois's "two-toned," and Bakhtin's "double-voiced," I am not suggesting congruence or succession of meaning. I intend rather to invoke the critical arguments that for at least the last century have suggested that African American writers, like all writers, have had inclination, ability, and reason to eschew the simple, the didactic, the literal.

37. The historical record is replete with examples of increasing racial tension during this period, but these particular incidents are discussed in Jordan, 116–23.

38. George Sheldon, "Negro Slavery in Old Deerfield," *New England Magazine* n.s. 8 (March 1893) 55.

39. Rayford W. Logan, "Lucy Terry Prince," *Dictionary of American Biography,* ed. Rayford W. Logan and Michael R. Winston (New York: Norton, 1982) 504.

40. Sidney Kaplan, *The Black Presence in the Era of the American Revolution, 1770–1800* (Greenwich, Conn.: New York Graphic Press, 1973) 211. Subsequent references are from this edition and found in the text.

41. William H. Robinson, *Phillis Wheatley and Her Writings* (New York: Garland, 1984), 27. Robinson, John Shields, and Julian D. Mason, Jr., are three of the leading Wheatley scholars and much of the biographical information cited may be found in any of these texts. For the convenience of the reader, I am using this edition of Robinson's work as the source of most biographical details about Wheatley. The page numbers in the text are preceded by *Her Writings.*

42. William Robinson informs us that the memoir was appended to the 1834 Boston reprinting of Wheatley's *Poems,* then published separately in 1836. The author was Margaretta Matilda Oddell (sometimes spelled Odell), the great grandniece of Susanna Wheatley. While the memoir is not without errors, it is considered the most authoritative of the early biographical accounts. Page references to Oddell's *Memoirs* are from the version reprinted in William Robinson's *Phillis Wheatley and Her Writings* and are indicated in the text as "Oddell."

43. Julian D. Mason, Jr., *The Poems of Phillis Wheatley,* rev. ed. (Chapel Hill: U of North Carolina P, 1989) 149. Unless otherwise indicated, quotations from Wheatley's writings are from this edition and the page numbers are found in the text.

44. *The Journey Back: Issues in Black Literature and Criticism* (Chicago: U of Chicago P, 1980), 23.

45. "'Our Modern Egyptians': Phillis Wheatley and the Whig Campaign against Slavery in Revolutionary Boston," *Journal of Negro History* 60 (July 1975) 409.

46. Quoted in Kenneth Silverman, "Four New Letters by Phillis Wheatley," *Early American Literature* 8 (1974) 261.

47. Several scholars, including Julian D. Mason, Jr., (30) and Robert C. Kuncio, in whose article "Some Unpublished Poems" the manuscript version was first printed, have pointed out that the 1768 version is less flattering to the king. I believe that the revisions of lines 14–15 and other changes, such as a de-emphasis of physical might to recognize that martial victories must be won with God's assistance, introduce more subtlety and complexity but continue to criticize King George. Our agreement, however, is that the published version is more politically astute.

48. Quoted in William H. Robinson, *Black New England Letters* (Boston: Public Library of the City of Boston, 1977) 28.

49. John Blassingame, *Slave Testimony: Two Centuries of Letters, Speeches, Interviews, and Autobiographies* (Baton Rouge: Louisiana State UP, 1977) 7.

50. Dorothy Sterling, *We Are You Sisters: Black Women in the Nineteenth Century* (New York: Norton, 1984) 108. Subsequent references are to this edition and found in the text.

51. Alice Brown, *Mercy Warren* (New York: Scribner's, 1896) 138. Subsequent references are to this edition and found in the text.

52. Quoted in Janet Wilson James, *Changing Ideas About Women in the United States, 1776–1825* (New York: Garland, 1981), 17.

53. Kenneth A. Lockridge, *Literacy in Colonial New England: An Enquiry into the Social Context of Literacy in the Early Modern West* (New York: Norton, 1974) 38. Subsequent references are to this edition and found in the text.

54. Emily Stipes Watts, *The Poetry of American Women from 1632 to 1945*

(Austin: U of Texas P, 1977) 4. Subsequent references are from this edition and found in the text.

55. Charles Francis Adams, *Familiar Letters of John Adams and His Wife Abigail Adams, during the Revolution* (New York: Hurd and Houghton, 1876) 149. Subsequent references are from this edition and found in the text.

56. Nancy F. Cott, *The Bonds of Womanhood* (New Haven: Yale UP, 1977) 199. Subsequent references are to this edition and found in the text.

57. Carl N. Degler, *At Odds: Women and the Family from the Revolution to the Present* (New York: Oxford UP, 1980) 28. Subsequent references are from this edition and found in the text.

58. See, for example, Anne Goodwyn Jones, *Tomorrow Is Another Day: The Woman Writer in the South* (Baton Rouge: Louisiana State UP, 1981). According to Jones the differences were both in the concepts of womanhood and also in the images of Southern womanhood. In the preface to *Tomorrow Is Another Day,* Jones admonishes: "Both my historical research and my experience of living outside the South lead me to issue a caveat at the outset: southerners and northerners seem to have—often unbeknownst to them—differing images of the southern woman" (xiii).

59. *The Life and Religious Experience of Jarena Lee, a Coloured Lady* (1836; reprinted in *The Female Autograph,* ed. Domna Stanton [New York: New York Literary Forum, 1984]) 156. Subsequent references are from this edition and found in the text.

60. *Religious Experience and Journal of Mrs. Jarena Lee* (1849; New York: Oxford UP, 1988). Subsequent references are to this edition and found in the text.

61. "Textual Note," *Sisters of the Spirit: Three Black Women's Autobiographies of the Nineteenth Century* (Bloomington: Indiana UP, 1986) 23.

62. (Princeton: Princeton UP, 1968) 5.

63. Solomon Bayley, reprinted in Dorothy Porter, *Early Negro Writing, 1760–1837* (Boston: Beacon Press, 1971) 591. Subsequent references are from this edition and found in the text.

64. The first version of John Marrant's narrative appeared in 1785. It was expanded in 1788. Quotations in my discussion are from the 1788 edition as published in Richard Vanderbeets, *Held Captive by Indians: Selected Narratives 1642–1836* (Knoxville: U of Tennessee P, 1973).

65. Robert Stepto, *From Behind the Veil: A Study of Afro American Narrative* (Urbana: U of Illinois P, 1979).

66. "Young Women in the Second Great Awakening in New England," *Feminist Studies* 3 (1975) 21.

67. *American Quarterly* 30 (Winter 1978) 638.

68. Nancy Hardesty, Lucille Sider Dayton, and Donald W. Dayton, "Women in the Holiness Movement: Feminism in the Evangelical Tradition," in *Women of Spirit: Female Leadership in the Jewish and Christian Traditions,* ed. Rosemary Ruether and Eleanor McLaughlin (New York: Simon and Schuster, 1979) 228.

69. James A. Handy, *Scraps of African Methodist Episcopal History* (1902; reprinted Ann Arbor, Mich.: University Microfilms, 1974), 120.

70. Daniel A. Payne, *History of the African Methodist Episcopal Church* (1891; reprinted New York: Arno Press, 1969) 189. Subsequent references are to this edition and found in the text.

71. Angelina Grimke, *Appeal to the Christian Women of the South* (1836; rpt. New York: Arno Press, 1969) 25.

72. "Woman's literature" is used here to include prose and poetry, fiction and nonfiction. But beyond a few (mostly structural) intrinsic generic restraints, this writing conforms to the definition that Nina Baym established in her seminal *Woman's Fiction: A Guide to Novels by and about Women in America, 1820–1870* (Ithaca: Cornell UP, 1978). Baym cites three conditions: "They are written by

women, are addressed to women, and tell one particular story about women" (22). The published literature by African American women writers of the antebellum period that this chapter discusses differs in one important way. It was not "addressed to women." Since her text is silent on the issue, one wonders if Baym considered writings by women of color when she formulated her definitions.

73. Mary E. Bryan, "How Should Women Write?" in *Hidden Hands: An Anthology of American Women Writers: 1790–1870* (New Brunswick, N.J.: Rutgers University Press, 1985), 370.

74. For an insightful analysis of the ways in which Stowe's text ultimately reaffirms the conventions of domestic feminism, see Jean Fagan Yellin's "Doing It Herself: *Uncle Tom's Cabin* and Woman's Role in the Slavery Crisis," in *New Essays on Uncle Tom's Cabin*, ed. Eric J. Sundquist (Cambridge: Cambridge UP, 1986).

75. "Discrimination Against Afro-American Women in the Woman's Movement, 1830–1920," in *The Afro-American Woman: Struggles and Images*. ed. Sharon Harley and Rosalyn Terborg-Penn (Port Washington, N.Y.: Kennikat Press, 1978) 17, 19.

76. See Joanne V. Hawks and Sheila L. Iskemp, eds., *Sex, Race, and the Role of Women in the South* (Jackson: UP of Mississippi, 1983) xiv.

77. Even this was fraught with charges of paternalism and racism. African Americans were quite aware that the restrictions that William Lloyd Garrison placed upon Frederick Douglass, to simply recite the facts of his slave experience and leave the philosophy to his white superiors, extended even more to the less educated and erudite among them.

78. *The Norton Anthology of Literature by Women: The Tradition in English*. compiled by Sandra M. Gilbert and Susan Gubar (New York: Norton, 1985) 184.

79. Harriet Jacobs, *Incidents in the Life of a Slave Girl* (1861; Cambridge: Harvard UP, 1987) 2. Subsequent references are from this edition and found in the text. There may have been other African American women who published writings directed toward a female readership, but this is the earliest extant text to date. This discussion of Harriet Jacobs's narrative would not have been possible were it not for the intrepid scholar Jean Fagan Yellin, who searched out and found the letters and other documents establishing Jacobs's authorship and many of the circumstances under which the book occurred.

80. Zipha Elaw, *Memoirs* (1846; reprinted in *Sisters of the Spirit*, ed. William L. Andrews (Bloomington: Indiana UP, 1986) 51. Subsequent references are to this edition and found in the text.

81. Ann Allen Shockley, *Afro-American Women Writers, 1746–1933: An Anthology and Critical Guide* (Boston: G.K. Hall, 1988) 51.

82. *A Narrative of the Life and Travels of Mrs. Nancy Prince*, 2nd ed. (1853; New York: Oxford UP, 1988) 3. Subsequent references are to this edition and found in the text.

83. Introduction to Harriet E. Wilson, *Our Nig; or, Sketches from the Life of a Free Black* (New York: Vintage, 1983) xli–xliii. Gates lists fifteen elements that characterize the overplot of woman's fiction. He calls *Our Nig* a "fictional third-person autobiography" that displays evidence of broad reading in nineteenth-century American and British literature and is a "complex response" to Stowe's *Uncle Tom's Cabin*.

84. (1859; reprinted New York: Vintage, 1983) 124–25. Subsequent references are from this edition and found in the text.

85. (1940; New York: Pageant, 1959) 270.

86. Reprinted in *A Brighter Coming Day: A Frances Ellen Watkins Harper Reader*, ed. Frances Smith Foster (New York: Feminist Press, 1990). Subsequent references to this and all other writings by Harper, unless otherwise noted in the text, are from this edition. In the "Two Offers," Harper handles race in such an

abstract way and the physical characteristics of the characters are so generic that some have assumed they are white. Given its author and its publisher, this is a mistaken assumption.

87. Harper's implication of the father's shared responsibility is fairly unusual. Most woman's fiction placed the burden of good behavior upon the woman and assumed that men's preoccupation with jobs and financial security was immutable and probably right.

88. Quoted in J. Saunders Redding, *To Make a Poet Black* (1939; Ithaca: Cornell UP, 1988) 39. Subsequent references are from this edition and found in the text.

89. Stone specifically notes the significance of such attitudes when the writers are not members of the dominant culture. Albert E. Stone, *Autobiographical Occasions and Original Acts* (Philadelphia: U of Pennsylvania P, 1982) 10.

90. Quoted in Claudia Tate, *Black Women Writers at Work* (New York: Continuum, 1983) 122.

91. Charles Ball, *Slavery in the United States: A Narrative of the Life and Adventures of Charles Ball, a Black Man* (1836; Detroit: Negro History Press, 1970). Subsequent references are from this edition and are found in the text. William Andrews and Phillip S. Foner have identified "Mr. Fisher" as Issac Fisher, a Lewistown attorney (see Andrews, *Free Story* 302).

92. The controversy over Hildreth's and Ball's works was based upon forthright declarations. Though published anonymously, *The Slave* was immediately recognized as a novel. Two years later, the controversy would be complicated by the exposure that the account that James Williams had dictated to John Greenleaf Whittier and which had been assumed to be a factual slave narrative was actually fictitious. The apparent fugitive was not a slave, but a free black who chose to test his own novelistic skill.

93. Richard Hildreth, introduction to *Archy Moore, the White Slave or, Memoirs of a Fugitive*, 1856. All book reviews related to the 1836 edition of *The Slave* are as quoted in Richard Hildreth's introduction. I have attempted to compare Hildreth's excerpts with the originals and am satisfied that he uses them appropriately. For the convenience of the reader, therefore, the pages cited here and in other references to reviews are from the Hildreth text.

94. *The Liberator* 7 (April 28, 1837) 72.

95. Jacobs used fictitious names and in summarizing the narrative or discussing its content I use those names. For example, since "Linda Brent" is the name that Harriet Jacobs calls herself in the narrative, "Linda Brent" is the term I will use to distinguish the character from its author.

96. Minrose C. Gwin, *Black and White Women of the Old South* (Knoxville: The U of Tennessee P, 1985) 5. Subsequent references are cited in the text.

97. For details of this see Jean Fagan Yellin, "Written by Herself: Harriet Jacobs's Slave Narrative," *American Literature* 53(1981) 479–86.

98. Robert B. Stepto, "Distrust of the Reader in Afro-American Narratives," in *Reconstructing American Literary History,* ed. Sacvan Bercovitch (Cambridge: Harvard UP, 1986) 303.

99. The British edition, that appeared the next year, is called *The Deeper Wrong; or, Incidents in the Life of a Slave Girl.* My examination of both editions reveals that both were set from the same plates, and with the exception of the titles that appear on their covers, the works are identical. Naming the text *The Deeper Wrong* calls attention to an implicit theme that requires the reader to assess the relative culpabilities within the story and implies that if Linda had done wrong, the fact ought to be judged against other, more grievous sins.

100. Karlyn Kohrs Campbell, "Style and Content in the Rhetoric of Early Afro-American Feminists," *Quarterly Journal of Speech* 72 (1986) 440–41.

101. The quote here is from William Andrews's *To Tell a Free Story,* 253. Andrews

is eloquent on Jacobs's manipulation of her ideal reader (women such as her friends Amy Post and Lydia Maria Child) and the more common reader.

102. Frances Smith Foster, "Adding Color and Contour to Early American Self-Portraitures: Autobiographical Writings of Afro-American Women," in *Conjuring: Black Women, Fiction, and Literary Tradition,* ed. Marjorie Pryse and Hortense Spillers (Bloomington: Indiana UP, 1985) 25–38.

103. Frances B. Cogan, *All-American Girl: The Ideal of Real Womanhood in Mid-Nineteenth Century America* (Athens: U of Georgia P, 1989) 4.

104. *Born for Liberty: A History of Women in America* (New York: Free Press, 1989) 114.

105. Elizabeth Keckley, *Behind the Scenes* (1868; New York: Arno Press, 1968) xii. Subsequent references are from this edition and are found in the text.

106. Here I am using the term as Joanne M. Braxton does in *Black Women Writing Autobiography: A Tradition within a Tradition* (Philadelphia: Temple UP, 1989) 31. Braxton supplements the *Webster's Dictionary* interpretation of impudent or disrespectful talk with reference to the West African associations of "sass" as a method of self-defense and ego preservation.

107. William L. Andrews, "Reunion in the Postbellum Slave Narrative: Frederick Douglass and Elizabeth Keckley," *Black American Literature Forum* 23 (1989) 7.

108. Francis J. Grimke, eulogy delivered at Home of the National Association for Colored Women and Children, May 28, 1907, Grimke Papers, Moorland-Spingarn Research Center, Howard University. Subsequent page references to this source are found in the text.

109. John E. Washington, *They Knew Lincoln* (New York: Dutton, 1942) 236. Jon Washington provides a very detailed chapter, "'Behind the Scenes': The Story of Mrs. Keckley's Book." While I have checked many of his sources and supplemented his history, I am indebted to him for much of the information on the production history of *Behind the Scenes.* Subsequent references to these details, unless otherwise noted, are from this source and noted in the text.

110. April 18, 1968, 4.

111. Quoted in Madeline B. Hern, *Imprints on History* (Bloomington: Indiana UP) 233. Subsequent references to this source are indicated in the text.

112. April 25, 1868, 4.

113. Fred Lewis Pattee, *A History of American Literature since 1870.* (1951; New York: Century Company, 1916) i–ii. Subsequent references are from this edition and are found in the text.

114. Nina Baym, Ronald Gottesman, and Laurence B. Holland, *The Norton Anthology of American Literature,* 2nd ed., vol 2 (New York: Norton, 1985) 2. Subsequent references are from this edition and are found in the text.

115. Quoted in William Still, *The Underground Rail Road* (Philadelphia, 1872) 770. Subsequent page references to *The Underground Rail Road* are from this edition and found in the text.

116. Kenny J. Williams, *They Also Spoke: An Essay on Negro Literature in America,* 1797–1930 (Nashville: Townsend Press, 1970) 121. Subsequent references are found in the text.

117. Reprinted in *Black Writers of America: A Comprehensive Anthology,* ed. Richard Barksdale and Keneth Kinnamon (New York: Macmillan, 1972) 234.

118. *Report of the Proceedings of the Eleventh National Woman's Rights Convention* (New York: American News Company, 1866) 47. Subsequent references to this essay are from this edition and page numbers are noted in the text.

119. Quoted in *The Underground Rail Road* 767.

120. *CLA Journal* 31 (1987) 19.

121. (New York: Oxford UP, 1988). Subsequent references to Graham's introduction are taken from this edition and noted in the text.

122. Roy Harvey Pearce, *The Continuity of American Poetry* (Princeton: Princeton UP, 1971) 194. Subsequent references are to this edition and found in the text.

123. Quoted in Richard Ruland, *The Native Muse: Theories of American Literature from Bradford to Whitman* (New York: Dutton, 1976) 345.

124. (Philadelphia: Temple UP, 1982) 36.

125. "Is Frances Ellen Watkins Good Enough to Teach?" *Legacy* 5 (1988) 31.

126. (Urbana: U of Illinois P, 1974) xxvii.

127. Walt Whitman, "The Poetry of the Future," *North American Review* (February 1881) 202. Subsequent references are from this source and are found in the text.

128. Introduction, *Collected Black Women's Poetry*, vol. 1 (New York: Oxford UP, 1988) xxxiii.

129. 1873; reprinted in *Collected Black Women's Poetry*, vol 1, 17. In 1974 when Joan Sherman published *Invisible Poets*, she indicated that Menken's race was "in doubt." While the controversy has not been fully resolved, the evidence seems to imply that Menken was an African American. In the introduction to the 1988 reprint, Sherman writes that "She probably was born to Autuste Theodore, a mulatto registered as a 'free man of color' and his wife Magdaleine Jean Louis Janneaux."

130. "Lifting as We Climb" was the official motto of the National Association of Colored Women, an organization which many of these writers helped found.

131. J. V. Ridgely, *Nineteenth-Century Southern Literature* (Lexington: UP of Kentucky, 1980) 2. Subsequent references are in the text.

132. Hugh Morris Gloster, *Negro Voices in American Fiction* (Chapel Hill: U of North Carolina Press, 1948) 8.

133. Quoted in Richard Yarborough, "The Depiction of Blacks in the Early Afro-American Novel," diss., Stanford University, 1980, 207.

134. Quoted in Louise Daniel Hutchinson, *Anna J. Cooper, a Voice from the South* (Washington, D.C.: Smithsonian Institution Press, 1981) 96.

135. Octavia Victoria Rogers Albert, *The House of Bondage* (1890; New York: Oxford UP, 1988) 161. Subsequent references are from this edition and are found in the text.

136. *The Narrative Act: Point of View in Prose Fiction* (Princeton: Princeton UP, 1981) 166. Subsequent references are found in the text.

137. *Narrative of the Life of Frederick Douglass, an American Slave* (1845; Cambridge: Harvard UP, 1960) 153.

138. *The Afro-American Press and Its Editors* (1891; New York: Arno Press, 1969) 226.

139. *The Incorporation of America: Culture and Society in the Gilded Age* (New York: Hill and Wang, 1982) 143.

140. John Herbert Nelson, *The Negro Character in American Literature* (1926; New York: AMS Press, 1970) 103. Subsequent references to this work are found in the text.

141. Quoted in Theodore L. Gross, *Thomas Nelson Page* (New York: Twayne, 1967) 27. Subsequent references are found in the text.

142. Thomas Nelson Page, *In Ole Virginia; or, Marse Chan and Other Stories* (1887; reprinted Chapel Hill: U of North Carolina P, 1969) 1–2. Subsequent references are to this edition and found in the text.

143. In subsequent editions, Page modified the dialect, rendering it even more divergent from standard written English. For example, in the quote cited above that begins "Dem wuz good old times," he changed "ever" to "uver," "nothin'" to "nuttin'," and after "waz po'ly" he added "an' all." Although in the introduction to the 1969 edition, Kimball King asserts that "Neither Page nor his publishers made substantive alterations in the texts of subsequent editions" (xviii), the further

linguistic manipulations suggest that Page was quite interested in having his language appear realistic.

144. Lucy A. Delaney, *From the Darkness Cometh the Light; or, Struggles for Freedom* (1891; New York: Oxford UP, 1988) vii–viii. Subsequent page references are from this edition and are noted in the text.

145. See, for example, Mary Helen Washington, *Invented Lives;* Hazel Carby, *Reconstructing Womanhood;* Barbara Christian, *Black Women Novelists: The Development of a Tradition, 1892–1976* (Westport, Conn.: Greenwood, 1980); Carole McAlpine Watson, *Prologue: The Novels of Black American Women, 1891–1965* (Westport, Conn.: Greenwood Press, 1985). Unfortunately, the relationship between African American women's literature and others has not received the same level of attention. Dickson Bruce's *Black American Writing From the Nadir* (Baton Rouge: Louisiana State UP, 1989), Elizabeth Ammons's *Conflicting Stories: American Women Writers at the Turn into the Twentieth Century* (New York: Oxford UP, 1991), and Richard Yarborough's *Ideology and Black Characterization in the Early African American Novel* (forthcoming) are notable exceptions.

146. Ida B. Wells, *Southern Horrors: Lynch Law in All Its Phases,* reprinted in *Selected Works of Ida B. Wells-Barnett,* ed. Trudier Harris (New York: Oxford UP, 1988) 14–15. Subsequent page references are from this edition and included in the text.

147. See my introduction to *Iola Leroy* in the Schomburg Library of Nineteenth-Century Black Women Writers series (New York: Oxford UP, 1988), my *A Brighter Coming Day: A Frances Ellen Watkins Harper Reader* (New York: Feminist Press, 1990), and "Frances Ellen Watkins Harper" in *African American Writers,* ed. Valerie Smith (New York: Scribners's, 1991).

148. The image of shadows being uplifted also suggests another context for interpreting "Iola." In Greek mythology, "Iola" is a derivation of "Iole," a personification of dawn and the consort of the sun who kills darkness in order to be with her. Given Harper's tendency to revise mythological narratives to increase the heroism of women, such an interpretation would not be too far-fetched.

149. Introduction, *A Voice from the South,* ed. Mary Helen Washington (New York: Oxford UP, 1988) xxxv. Subsequent page references are included in the text.

150. Sandra M. Gilbert and Susan Gubar, "Turn of the Century Literature" in *The Norton Anthology of Literature by Women: The Tradition in English* (New York: Norton, 1985) 948.

Index

Abolitionism: and Harper, 133; and Jacobs, 101; writers, 101. *See also* Anti-slavery; Slavery
Ada: pseudonym for Sarah Forten, 81
Adam: role in slave narrative, 2
"Adam Negro's Tryalls," 2
Adams, Abigail, 70; on women's rights, 49–51
Adams, John, 49–50
"An Address to the Deist," 57
"Advice to Young Ladies," 53–54
African Americans: racial discrimination, 10; spiritual narratives, 60–61; whites' attitudes about their intelligence, 31, 32
African American women: discrimination, 14; faith in power of Word or *Nommo*, 16–17; increase in literacy, 45; as professionals, 154; testifying experiences, 3
African American women's literature: post-revolution, 44–55; 1800–1850, 53; antebellum period, 76–94; discrimination, 80; ecumenism, 20–21; literary tradition, 2–15; as part of literature of world, 21; publishing problems, 78–79; scarcity of publications, 9–10; separate sphere ideology, 53; tradition, 15
African American women writers: 1800–1850s, dedicated to moral improvement, 53; publishing in 1820s, 1830s, 46; and American literature, 19; antebellum period, 83; anti-slavery movement, 81–82; color line between whites, 82; conversions to Christianity, 2; faith in power of the Word, 16; female audience, 53; historical context, 11; moral fables, 90; psychological barriers, 13; struggle compared to white women, 13; true womanhood ideology, 54; western literary influence on, 19–20; writing for publication, 9–10
African American writers, 192n; ambiance, 13–14; freedom in stories, 18–19; identified by race in titles, 65–66; usable past, 133
African culture, 16
African Methodist Episcopal church, 68; Book Concern, 74–75
Albert, Octavia Victoria Rogers, 163, 165–72, 174–77; death, 162; discourse of distrust, 164; and Page, 173; similarity to Harper's writing, 160–61
Aldridge, William, 65
Alice: role in women's literary tradition, 2, 14; testifying experiences, 3
Allen, Eunice, 29, 30
Allen, Richard, 63, 67, 68, 71, 74
Allen, Samuel, 29
American Anti-Slavery Society, 98

American Literary Gazette and Publisher's Circular, 129
Amsden, Simeon, 29
Andrews, John, 30, 37
Andrews, William, 18, 57, 111, 124
The Anglo-African, 171
Anglo-African Magazine, 93
Anglo American males: in American literature, 12
Anti-slavery: African American women writers, 81–82; novel, 99–100. *See also* Abolitionism; Slavery
An Appeal to the Christian Women of the South, 76
An Appeal to the Women of Nominally Free States, 81
Archy Moore, the White Slave; or Memoirs of a Fugitive, 99
"Aunt Chloe," 146
"Aunt Chloe's Politics," 148
Authenticating affidavits, 181
Authoritative references: *Incidents in the Life of a Slave Girl,* 110
Autobiographies, 83–84. *See also* Spiritual autobiographies

Baker, Houston, 32
Ball, Charles, 97, 196n91
"Bar's Fight," 8, 23, 27; author's influence, 24–25; author's persona, 29–30; historical significance, 28; interpretation, 29–30
Bayley, Solomon, 60, 68
Baym, Nina, 89, 194–195n72
Behind the Scenes, 122, 124, 126–28, 197n105; advancement via individual determination, 131; advertising, 129–30; difference from *Incidents,* 120–21; physical resistance in, 123; as prototype for later stories, 123; reunion scene, 125; theme of, 118–19
Belinda of Boston: autobiographical statement, 44–45
Beryl Watson's Ambition, 156
Bible: as source in Wheatley's poems, 41–42. *See also* Corinthians; New Testament
Biography of an American Bondman, 161
Black and White Women of the Old South, 105
The Black Man, His Antecedents and His Genius, 128
Blake; or, The Huts of America, 93
Bontemps, Arna, 15, 132
Book Concern: African Methodist Episcopal church, 74–75
Bradstreet, Anne, 34, 38, 48
A Brand Plucked from the Fire, 160
Brooks, Mary E., 128
Brown, Alice, 47, 48

FRANCES SMITH FOSTER is Professor of Literature at the University of California, San Diego. She is the author of *Witnessing Slavery: The Development of the Ante-Bellum Slave Narrative* and editor of *A Brighter Coming Day: A Frances Ellen Watkins Harper Reader.*